IMAGES
of America

LEGEND CITY

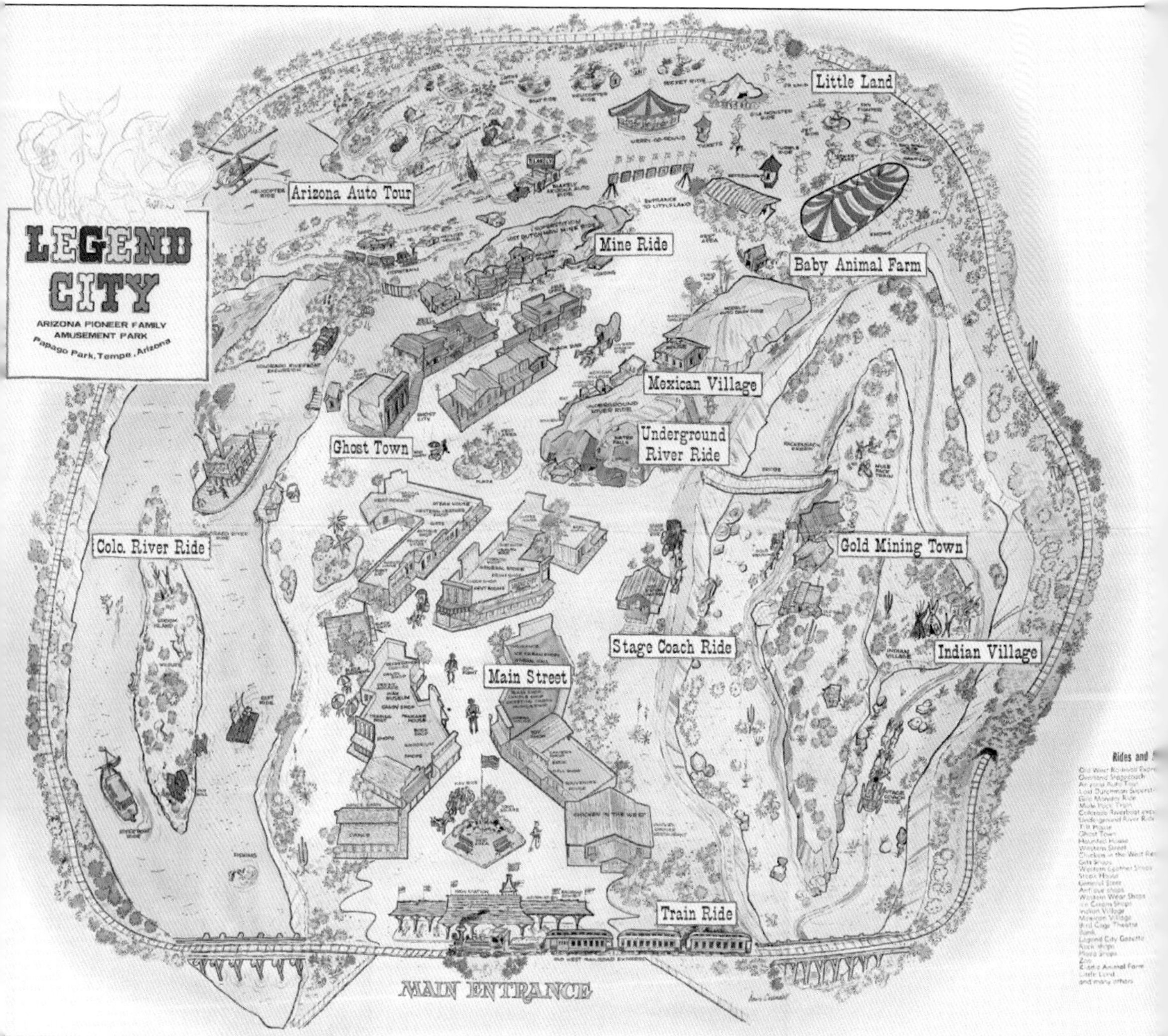

Louis Crandall himself drew up the first Legend City map in 1961, soon after the board of directors had acquired the land for the park. Interestingly, the map includes attractions that did not appear in the final configuration of the park, such as a stagecoach ride, baby animal farm, and "Little Land," an area of rides designed for the very youngest park visitors.

ON THE COVER: A 10-member contingent of the Legend City Band pauses to interact with a very young park visitor in the summer of 1963, shortly after the park's opening.

IMAGES
of America

LEGEND CITY

John Bueker

ARCADIA
PUBLISHING

ISBN 978-1-4671-3071-4

Published by Arcadia Publishing
Charleston, South Carolina

Printed in the United States of America

Library of Congress Control Number: 2013937855

For all general information, please contact Arcadia Publishing:
Telephone 843-853-2070
Fax 843-853-0044
E-mail sales@arcadiapublishing.com
For customer service and orders:
Toll-Free 1-888-313-2665

Visit us on the Internet at www.arcadiapublishing.com

To my mother and father, who brought me to the magical place that was Phoenix in the 1960s.

Contents

Acknowledgments

I wish first to thank Louis E. Crandall for his wonderful friendship, his unwavering assistance and support, and his touching and still undying enthusiasm for the theme park he so lovingly brought to life so long ago. Unless otherwise noted, the photographs in this book are courtesy of Mr. Crandall.

Much credit must also be accorded to Jan Rush, who did extensive preliminary research for a Legend City book and generously shared her materials with the author.

I have also drawn extensively on the photographs and recollections of Dick Kraus, who worked at the park during its formative years and devised many of the wonderful animated effects on the mine and river rides.

Jim Madden has kindly provided me with unfettered access to his invaluable photograph and video collection documenting the final days of the park, making possible a poignant conclusion to the narrative. Important input was also provided by Serge Huff regarding the early days of the park, and by Bill Capell Jr. regarding the twilight years.

I sincerely wish to acknowledge and thank the many loyal Legend City fans and employees who came out and supported their amusement park for 20 years and who have lamented its passing ever since. I am deeply grateful for the many priceless photographs and memories these folks have contributed to the Legend City website over the years.

Above all, I extend my eternal gratitude and love to my wife, Sue, for her constant support, encouragement, ideas, suggestions, and exemplary tolerance for my endless Phoenix nostalgia trip.

Introduction

The story of Legend City is not in fact a happy one, when viewed in terms of its persistent financial turmoil, squandered potential, and ultimate fate. But the passage of time has a way of softening perceptions, and hindsight has been rather kind to the ill-fated Phoenix-Tempe amusement park.

Legend City was fun. It was an imaginative and visionary enterprise, worthy of the broadly ambitious dreams that brought it into being. The park was possessed of a uniquely charming character that was never quite extinguished in the swirl of ownership changes, bankruptcies, chronic mismanagement, and conceptual meanderings that characterized its eventful, 20-year run. Legions of current and former Phoenix residents continue to nurture remarkably fond memories of their long-lost theme park. In this regard, at least, Legend City may be regarded as a grand success.

What makes this success so remarkable is that it persists in the aftermath of inarguable failure. Legend City developed financial problems of lasting consequence almost from the moment the gates first swung open on June 29, 1963. The early economic disarray and resulting bankruptcy prevented the business from establishing any initial traction, and it never truly recovered from these disastrous beginnings. The tragedy of Legend City is one of a beautifully conceived and skillfully executed theme park that was poorly administered and built slightly ahead of its time. The park's fate was sealed early on.

Clearly, however, there is much more to this story than dismal failure and wistful regret. When viewed within its proper cultural and historical context, the inherent beauty and historical importance of Legend City becomes apparent.

The construction of a major theme park in early-1960s Phoenix was in itself an astonishing feat. It is difficult, 50 years later, to adequately appreciate the enormity of this achievement. The park's ability to then withstand two decades' worth of organizational and financial instability, in addition to the blazing Phoenix summer heat, before finally succumbing to the stark economic realities is more remarkable still. With 30 years now separating us and the park's demise, Legend City's place in the cultural history of Arizona is coming into sharper focus.

Phoenix in 1960 was a city very much in transition. Perched precisely between its past as a small Arizona town and its future as a Southwest metropolis, the city manifested elements of both settings. The Valley of the Sun was in the throes of rapid change, and its leaders were uncertain about what should come next. The population was expanding and streaming outward to the suburbs, altering the blueprint for shopping and entertainment venues. The city was beginning to shed its reputation as a culturally devoid backwater, constructing a modern library, little theater and art museum, and adding a symphony orchestra. Phoenix was becoming a major American city, and its residents were beginning to expect the amenities that such a place entails.

Meanwhile, next door in California, events were changing the face of American culture forever. The scope of Disneyland's cultural impact simply cannot be overstated. The entire concept of the amusement park, and entertainment in general, changed decisively in 1955. The creation of a park organized around discrete and highly imaginative themes was revolutionary at the time, even if it is now taken completely for granted. The reverberations were felt across the country and indeed around the world. That such a project would be considered for the fast-growing Phoenix area was an inevitability.

A few modestly sized amusement parks came and went in Phoenix during the 1940s and 1950s, most notably Kiddieland, which was built in Encanto Park in 1946. However, nothing on the scale of Legend City had ever been contemplated, let alone attempted. Why would it? The conventional wisdom in 1960 was that Phoenix had not developed an adequate population base or tourism industry to support a park remotely on the scale of a Disneyland. In hindsight, this appraisal proved accurate.

In any event, with the matchless Disneyland less than a day's travel away, what sort of amusement park could possibly be built in Phoenix to keep people home and patronizing their own local version of such a place? The answer was pretty simple: a park that incorporated the wonderful new theme-park paradigm into a context that would have unique meaning for someone living in Arizona. Legend City would have mixed results in this regard, but the place nevertheless attracted a loyal fan base and lasted much longer than it had any right to. Despite all its failings and inadequacies, Legend City was loved. As a former employee has remarked, "No, it wasn't Disneyland. But it was there, and so were we."

The downfall of Legend City has traditionally been attributed to the unforgiving heat of the Phoenix summers, but the importance of this factor is overrated. Far more crucial was the relatively small population of Phoenix when the park was built, combined with the ensuing financial mismanagement that plagued the enterprise from the very beginning. The truth is that Phoenix in the 1960s was not quite ready to host a world-class theme park, and that is precisely what Legend City aspired to be.

Still, the park was built, and it stood for 20 years. It is perhaps useful to view the Legend City experience as an essential element in the overall process of Phoenix's development, a mirror for the maturation of the city itself. An entire generation of Arizonans can track their childhood, teen years, and early adulthood precisely with the run of their local theme park. According to this perspective, the whole area came of age alongside Legend City, and once this process had played out, the old park became an afterthought. It served its purpose and then scattered to the four winds.

Yet Legend City is far from forgotten. Nostalgia aside, one fundamental reason for the renaissance of interest in the park stands out immediately—the amazing fact that nothing has ever been built to take its place, despite the massive population growth and continuing cultural development that has occurred in the Phoenix area in the years since the park's heyday. The reasons for this conspicuous entertainment vacuum are fairly complex and certainly debatable, but it is difficult to believe that the perceived catastrophe of Legend City is not a big part of the picture.

In the final analysis, of course, the Legend City story is a story about people. Enter one Louis E. Crandall.

One

CRANDALL'S DREAM

Louis Crandall was a man with a mission. A Mesa native, Arizona State University graduate, artist, and dreamer, Crandall was running his own Phoenix advertising agency in the late 1950s when he became consumed with the idea of building a Disneyland-style amusement park for the Valley of the Sun. A series of visits to the Magic Kingdom years earlier had made such an overwhelming impression on the young man that he soon became passionately determined to bring a similar entertainment venue home to Arizona.

Amazingly enough, he actually pulled it off. Crandall's dynamic personality and early business success prepared him for the challenges he would face in translating his theme-park dream into reality. Undeterred by a chorus of naysayers, he moved aggressively ahead with his plans, touring major amusement parks across the country over a period of several years. There he absorbed key ideas for his new park, most notably the saloon shows he witnessed at Six Flags over Texas and the Victorian train station and mine ride attraction he encountered at Frontier Village in California. The notion of a theme park dedicated to Arizona legends and lore methodically took shape in his mind. Taking a cue from his own initials, Crandall settled on "Legend City" as the ideal name for his proposed park. All that remained was to actually build the thing.

In 1961, Crandall, then a mere 32 years of age, assembled a group of prominent Arizona businessmen as officers and directors, forming Legend City Inc. A million shares of stock were sold at $2 apiece, and a down payment was made on an 87-acre parcel of land on East Washington Street, on the border of Phoenix and Tempe. Laurence Hollings, an accomplished theme-park designer and Hollywood set designer who had worked on the Frontier Town and Frontier Village parks in California, was hired to design the new park.

Ground was broken at the end of 1961, and construction began almost immediately thereafter. The project rapidly generated immense excitement among the local population and clearly held great promise. What could go wrong?

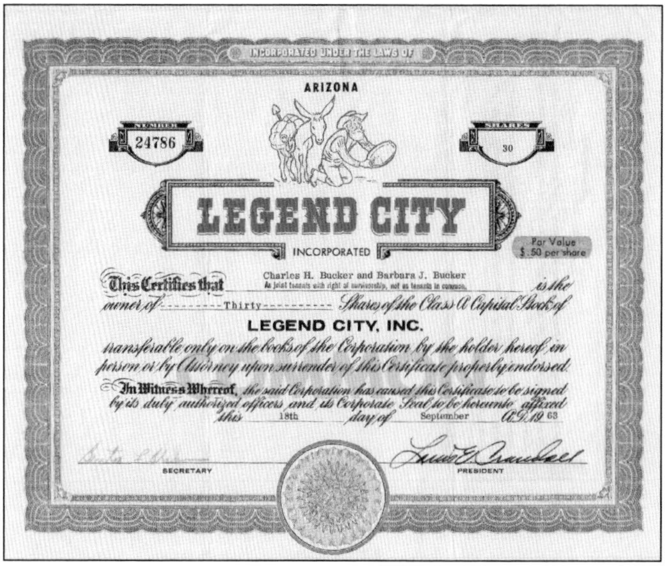
INCORPORATED UNDER THE LAWS OF
ARIZONA
NUMBER 24786
SHARES 30
LEGEND CITY
INCORPORATED
Par Value $.50 per share
This Certifies that Charles H. Bucker and Barbara J. Bucker As joint tenants with right of survivorship, not as tenants in common, is the owner of ---------Thirty---------- Shares of the Class A Capital Stock of
LEGEND CITY, INC.
transferable only on the books of the Corporation by the holder hereof in person or by Attorney upon surrender of this Certificate properly endorsed.
In Witness Whereof, the said Corporation has caused this Certificate to be signed by its duly authorized officers and its Corporate Seal to be hereunto affixed this 18th day of September A.D. 19 63
SECRETARY
PRESIDENT

The first stock issue for Legend City was offered on June 27, 1961, and completely sold out in the span of just 11 months. A second issue for the same amount took place the following May. In November 1961, Crandall's group purchased 87 acres of land south of Papago Park for $811,000, with nine acres sold to the City of Phoenix for a new municipal stadium. All told, 10,000 Arizonans purchased $4 million worth of stock. Legend City cost about $5 million to construct. (Courtesy of Barbara Bueker Stewart.)

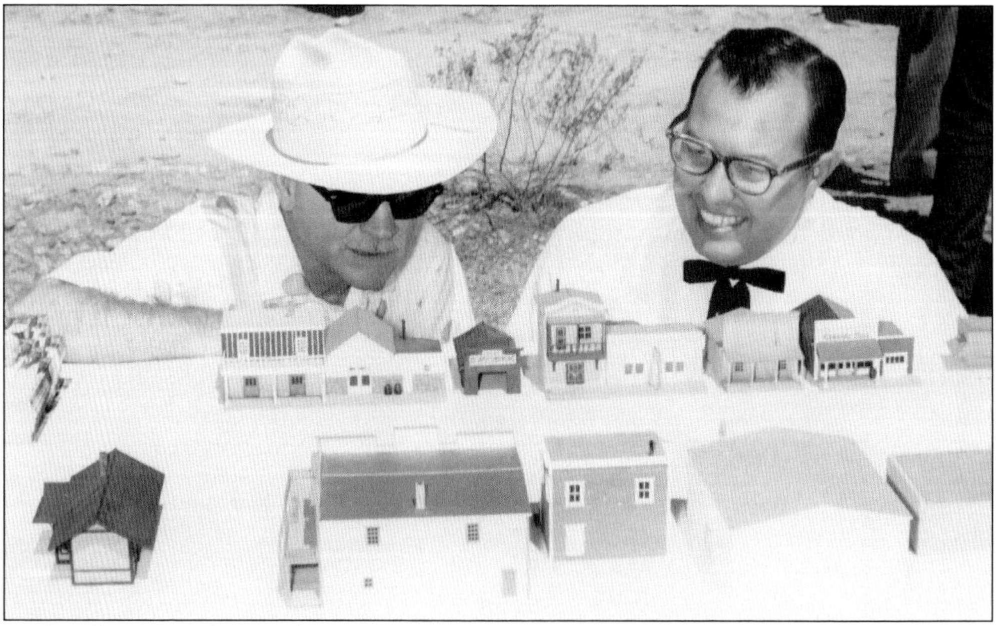

Within days of purchasing the property, Louis Crandall was busy creating a Legend City map based on the area's distinctive topography, which featured a pair of prominent ravines. Meanwhile, Louis's wife, Mabel, began weaving a Legend City flag. A few weeks before ground was broken, Crandall organized a small event on the still-vacant site for a flag-raising and map unveiling, along with the presentation of a scale model of the proposed "Boom Town" area of the park. Here, a beaming Crandall (right) inspects the Boom Town model.

Louis Crandall (far right) and friends raise the Legend City flag for the first time. The flag pole was believed to be the tallest in Arizona at that time. Benton Blake, member of the board of directors, is standing second from the left. Crandall's close friend Robert Shinn, who would later operate the Legend City Queen riverboat ride, is on the right, beside Crandall.

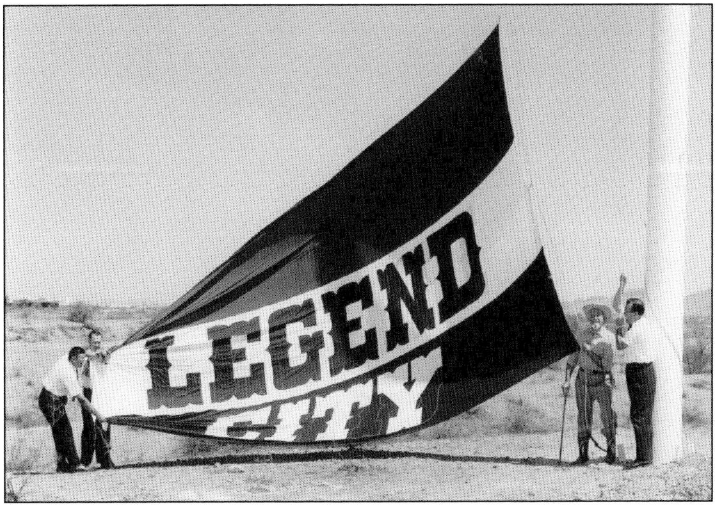

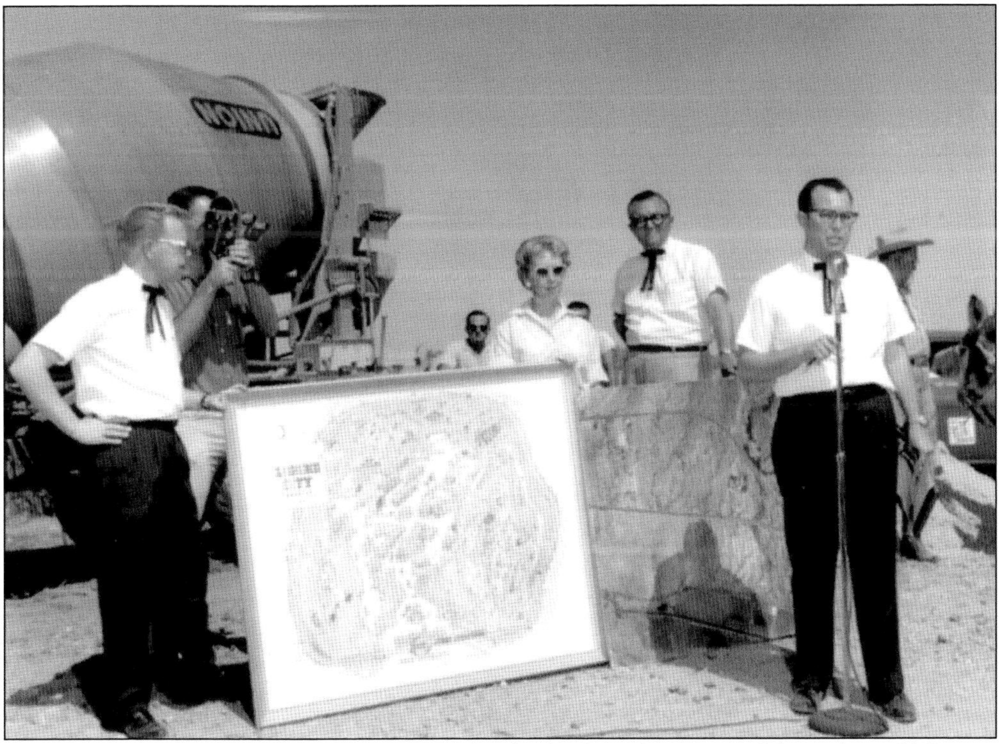

Crandall presents his proposed map of the park. The final configuration of the park would deviate somewhat from this original design, but most of the familiar elements are already present in some form. The mine ride, river ride, mule ride, Indian village, Mexican village, and car ride all appear on the original map. Interesting attractions that were dropped from Crandall's original vision included a baby animal farm and stagecoach ride.

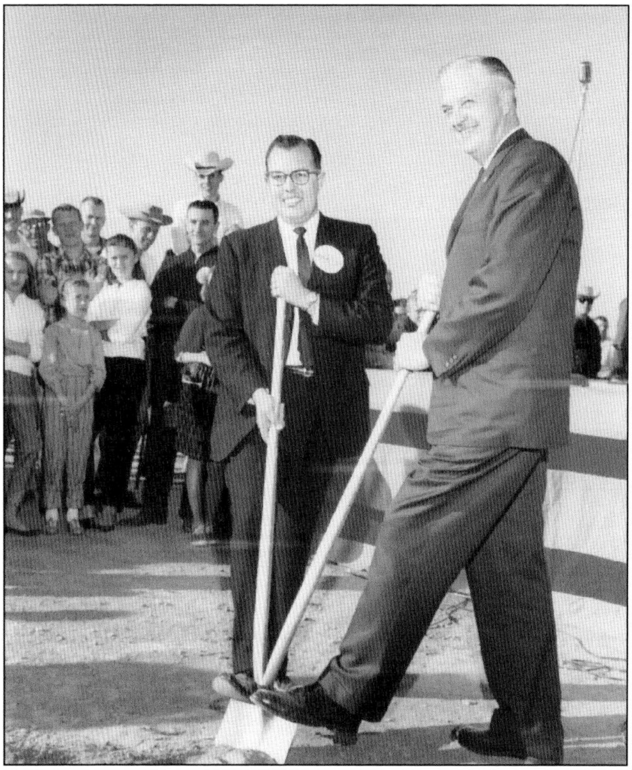

Ground was formally broken for Legend City on December 30, 1961. The festivities included a free stage show featuring Wallace and Ladmo, Dolan Ellis, and other prominent local entertainers of the day. Refreshments, prizes, and free stagecoach rides were also provided for attendees. Here, Louis Crandall (left) officially breaks ground with Arizona secretary of state Wesley Bolin.

A local dance troupe entertains the crowd at the ground-breaking ceremonies. Many of the performers who appeared at the event would work at the park 18 months later, when Legend City finally opened to the public.

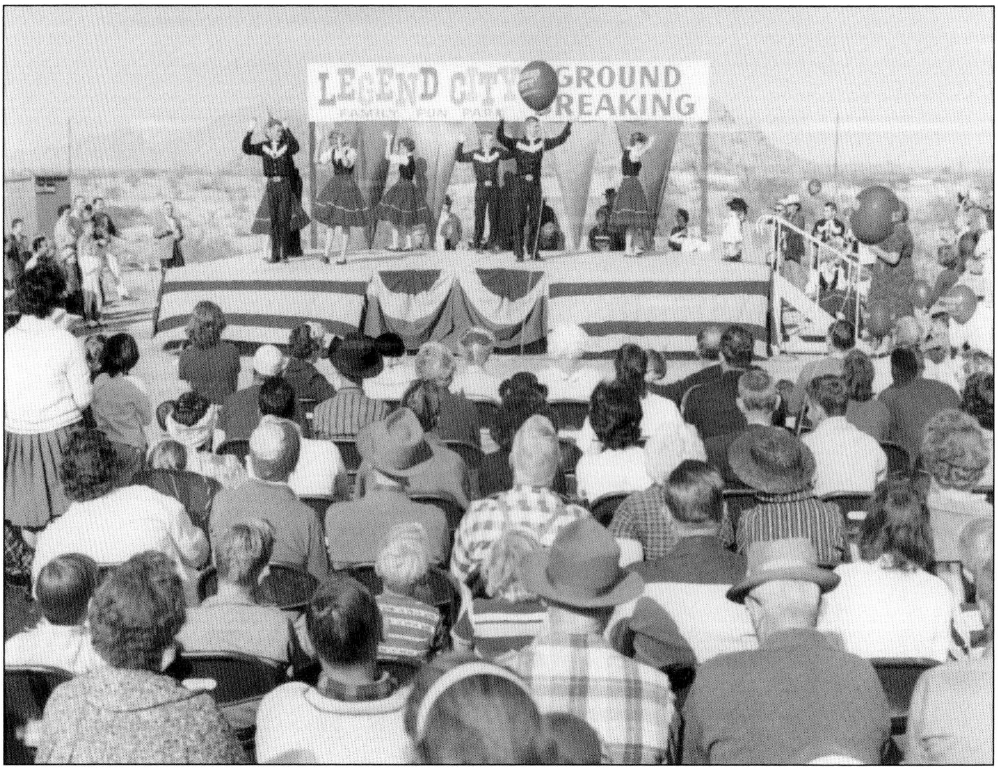

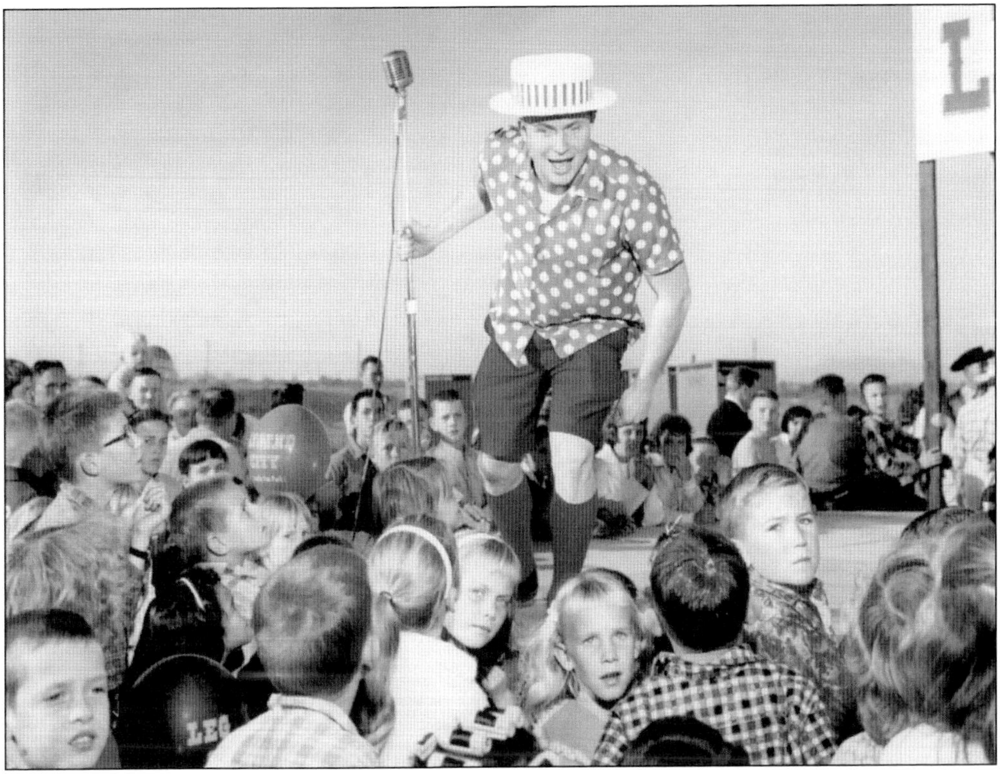

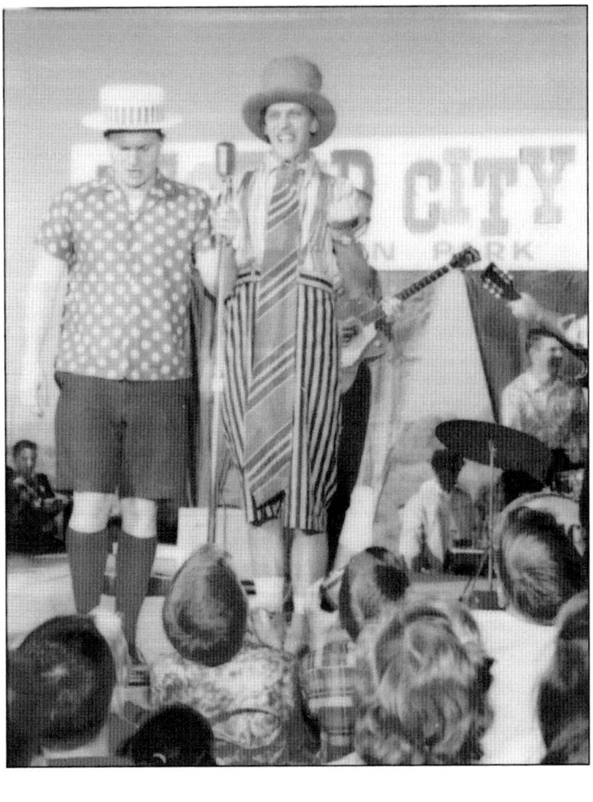

Legends in their own right, Wallace and Ladmo were the hosts of the longest-running daily television kid's show in history, an eclectic blend of cartoons, skits, music, and general silliness that included Pat McMahon's unforgettable characters of Aunt Maud, Captain Super, Marshal Good, and the quintessential spoiled brat, Gerald. This remarkable show aired on KPHO-TV in Phoenix for 35 years, from 1954 to 1989. Wallace and the gang brought their stage show to the Lagoon Amphitheater in Legend City on weekends for almost the entire run of the park, and they tirelessly promoted Legend City on their weekday television program. Above, Wallace (Bill Thompson) entertains the kids at the groundbreaking celebration. At right, he delivers a routine with lovable sidekick Ladmo (Lad Kwiatkowski)

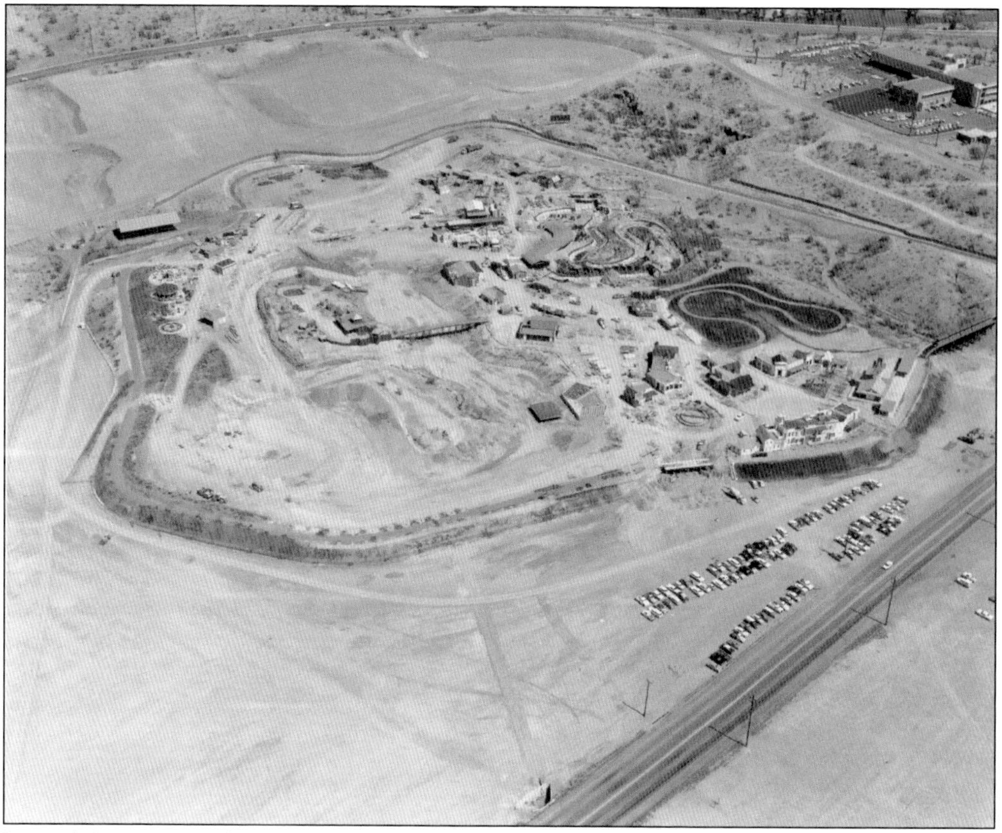

Legend City in its early stages of construction is revealed in this 1962 aerial photograph looking north. The outlines of the Antique Car Ride track and river ride are visible at right center. At right bottom, most of the Gay '90s section has been constructed, including the train station. The western half of the park, which would include the Modern section and Indian Island, has barely been started. Washington Street is visible at the bottom of the photograph.

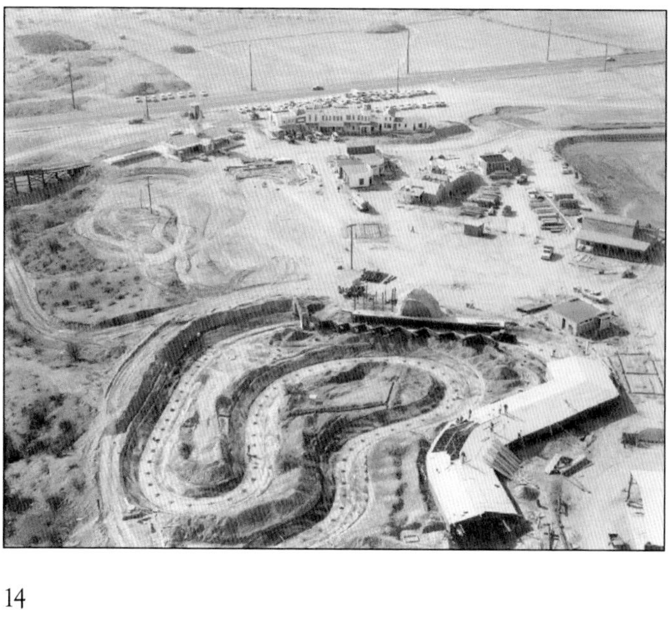

In October 1962, park designer Laurence Hollings suddenly resigned over a disagreement on the final park configuration. Designer Randall Duell and a general contractor called Skylim were brought in to complete the building of Legend City. In this remarkable close-up aerial photograph, the River of Legends ride is under construction. Workers are busy completing the outer shell for the "haunted cave" portion of the ride (bottom right). (Courtesy of Carol Risch.)

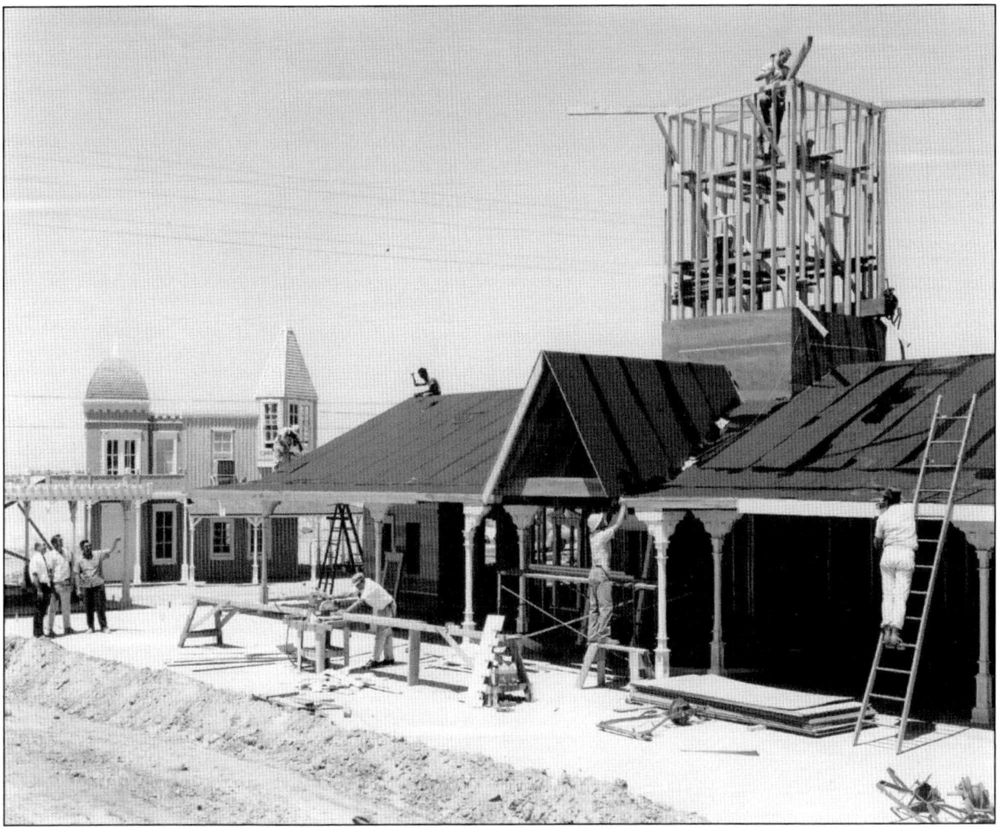

The Legend City train station is shown here under construction in early 1962. Crandall was deeply impressed with the Victorian-style architecture of the train station he observed at the Frontier Village theme park in California, and he closely followed the design, albeit on a somewhat larger scale.

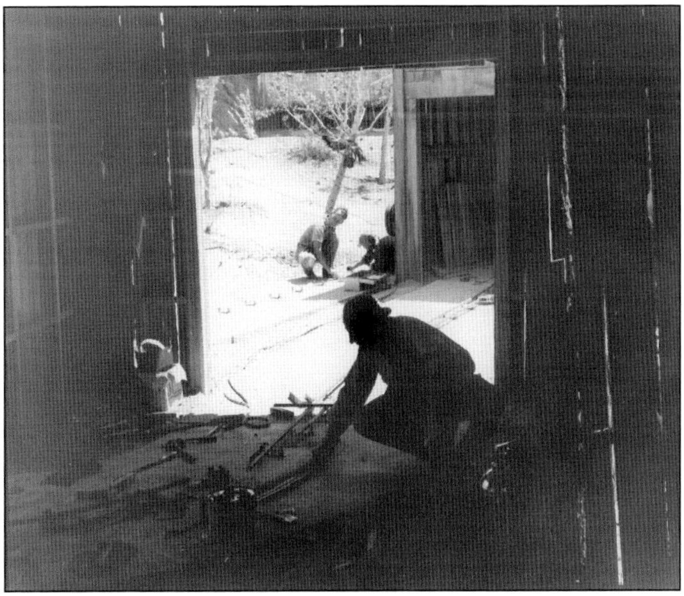

Destined to become the most popular and enduring ride at Legend City, the Lost Dutchman Mine was constructed in the summer and fall of 1962. Originally called the Superstition Mountain Mine Ride by Crandall, the ride was renamed before the park opened to more precisely reflect the Arizona legends theme.

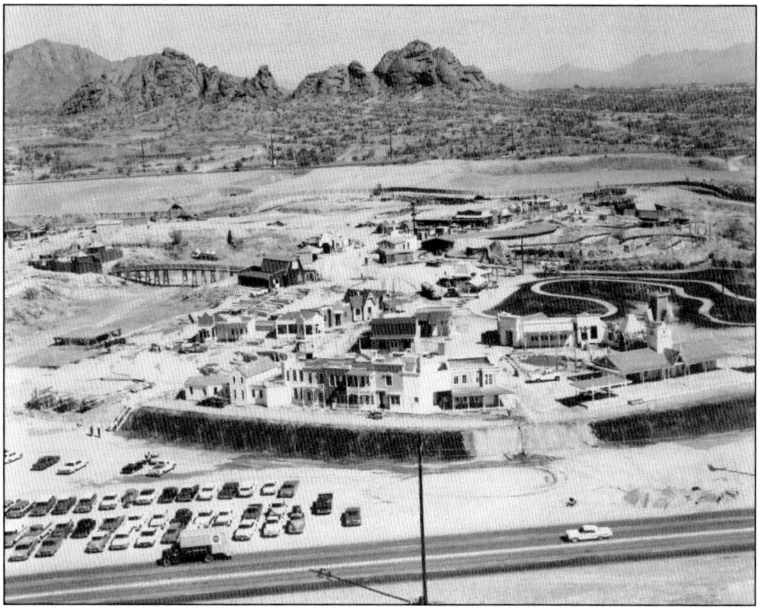

Papago Park is clearly visible in the distance in this 1962 photograph looking north. The Antique Car Ride (right) is now well defined, and the Boom Town section is taking shape in the middle distance. (Courtesy of Carol Risch.)

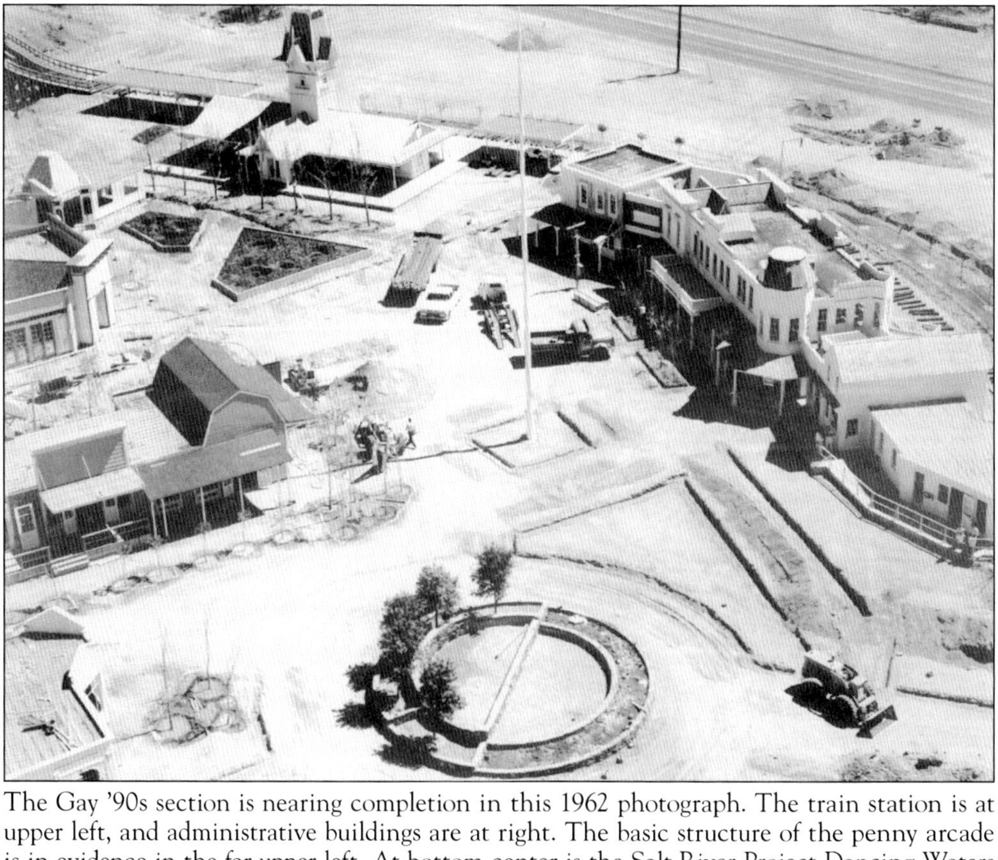

The Gay '90s section is nearing completion in this 1962 photograph. The train station is at upper left, and administrative buildings are at right. The basic structure of the penny arcade is in evidence in the far upper left. At bottom center is the Salt River Project Dancing Waters fountain under construction. (Courtesy of Carol Risch.)

Louis Crandall (second from left) inspects work on the Legend City tilt house, here under construction in late 1962 or early 1963. The park's tilt house was probably inspired by the Casa Magnetica, a similar amusement that Louis Crandall had admired at Six Flags Over Texas. Casa Magnetica opened in 1962.

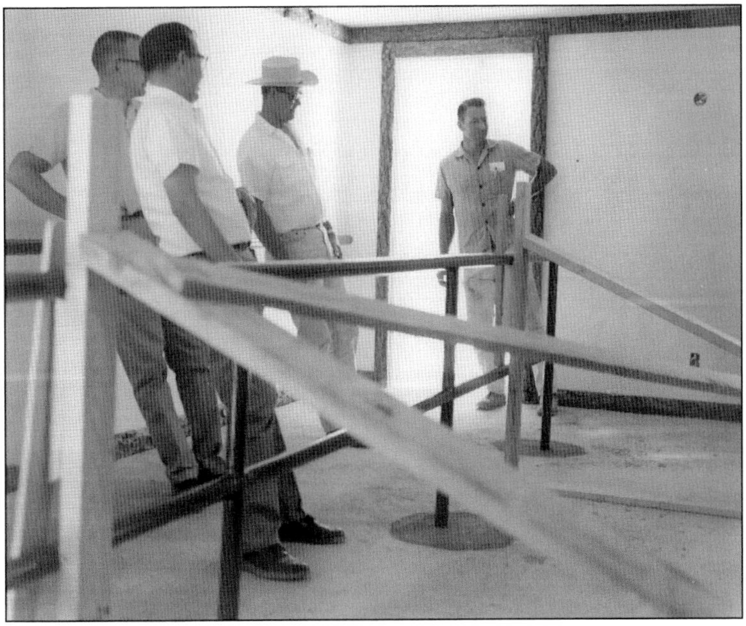

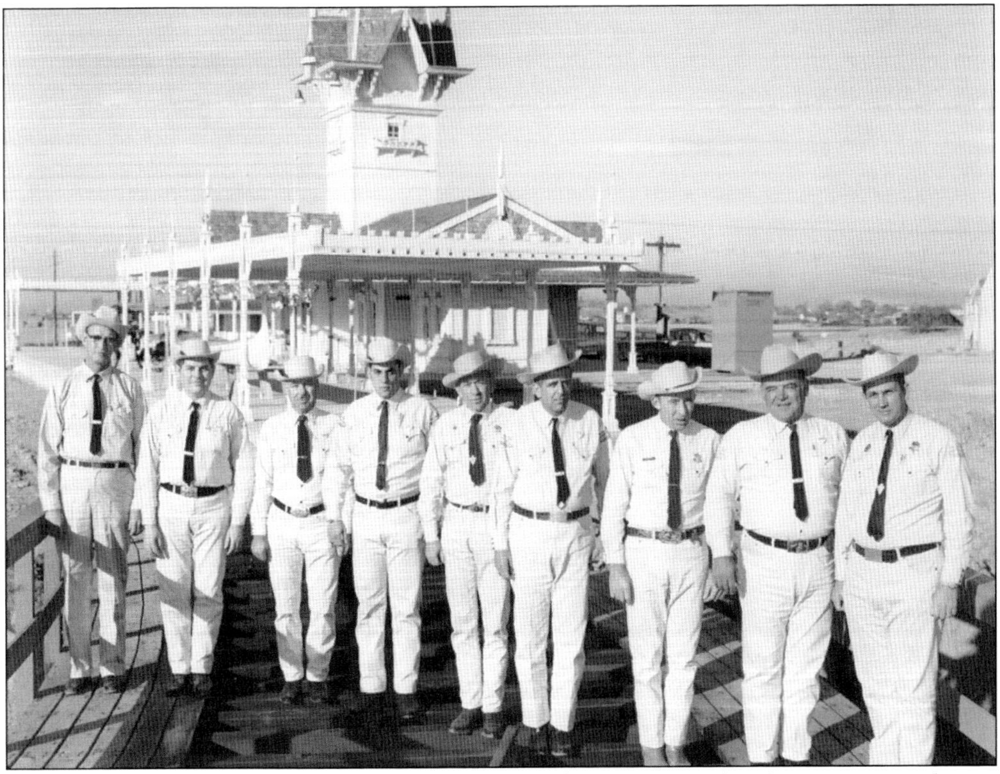

In this photograph from the spring of 1963, the Legend City security detail goes on active duty as opening day approaches. Taking a moment to pose near the train station are head of park security Bill Gunn (far right) and his team. (Courtesy of Carol Risch.)

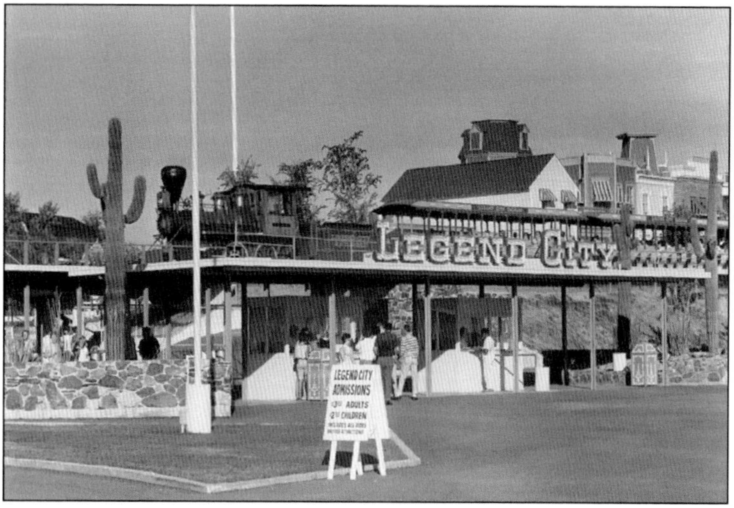

After a highly successful dress rehearsal the night before, Legend City officially opened its doors to the world on Saturday, June 29, 1963. It was the fifth-largest theme park of its kind in the United States. By 1:00 that afternoon, 4,100 people had passed through the gates. The park entrance is seen here on opening day.

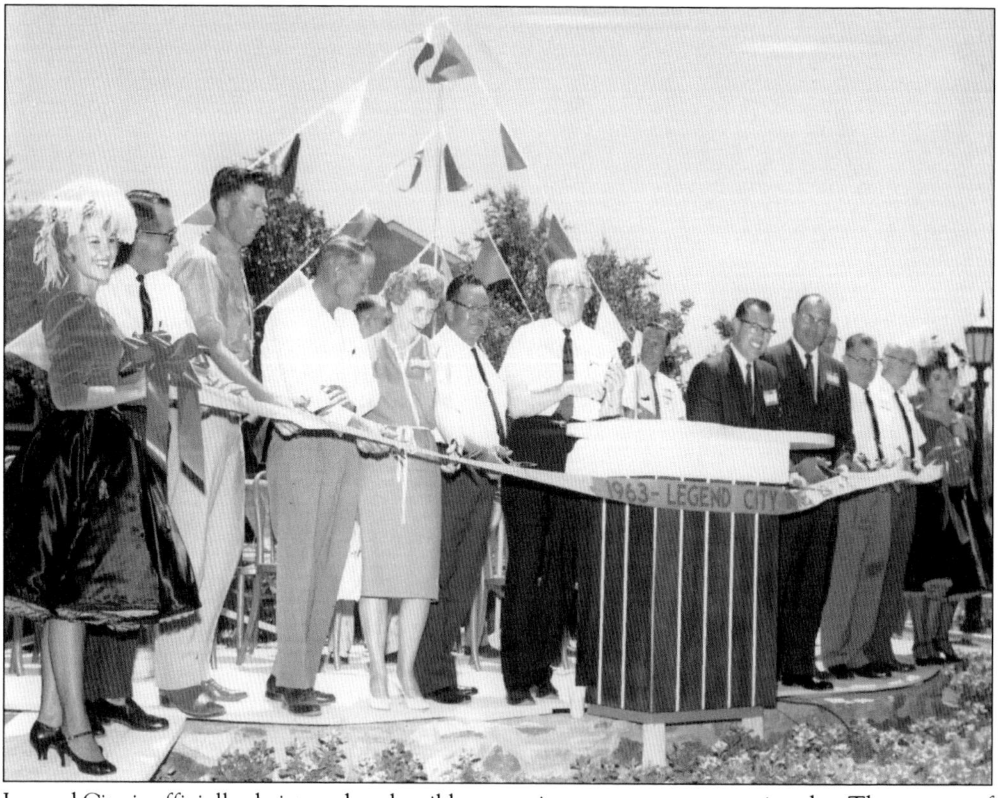

Legend City is officially christened at the ribbon-cutting ceremony on opening day. The mayors of seven Arizona cities were in attendance, including Phoenix mayor Sam Mardian, who is standing immediately to the right of Crandall (behind podium). At far left is Printy Crandall, sister of Louis and a can-can dancer at the Golden Palace Saloon. Louis Crandall announced to the crowd, "Legend City will never be completed. Every year, something will be added to it."

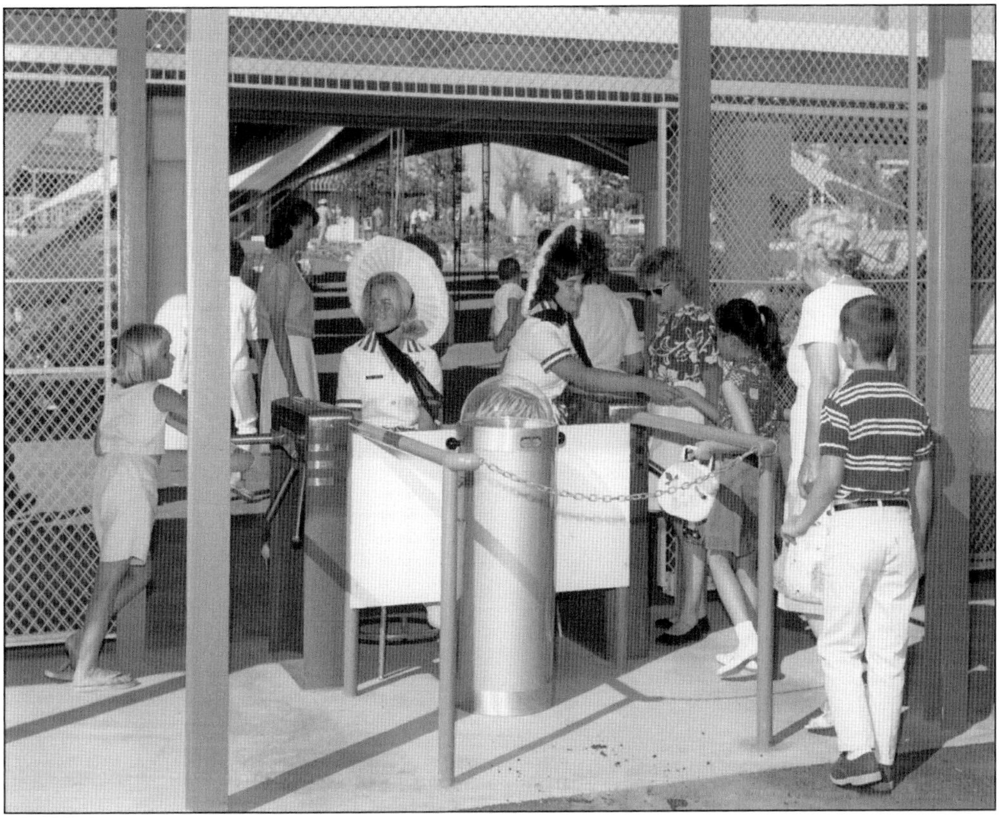

Excited visitors enter Legend City for the first time. Free trams transported visitors to and from the parking lot. Admission was $3 for adults and $2.50 for children. First in line when the gates opened were Mrs. Joseph P. Doyle of Phoenix and her daughter Kristen. They arrived at the park around 5:30 that morning. The park opened at 9:00 a.m. sharp.

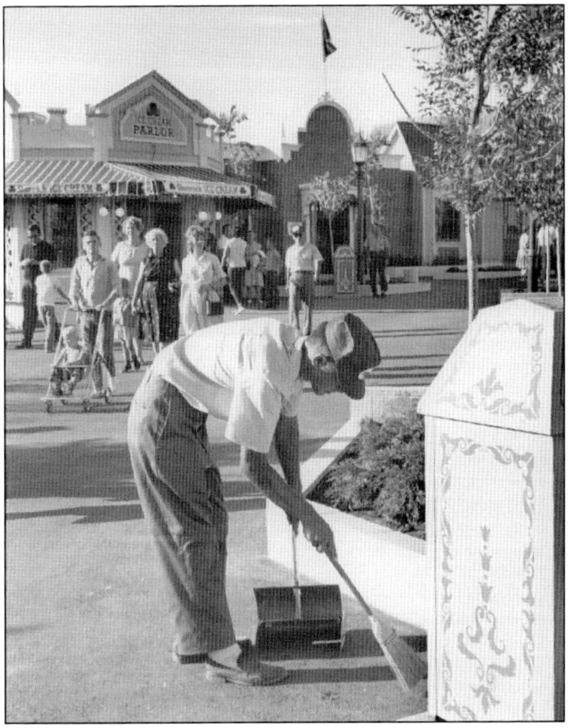

A Legend City custodian tidies up on opening day. The park opened with a staff of no fewer than 450 employees, 90 percent of whom were college students or teachers. The park's director of personnel, Jim Thetford, interviewed 6,000 applicants, mostly from nearby Arizona State University. The park payroll that first year was about $1.2 million.

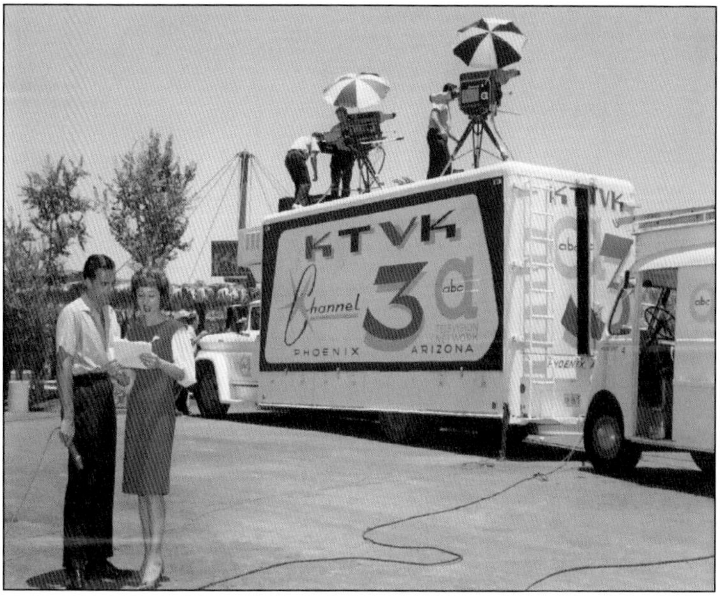

Legend City was big news in the Phoenix area, and the local media flocked to the grand opening. The ABC affiliate in Phoenix, KTVK-TV, channel 3, sent a remote broadcasting truck and a pair of on-air personalities. Here, reporters do a last-minute review of their copy immediately before the dedication ceremony commences.

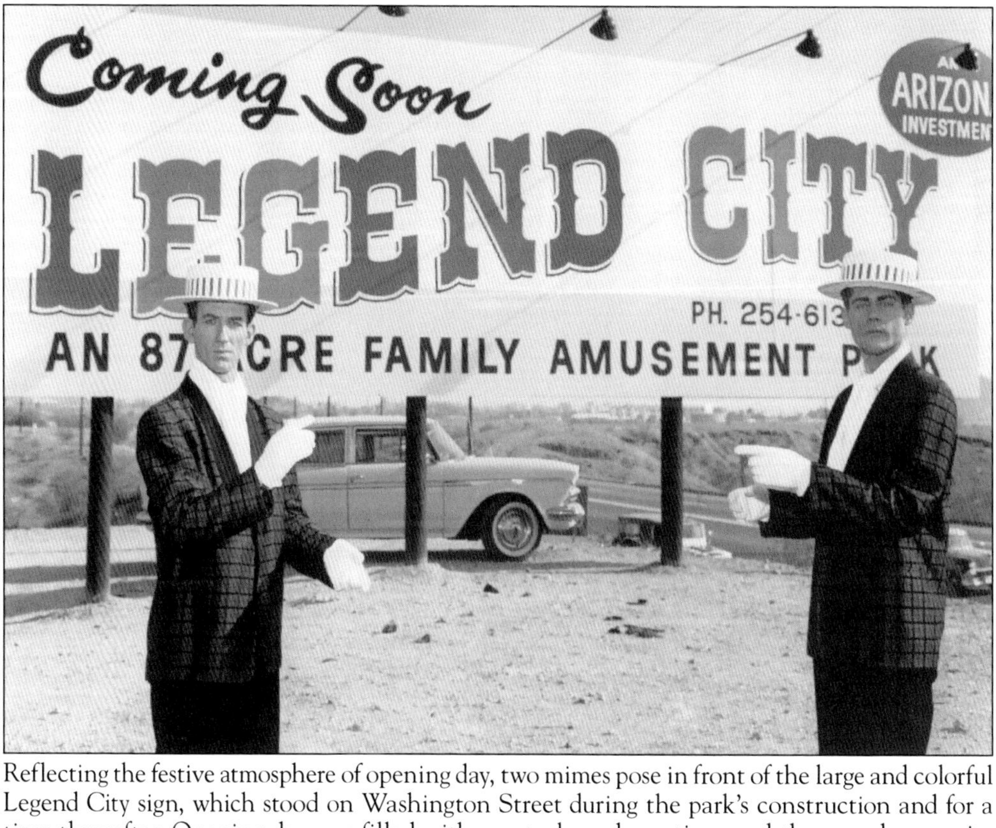

Reflecting the festive atmosphere of opening day, two mimes pose in front of the large and colorful Legend City sign, which stood on Washington Street during the park's construction and for a time thereafter. Opening day was filled with spectacle and emotion, and the crowd was quite enthusiastic. Attendance, however, was disappointingly below expectations.

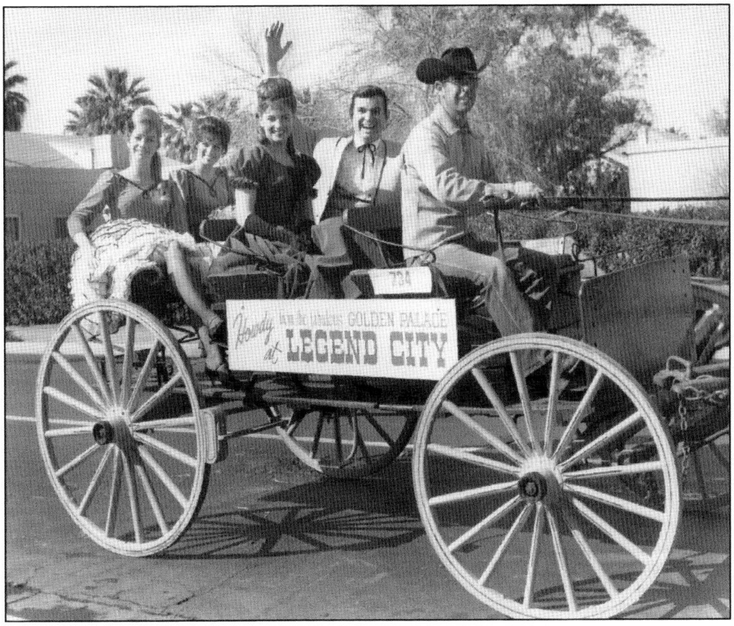

Legend City was promoted in a variety of ways from the beginning, one of the most popular being parades. Here, the primary performers from the Golden Palace Saloon ride in their horse-drawn carriage during a Fourth of July parade in Phoenix just days after the park's opening. From left to right are Barbara Rebeske, Sandy Dirickson, Vonda Kay Van Dyke, and Sandy Gibbons. The driver's name is lost to history.

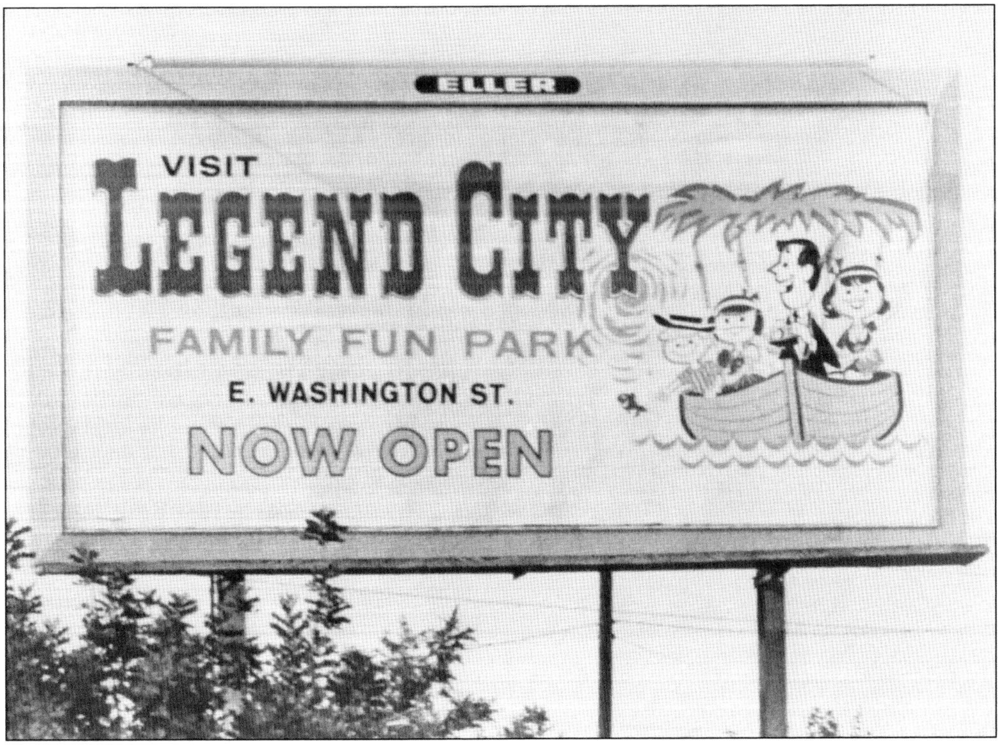

One year before Legend City opened, Karl Eller purchased the Arizona operations of a New York–based billboard company. Eller billboards soon became ubiquitous throughout the Phoenix area. The Eller Legend City billboard seen here was erected to coincide with the park's grand opening in June 1963.

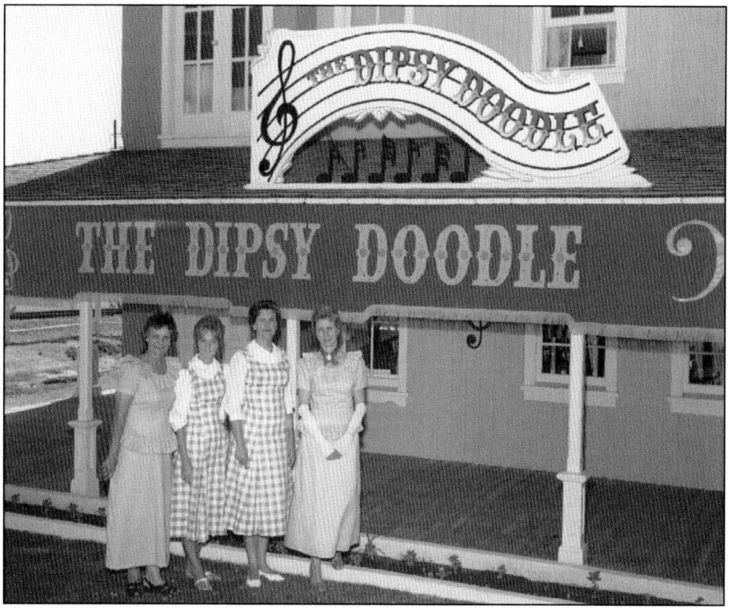

The Dipsy Doodle was one of several gift shops open for business at Legend City in the early days of the park. The shop was located near the park entrance, in the Gay '90s section. It offered various trinkets and park souvenirs for sale. In this photograph, the staff of the Dipsy Doodle proudly poses in front of their store on opening day.

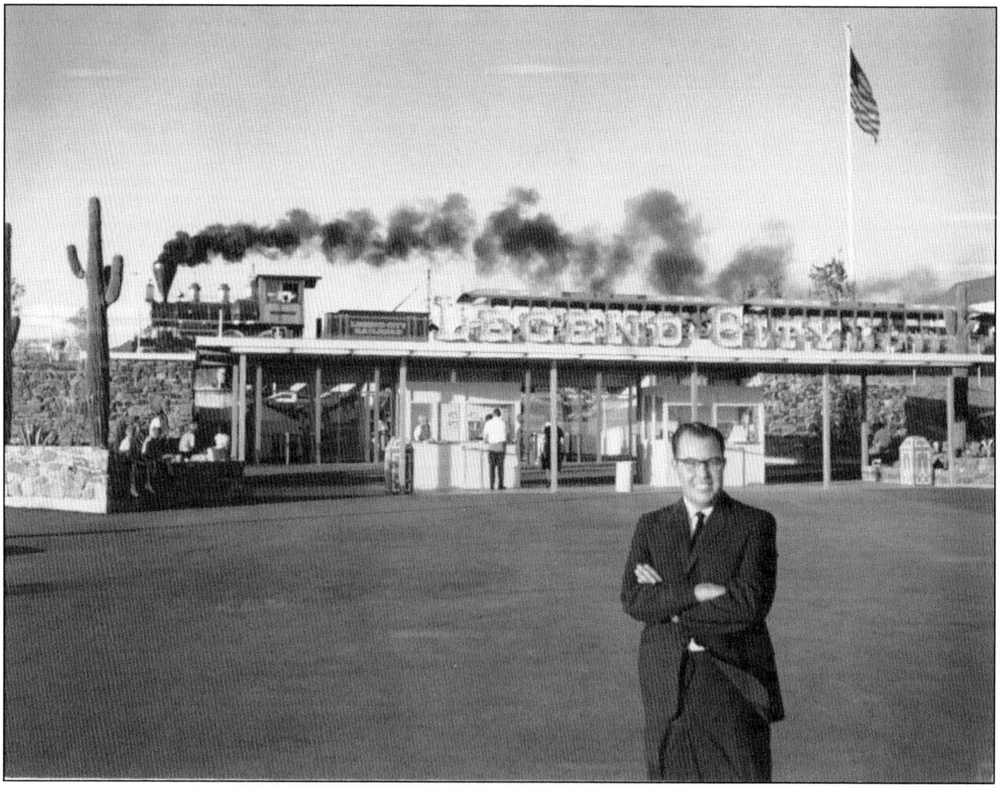

On opening day, Louis Crandall stands triumphantly in front of his dream that has now become reality: his fabulous family fun park, Legend City. Park music director Serge Huff would later say of his friend, "Louis was an artist and dreamer of the highest quality. Unfortunately, he was a trusting, kind-hearted individual who assumed everyone else was as honest and dedicated as he was. A businessman he was not."

Two

A Tour of the City

Although they borrowed key ideas from other theme parks of the day, above all Disneyland, the creators of Legend City were determined to forge a unique identity for their new park.

Louis Crandall's vision was for a family fun park extolling famous legends in Arizona history, in essence a Disneyesque "Frontierland" expanded to full-park size. This concept would ultimately be modified to embrace a more versatile entertainment model that included non-frontier attractions like sky rides and modern car rides.

Legend City was originally divided into six "sections" that were roughly analogous to the themed "lands" found in Disneyland: Gay '90s, Boom Town, Ghost Town, Indian Village, Mexican Village, and the Modern section.

The Gay '90s section was located inside the park entrance and offered guests turn-of-the-century amusements like the Antique Car Ride, Kapp's Penny Arcade, a miniature golf course, and eateries like the Shamrock Ice Cream Parlor and Beech-Nut Coffee House. Directly adjacent to the Gay '90s section was the River of Legends ride.

The Boom Town and Ghost Town comprised the primary showcase for the park's Arizona legends theme. Home to an Old West Main Street featuring gunfights, bank robberies, saloon brawls, bullwhip exhibitions, and a sheriff's office, this area also provided a gateway to Indian Island, the Fort, and the legendary Lost Dutchman Mine ride.

The Modern section represented a significant deviation from the Arizona legends theme, a concession made to create a more eclectic park experience. Here was found the Blakely Modern Car Ride, a variety of modern-day amusement thrill rides, and access to the Sky Ride.

Live entertainment at Legend City was presented primarily in two venues, the Golden Palace Saloon in Boom Town, and the Amphitheatre, which was perched on the edge of the lagoon on the west side of the park near the Gay '90s section. Encircling the new theme park was the Legend City Railroad, powered by a replica 1860s steam-engine locomotive dubbed the "Iron Horse."

Legend City opened as a beautiful, well-designed theme park with a seemingly stellar future. Sadly, this was as good as things would get.

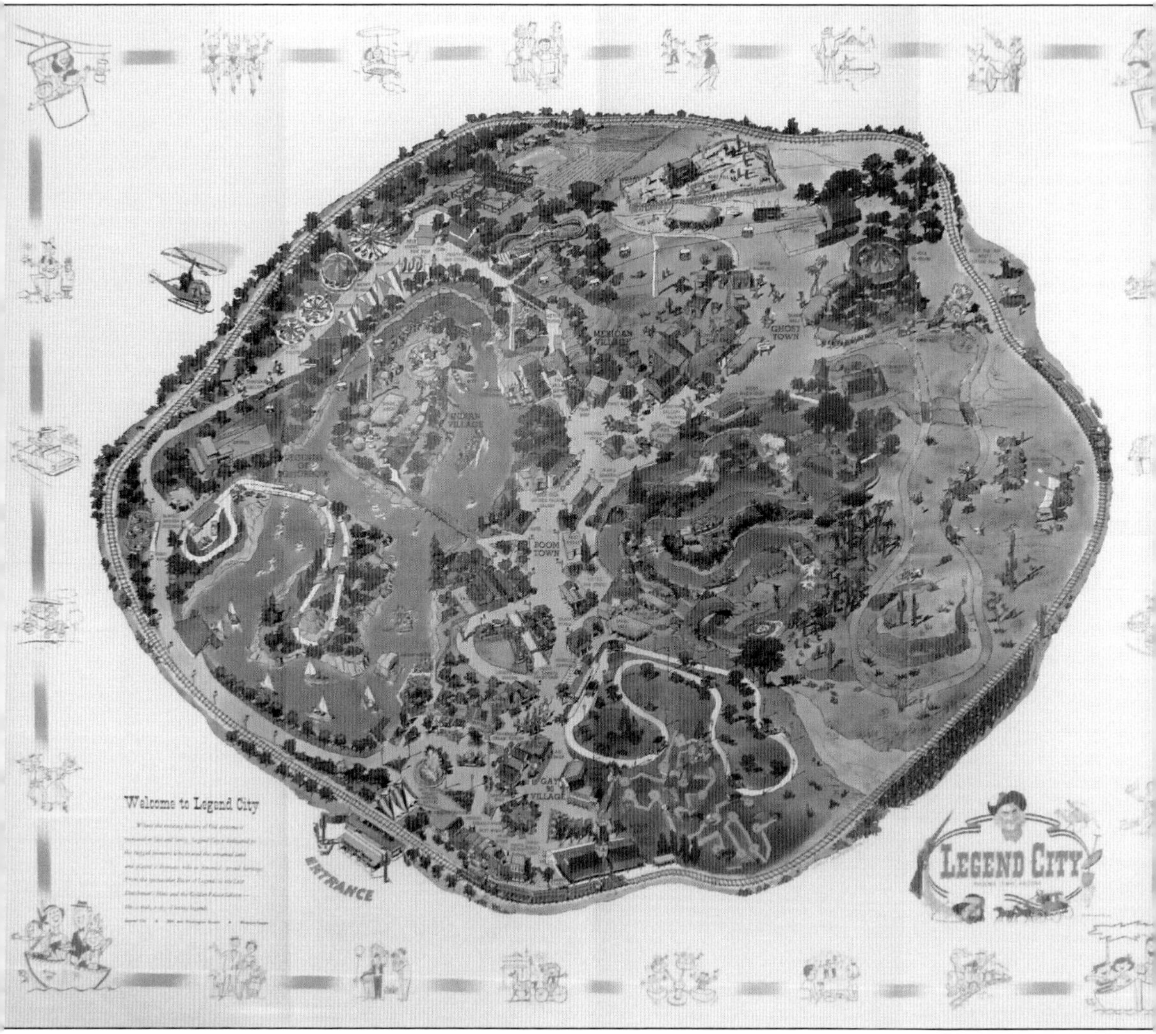

The official Legend City map, designed by Disney artist Chic Albertson, provided an accurate and colorful representation of the park layout on opening day. Copies of the map were made available at the Legend City print shop in the Boom Town section and were also mailed out to stockholders. The text at lower left neatly summarizes Louis Crandall's vision for the park: "Welcome to Legend City . . . Where the exciting history of Old Arizona is recreated in fact and fancy. Legend City is dedicated to the rugged pioneers who braved this untamed land and played a dramatic role in America's proud heritage. From the spectacular River of Legends to the Lost Dutchman's Mine and the Golden Palace Saloon—this is truly a city of living legends."

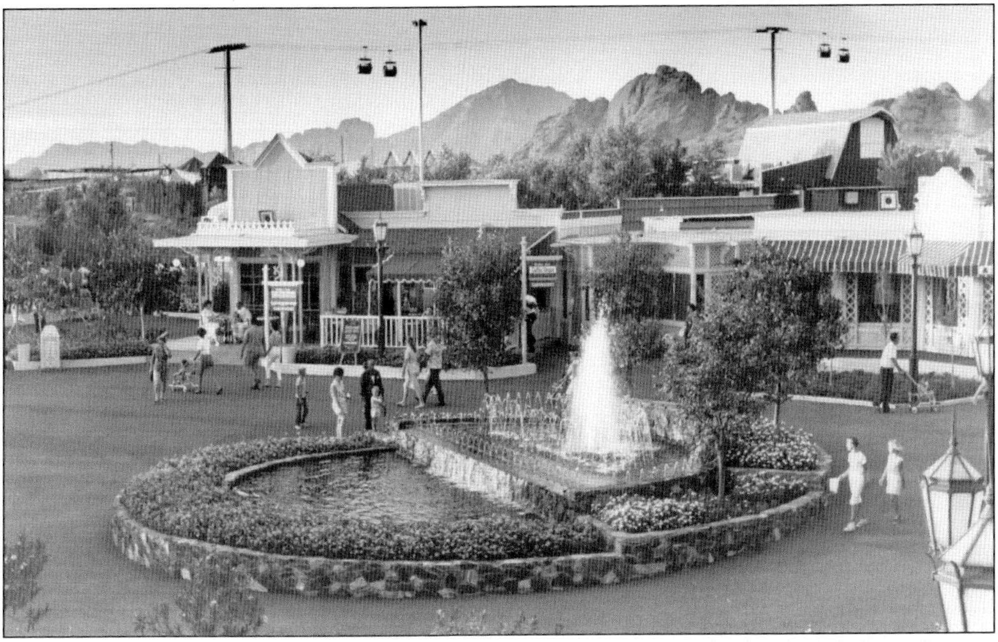

Upon entering the park, Legend City guests would first encounter the lovely Salt River Project Dancing Waters fountain. The fountain ran continuously and was illuminated at night by multicolored lights. Ironically, 20 years later, SRP would acquire the property and demolish Legend City to make way for its new corporate headquarters on the site.

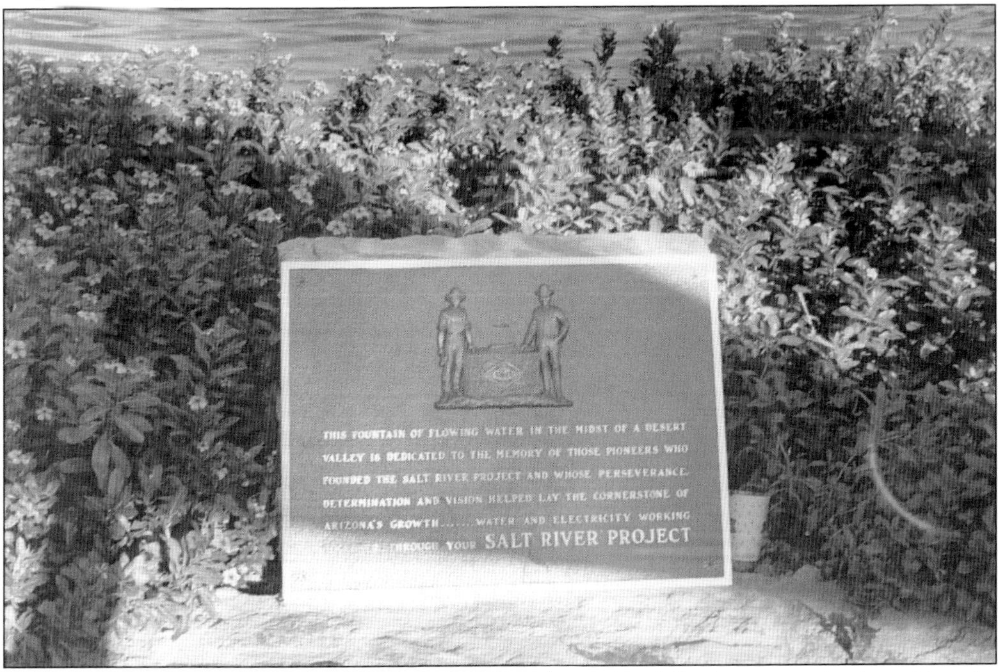

The Dancing Waters fountain plaque reads: "This fountain of flowing water in the midst of a desert valley is dedicated to the memory of those pioneers who founded the Salt River Project and whose perseverance, determination and vision helped lay the cornerstone of Arizona's growth . . . water and electricity working together through your Salt River Project."

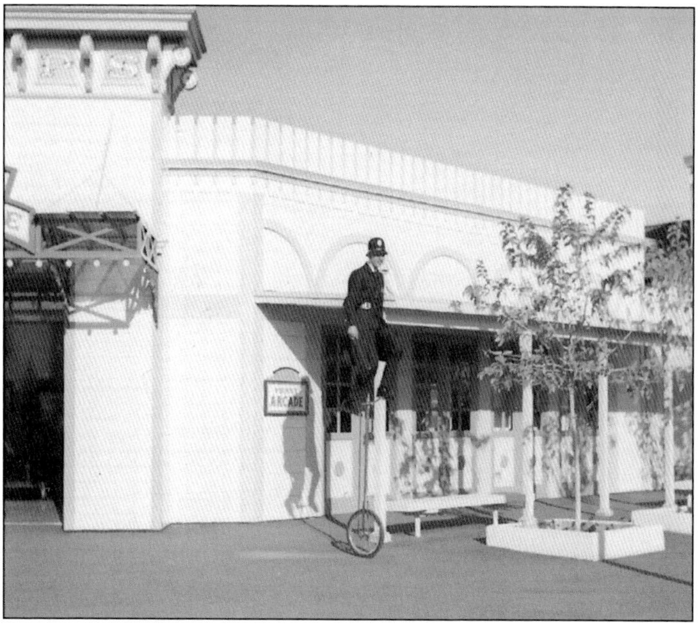

Kapp's Penny Arcade was a popular attraction in the heart of Legend City's Gay '90s section. The arcade originally featured old-time amusements such as kinetoscopes, but it evolved through a series of incarnations over the years. Posing in front of the arcade building in this early photograph is Larry Chebowski, who worked as an entertainer at the park in its first two seasons. His primary shtick involved patrolling the streets of Legend City as a unicycle-borne police officer. (Courtesy of Larry Chebowski.)

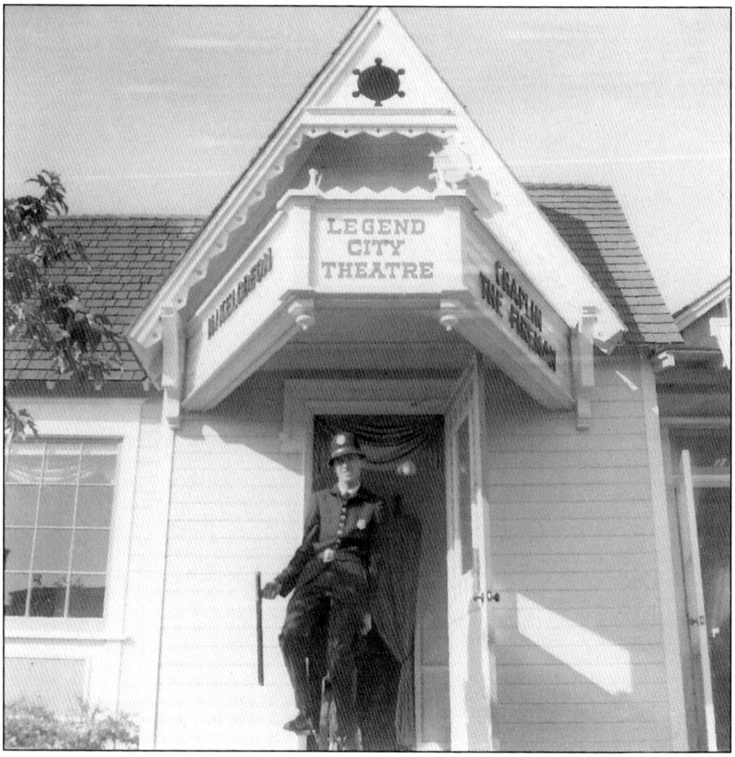

The Legend City Theatre was a curiously small cinema located in the Gay '90s section, near the ice-cream parlor. This nickelodeon continuously ran vintage silent films for the viewing pleasure of any park guests who happened to wander inside. According to the marquee, Chaplin's *The Fireman* is currently showing. (Courtesy of Larry Chebowski.)

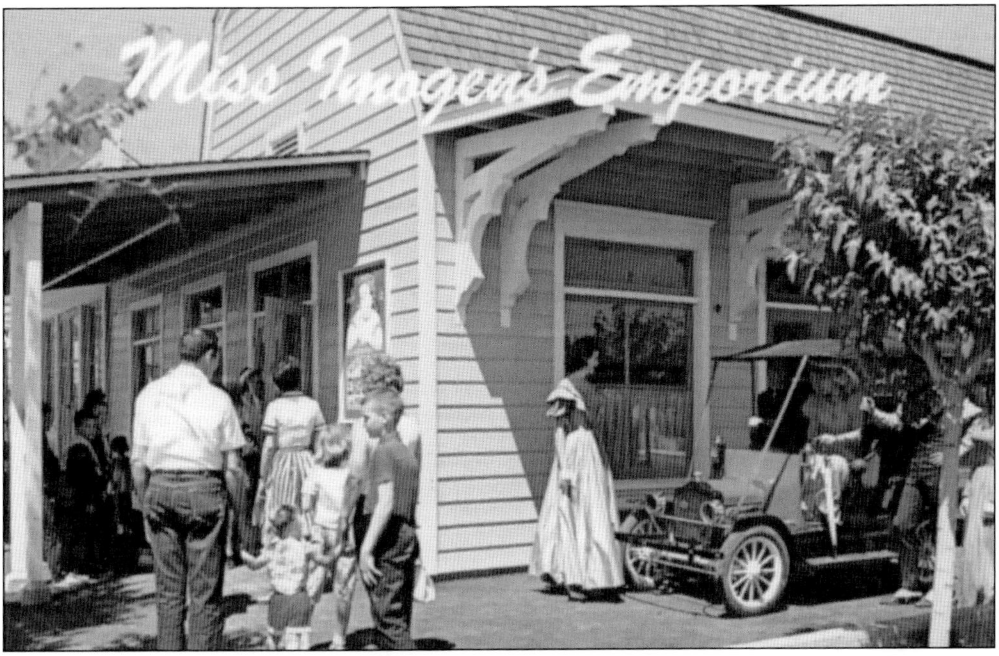

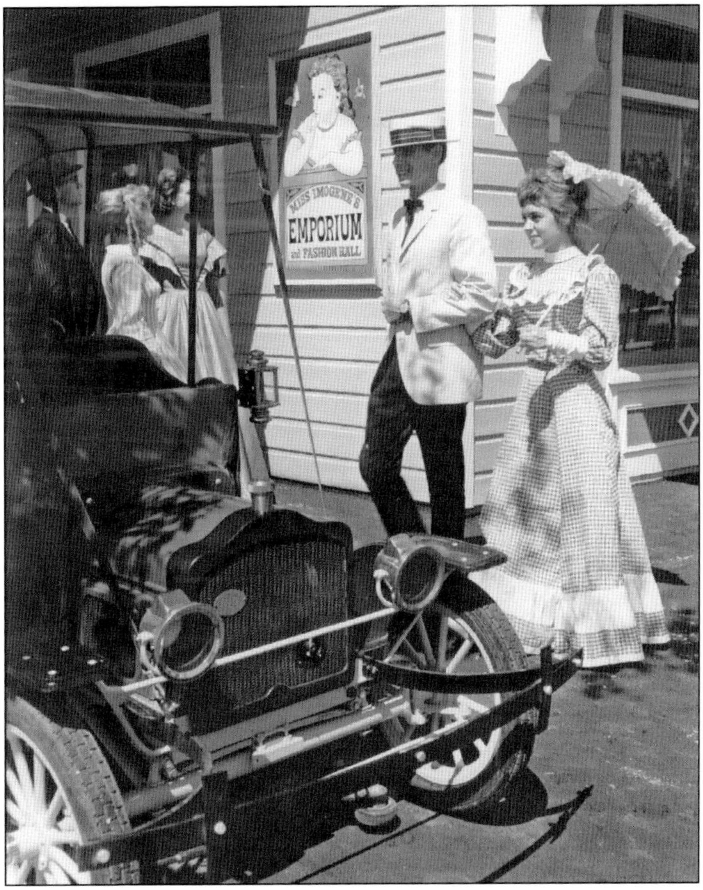

Miss Imogene's Emporium was located in the Gay '90s section, directly across from the ice-cream parlor and adjacent to the Antique Car Ride. This shop offered park guests a wide variety of gifts and souvenirs from which to choose. In the early postcard above, the name of the emporium is misspelled, as it also appears to be on the front of the building. Or was this the correct intended spelling? At right, Copper Tone Jack Hanf escorts can-can dancer Linda Warner to a waiting antique car outside of Imogene's in a posed publicity shot. Jack and Linda were eventually married.

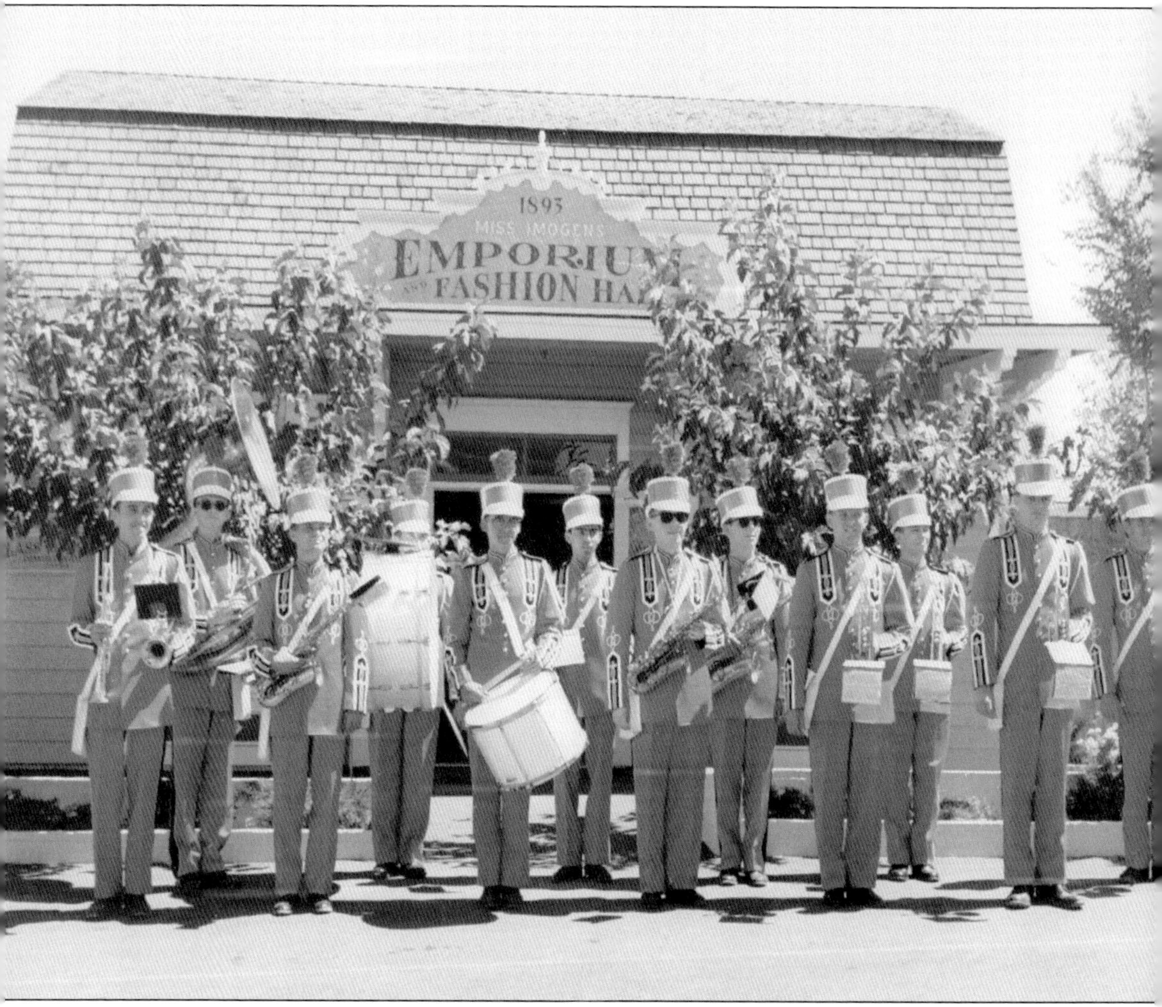

The Legend City Band poses in front of Miss Imogene's Emporium. The band was composed of 20 players who were routinely divided into two groups of ten. The two groups alternated daily, marching around the park and performing upbeat tunes appropriate to the area in which they happened to be playing at the moment. At the evening amphitheater shows, the band arrived from upstream on a motorized barge and became the pit band for the show. Musical director Serge Huff recruited 18 of the original 20 band members from the ASU Sun Devil Band, with the other two members coming from the Phoenix College Band. Highly talented musicians, many of the band members went on to play in professional local groups and to direct their own band programs in high schools. The band uniforms were of extremely high quality, purchased from an upscale costume house in Los Angeles. Louis Crandall insisted on acquiring the heaviest and most expensive weave material available. The result was a great-looking band that struggled mightily with the heat of the long summer days in Phoenix.

Shamrock Dairy was founded in Tucson in 1922, with 20 cows and a Model-T Ford for deliveries. By 1963, when it sponsored the ice-cream parlor at Legend City, Shamrock was one of the largest dairies in Arizona, becoming the largest in 1967. Here, the surprisingly large staff of the Shamrock Ice Cream Parlor poses in front of the popular eatery in the summer of 1963.

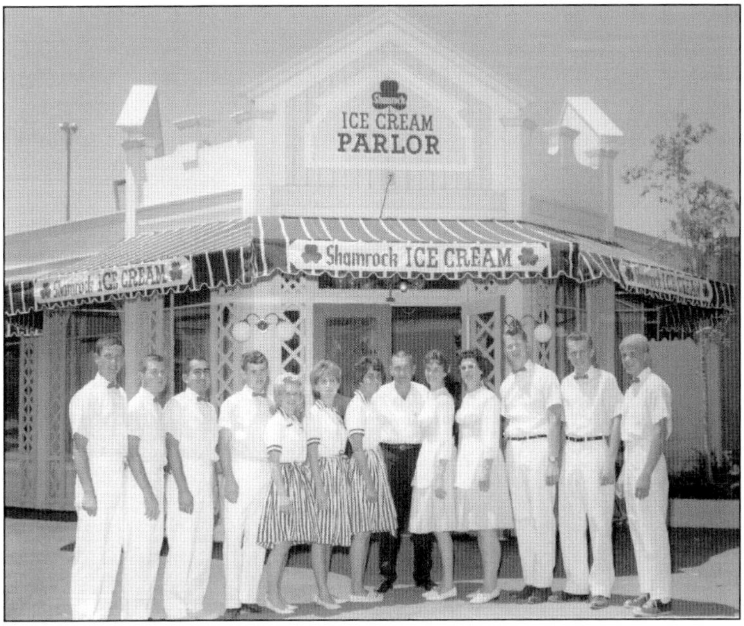

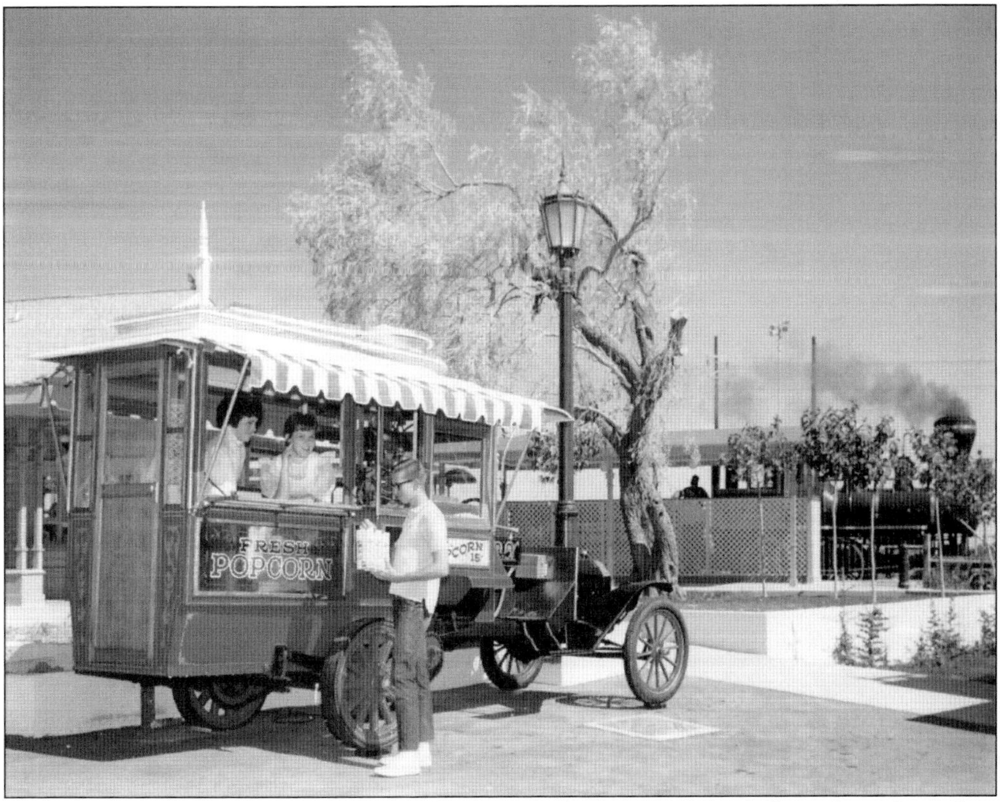

The mobile popcorn vendor trucks could be positioned at strategic points throughout the park as management dictated. The Iron Horse and train station can be seen in the immediate background of this photograph.

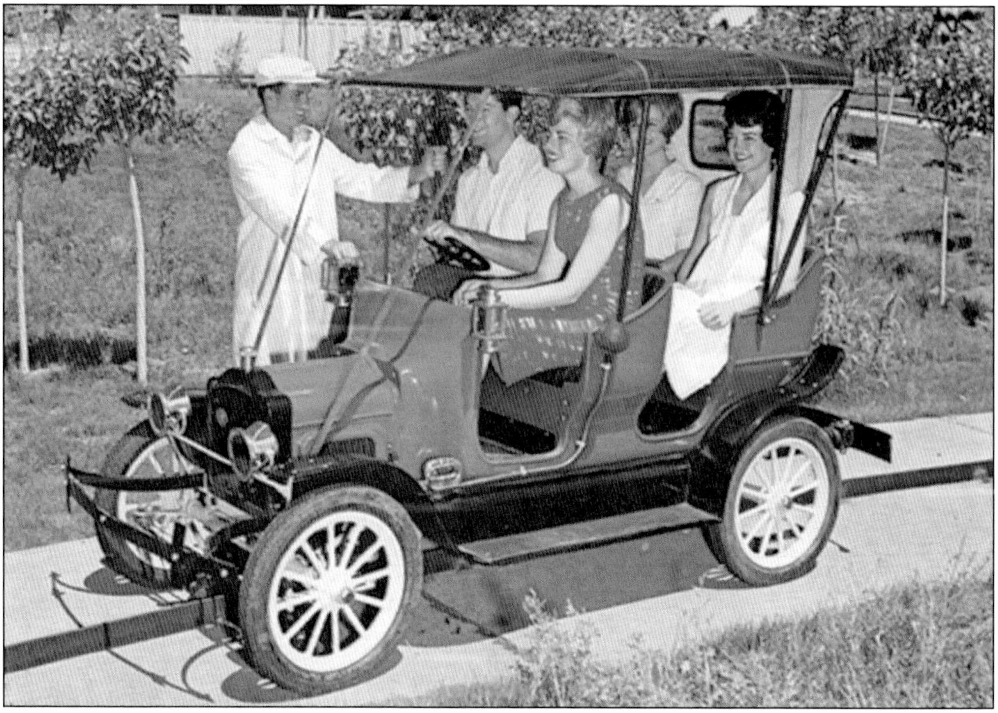

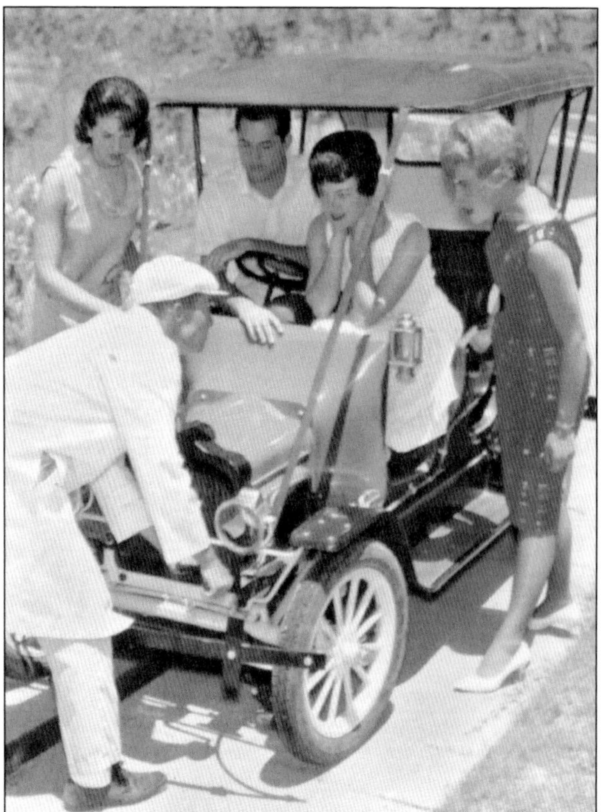

The Antique Car Ride was unquestionably the most popular attraction in the Gay '90s section. Safely tethered to a concrete track, the cars were real, functioning automobiles manufactured by Arrow Development Co. of Mountain View, California. One consequence of the ride's popularity, however, was constant wear and tear, and the cars regularly required expensive repairs.

Johnny Franklin was a prolific Phoenix photographer who captured extraordinary images of local entertainers and popular musicians of the 1960s as they rolled through town. His photographs of Wallace and Ladmo cavorting at Legend City were later used to create a popular coloring book. Gerald, the spoiled brat from the television show, displays his penchant for mischief, leaking air out of an antique car occupied by his oblivious pals Ladmo (left) and Wallace (right). (Courtesy of the Johnny Franklin collection.)

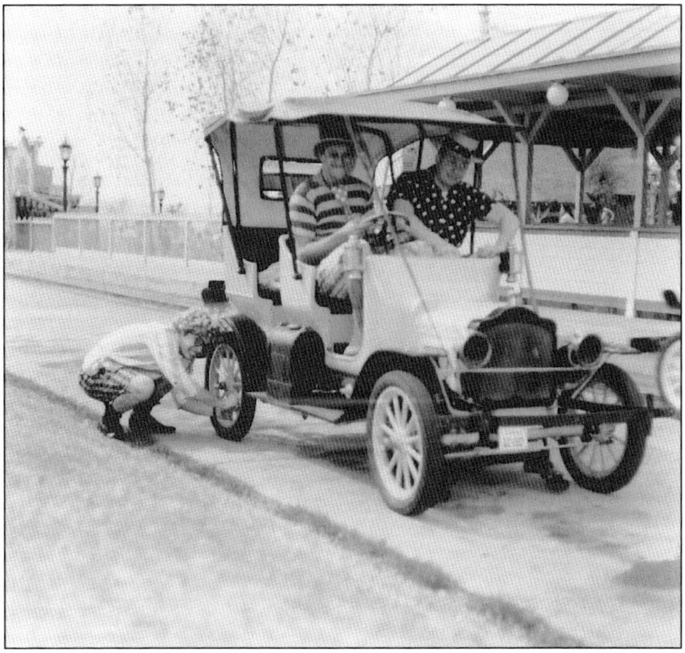

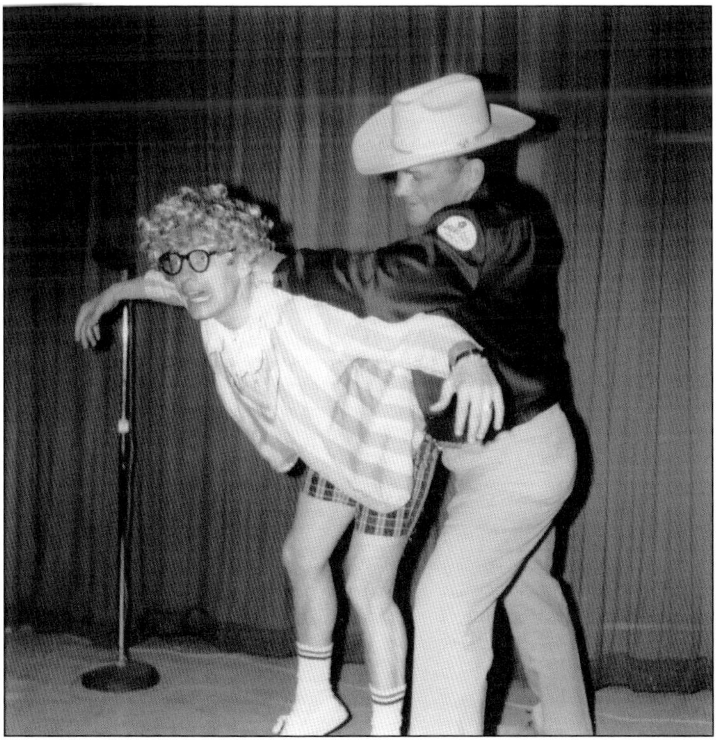

It is difficult now to properly convey the unmitigated pandemonium that was unleashed when the character of Gerald would appear during the Wallace and Ladmo stage shows. Kids went absolutely bonkers, and more than a few were determined to actually physically attack Gerald. The management at Legend City quickly learned to have security guards assigned to protect Pat McMahon. Here, a Legend City security guard is showing Gerald to the exit. (Courtesy of the Johnny Franklin collection.)

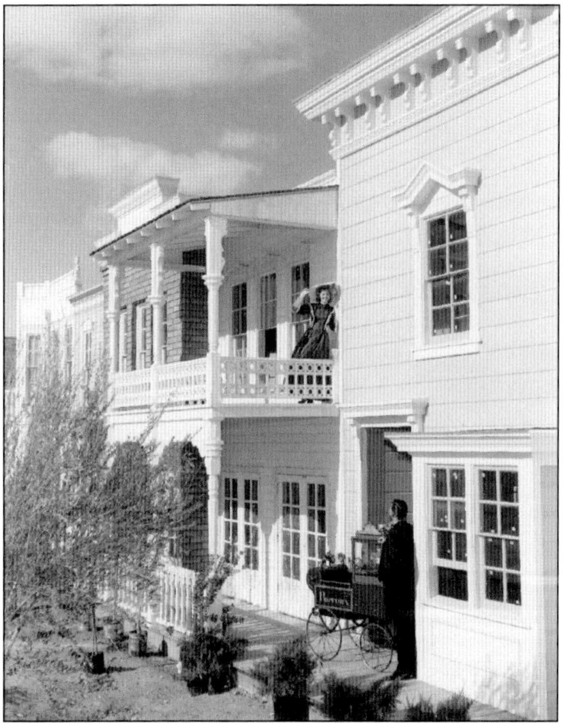

These Victorian-style buildings in the Gay '90s section near the park entrance originally housed various administrative offices and living quarters for select park executives. Posed promotional shots, like this one, were created around the time of the park's opening to emphasize the romantic, turn-of-the-century feel of the Gay '90s section.

The House of Sweets candy shop was located next door to the Legend City Theatre nickelodeon. It offered a variety of sweet treats, including caramel corn, cheese corn, dates, preserves, peanut brittle, and fudge. Note the rather elaborate chandelier hanging from the ceiling.

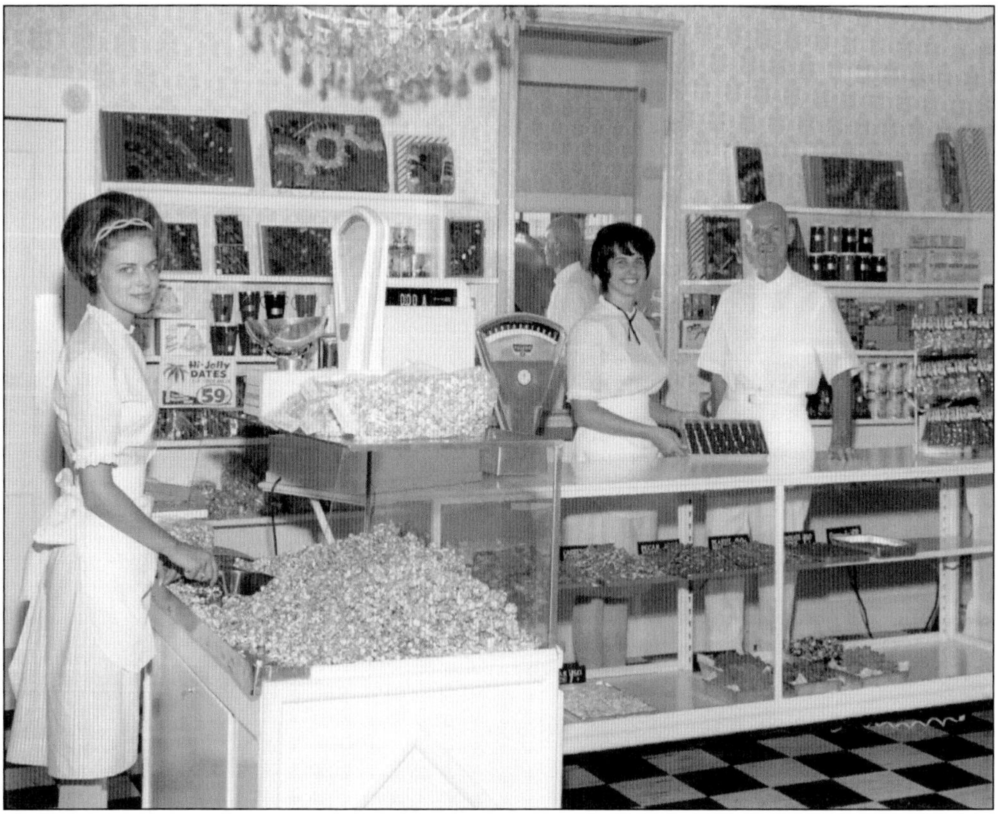

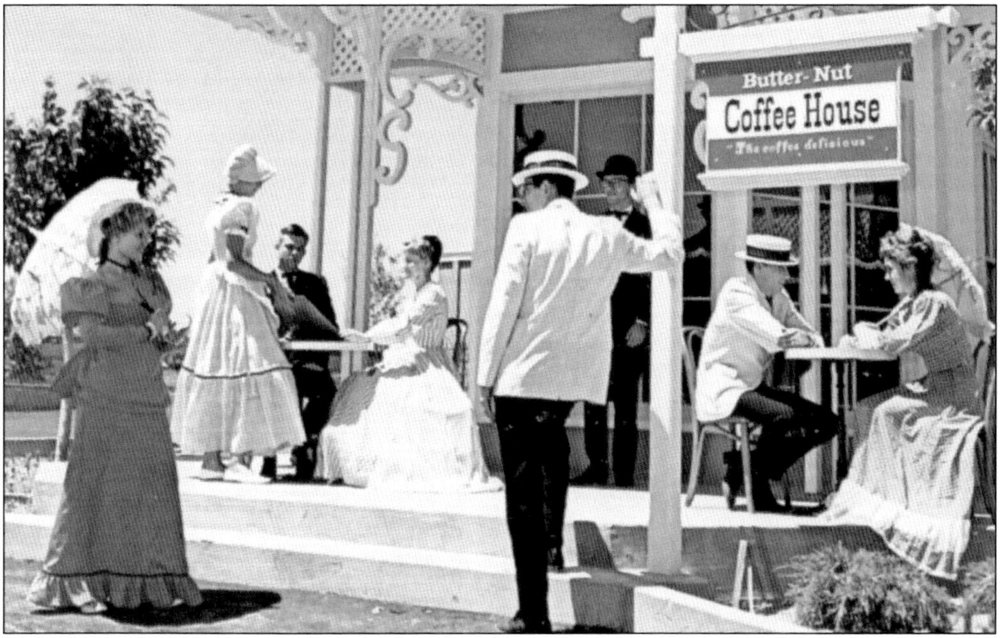

The quaint Butter-Nut Coffee House was located near the lagoon amphitheater on the far west end of the Gay '90s section. Here, Legend City sold its own special blend of Butter-Nut coffee, which was a popular brand of the day. The coffeehouse also served freshly baked pastries. In the postcard photograph above, the Copper Tones and can-can girls from the Golden Palace Saloon strike various poses in front of the coffeehouse. Below, Printy Crandall strolls by the establishment, shading herself with a parasol.

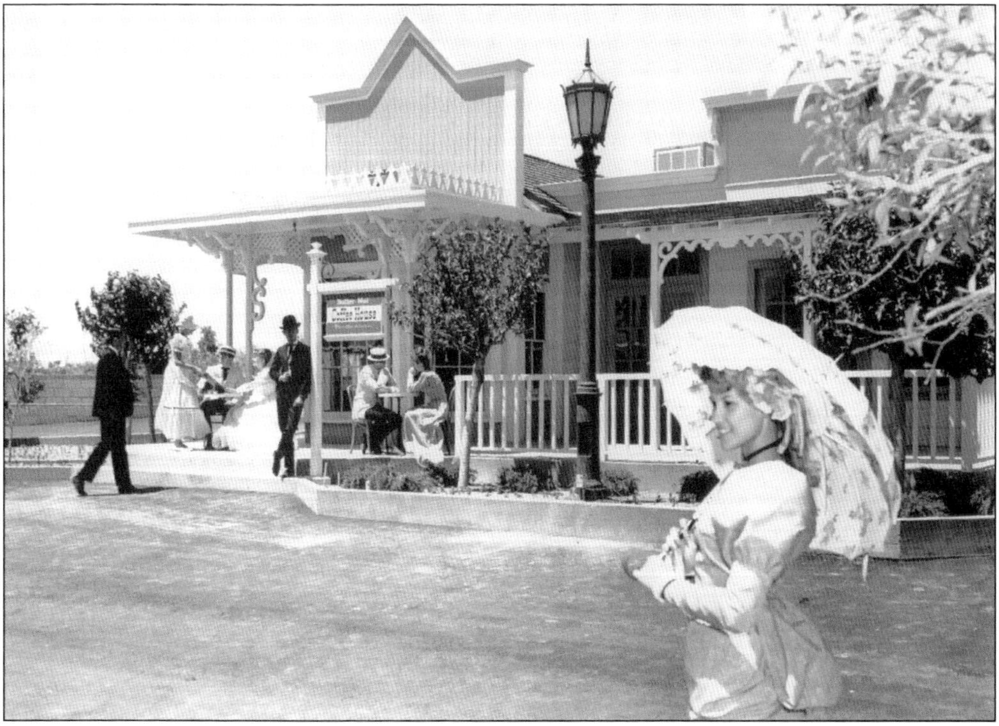

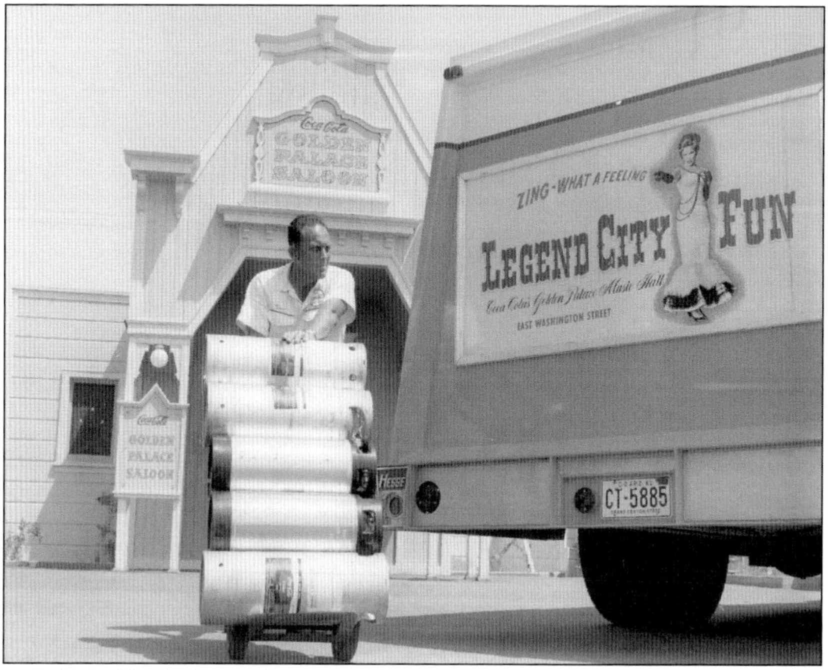

The Coca-Cola Golden Palace Saloon was at the entrance to the Boom Town section of Legend City, and it quickly emerged as the most popular attraction in the early days of the park. Coca-Cola's sponsorship of the saloon was useful in assuring nervous parents that nothing stronger than soda pop would be served in the venue, keeping with Crandall's vision of a family fun park. Entertainment at the Golden Palace was comprised of a more or less continuous frontier variety show that routinely packed the venue. The above photograph shows a delivery of soda being made to the saloon. Below, the original saloon cast and crew pose at the bar.

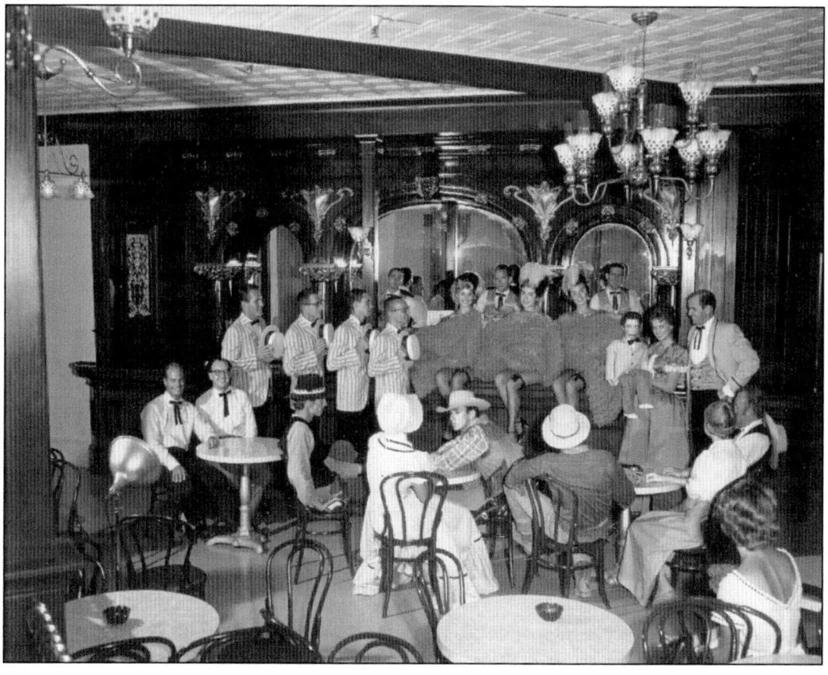

Crandall hired his friend, West High School music teacher Serge Huff, to manage the musical productions at both the Golden Palace Saloon and Lagoon Amphitheater. With a sharp eye for talent, Huff brought in superb performers, including future Miss America Vonda Kay Van Dyke. She performed at the Golden Palace as both singer and ventriloquist, talents she would hone there and then display to great effect in beauty pageants. At right, Van Dyke performs onstage in 1963 with her mannequin pal Kurley-Q. Below, she sings for an enchanted saloon audience. Vonda Kay Van Dyke was crowned Miss America in 1965.

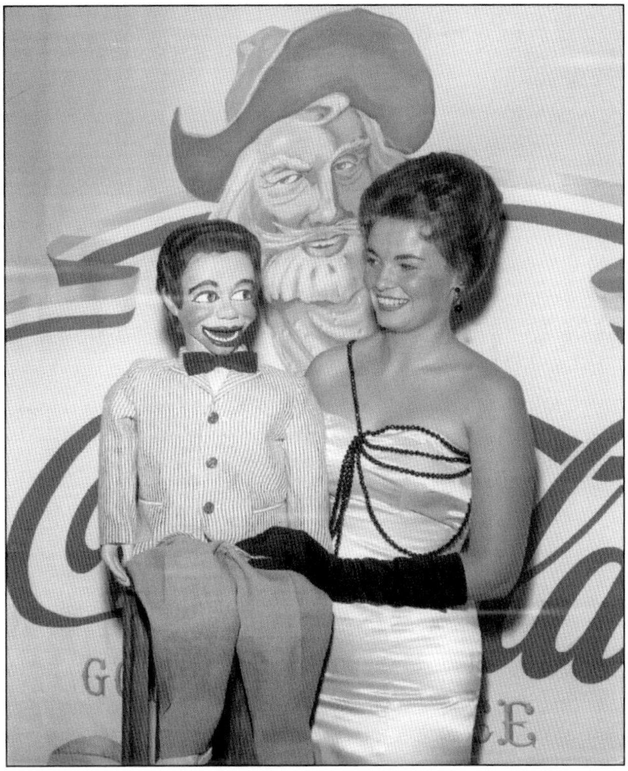

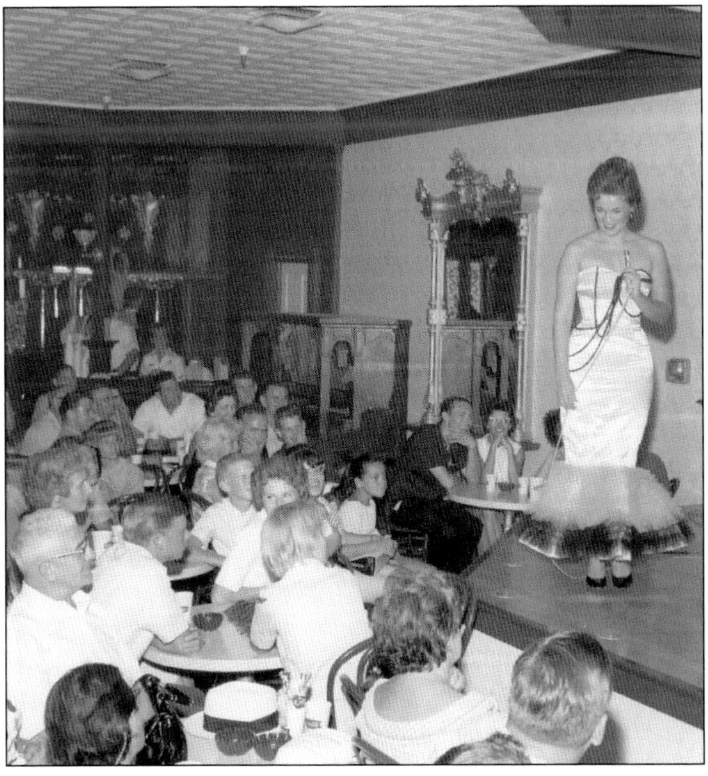

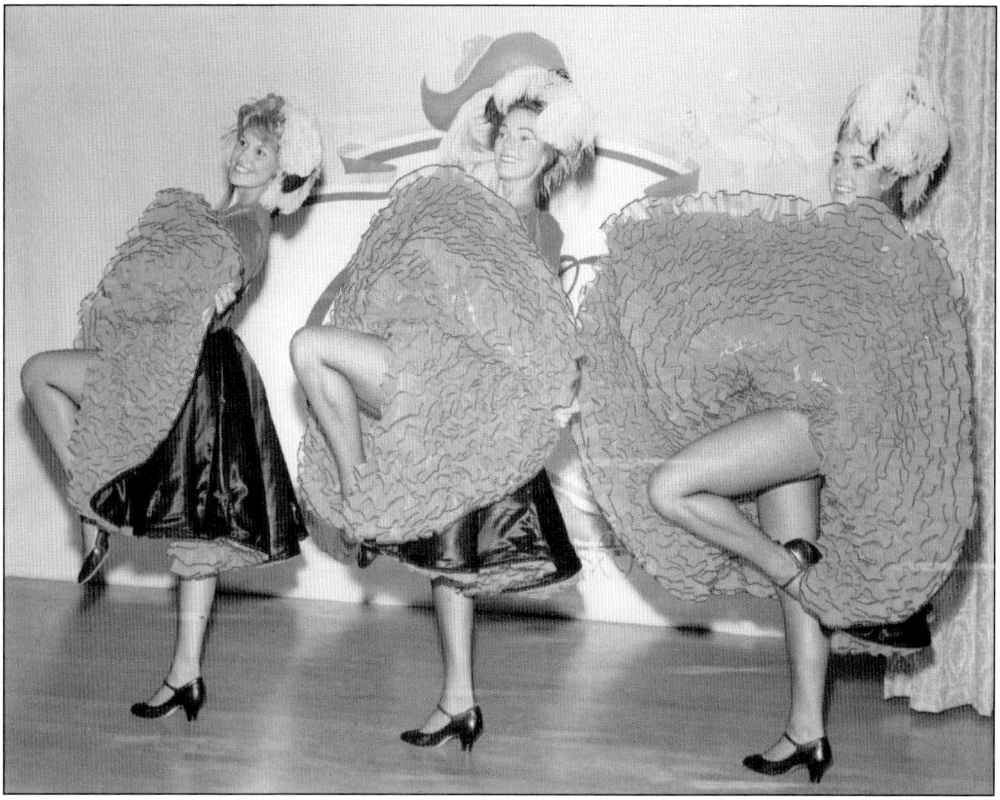

The Golden Palace can-can dancers run through their routine. Prior to the park's opening, Serge Huff hired Clair Folk, co-owner and operator of the Folk School of Dance in East Phoenix, to stage and choreograph the amphitheater show and to supply can-can dancers from his studio for the Golden Palace show. Leila Parriot created the costumes for the can-can dancers as well as for the amphitheater show. With the assistance of her daughter, Parriot came up with gorgeous costumes, often on very short notice, including Sandy Gibbon's period coat and Vonda Kay Van Dyke's dresses. Shown here are, from left to right, Printy Crandall, Donna Caferty, and Linda Warner.

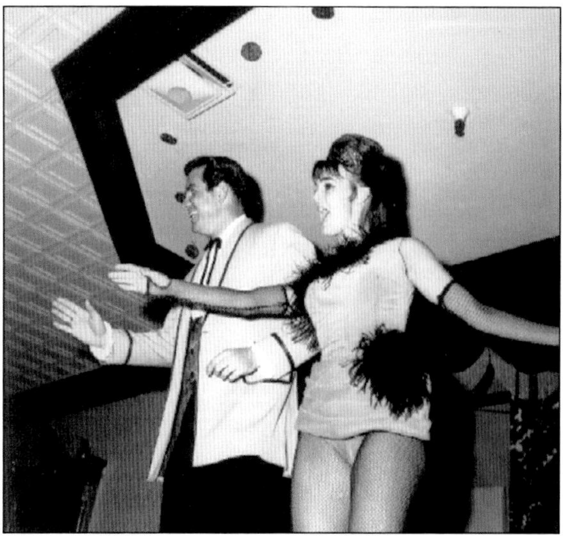

Sandy Gibbons, a local radio personality, signed on as emcee at the Golden Palace, bringing a raucous charm to the proceedings. He often entertained the crowd with the assistance of sidekick Sandra Dirickson (right). Sandy also starred on the Golden Palace stage as the villain in a half-hour version of the classic melodrama *The Drunkard*. In the first six months of park operations, the frontier variety show gave 95 performances at the Golden Palace, to about 200,000 people. (Courtesy of Nanci Keener.)

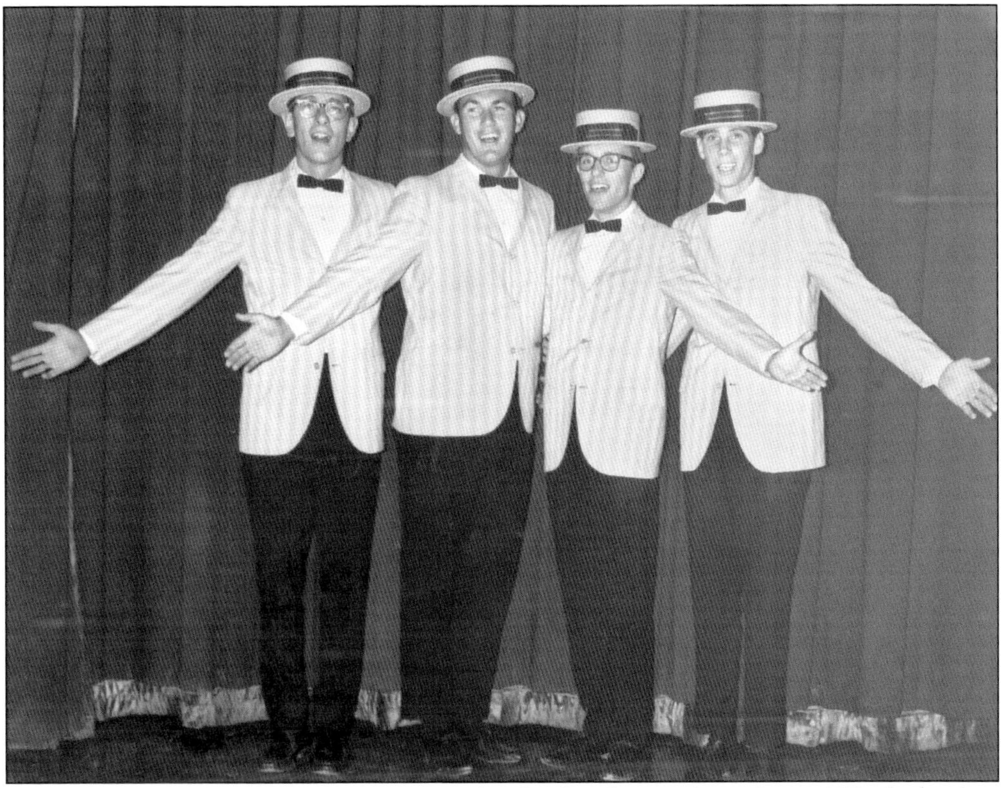

Serge Huff recruited some of his own West High School students to form a Legend City barbershop quartet called the Copper Tones. The Tones performed 477 shows at the Golden Palace and made several appearances at the Lagoon Amphitheater. The Copper Tones' forte was slapstick comedy, and their musical repertoire included popular tunes like "Lida Rose," "In the Good Old Summertime," and "Goodbye My Legend City Baby." Shown in both photographs are, from left to right, Dave Zorn, Pat Lebs, Rick Mitchell, and Jack Hanf. (Courtesy of Rick Mitchell.)

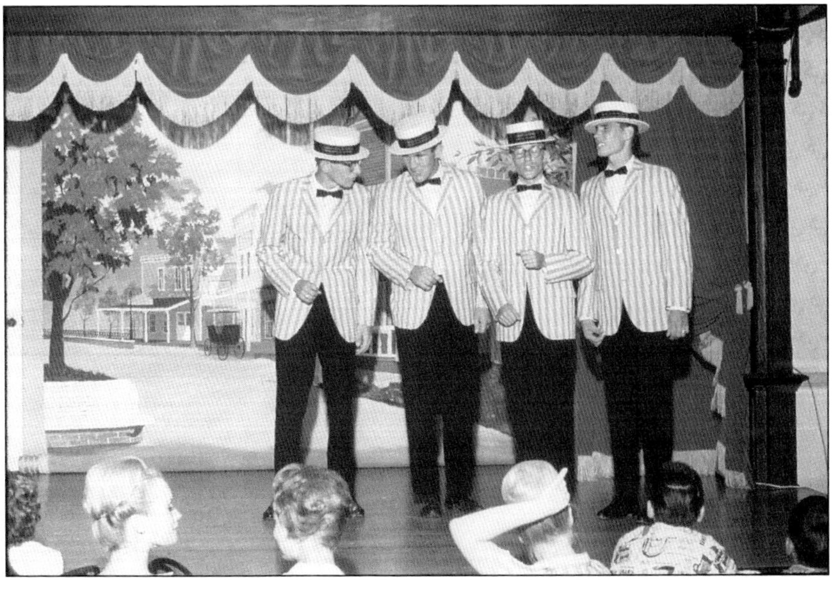

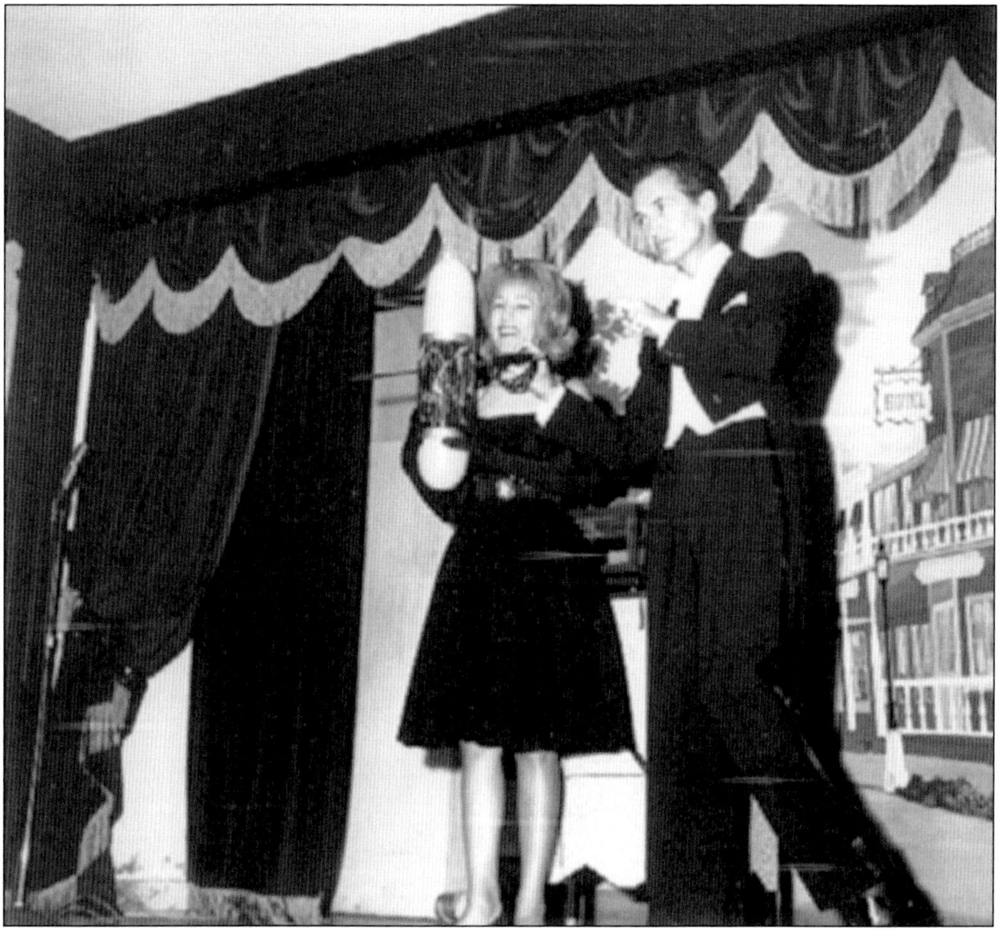

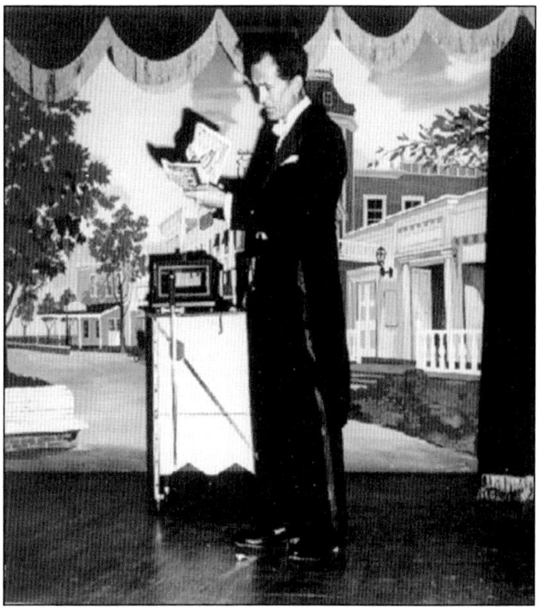

Ed and Nanci Keener performed their magic act at Legend City during the second season of shows at the Golden Palace. The pair perfected their "Summer Magic" show by giving four to five performances an evening, six nights a week. Ed Keener invented an original method for shooting a silk into a balloon and created other original effects that made the act genuinely unique. Ed made good use of a Phoenix magic shop founded by Bert Easley, a retired vaudevillian magician. Easley's also proved to be an ideal environment for making new friends in magic and giving a boost to the Keeners' dreams. After Legend City, the Keeners crossed the Atlantic and enjoyed a fabulous career in Europe, giving 7,621 performances during 21 years of nonstop work. (Courtesy of Nanci Keener.)

The Copper Tones departed Legend City after the first season and were replaced by a somewhat older barbershop quartet called the Devilaires. To make extra money, the quartet doubled as waiters for the Golden Palace patrons, hence the trays they are all holding as they belt out a number in this photograph. (Courtesy of Nanci Keener.)

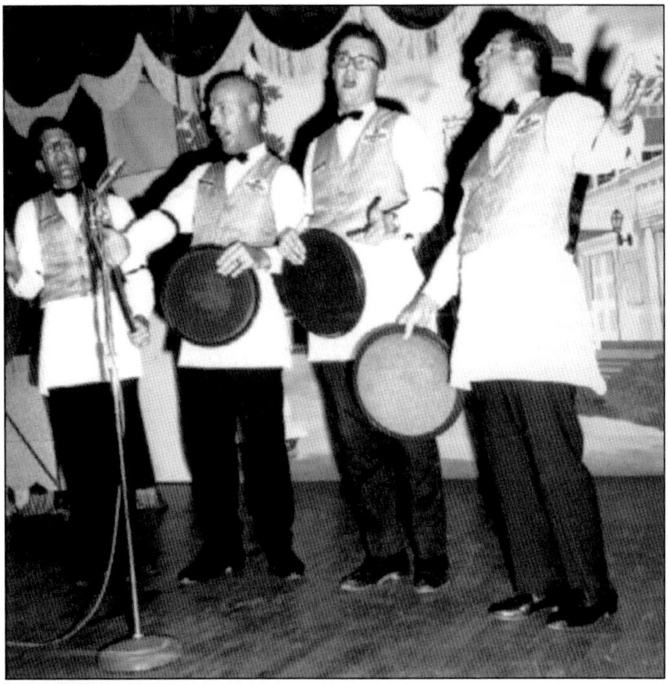

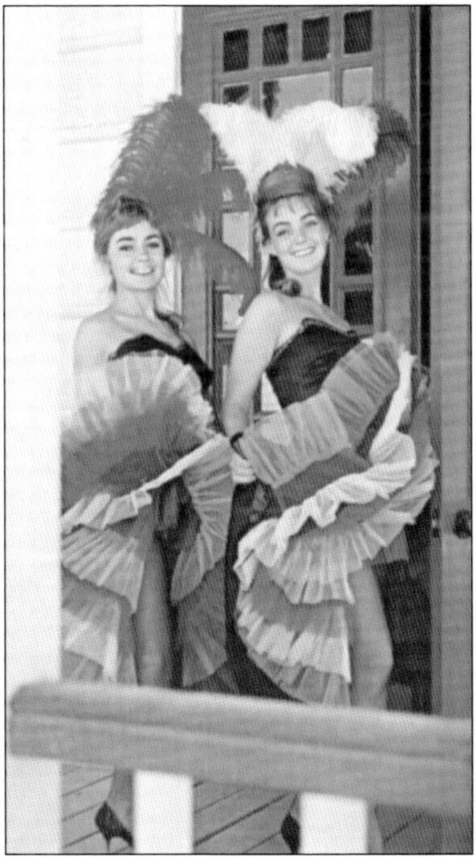

The Golden Palace Saloon girls, evocative of the roaring boom towns of Arizona's mining days, also helped out with the serving of food and drink at the saloon. Here, a pair of smiling saloon girls poses for a postcard photograph on the porch outside the establishment.

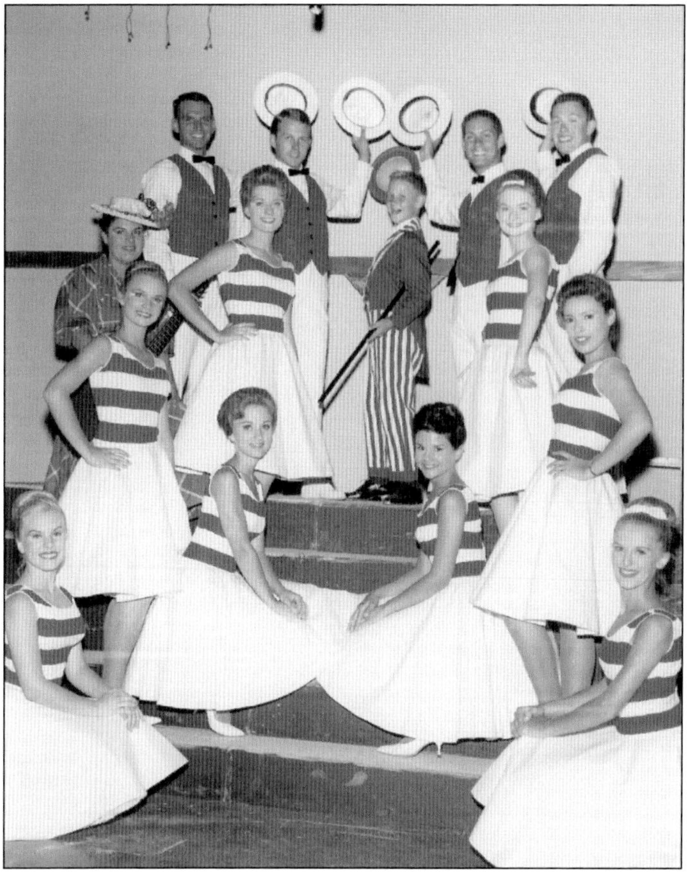

The Lagoon Amphitheater show was originally a light-hearted play with music interspersed throughout. Playwright Tim Kelly wrote the play around the musical numbers that Serge Huff selected. However, cast members soon became dissatisfied with the show, and after two weeks, the format was changed into a variety show. The performers changed often, as family vacations and other job opportunities arose. Shown here is an early lineup of the amphitheater show cast.

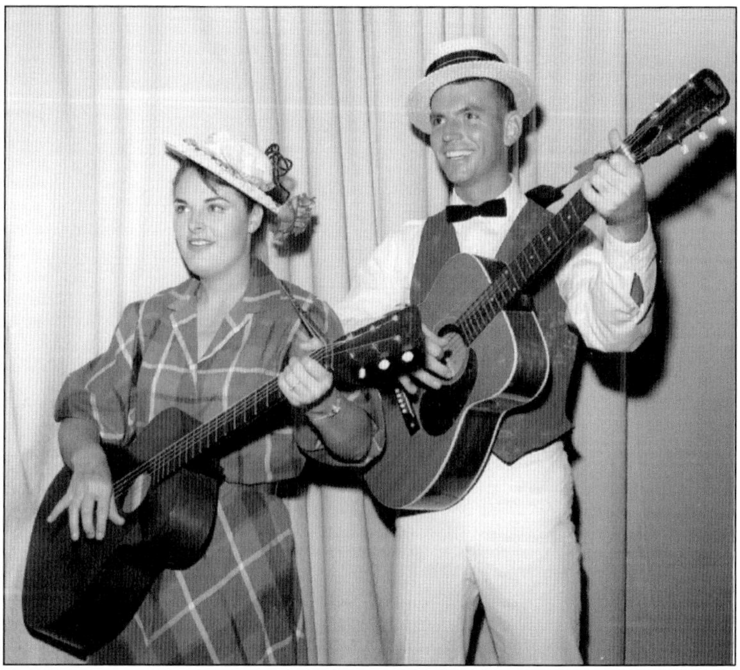

Ed Humphrey (right) was featured in an exceptional folk music segment of the Lagoon Amphitheater variety show. He was active in musicals at Arizona State University at the time, and later performed in Las Vegas as a singer and dancer. By the fall of 1963, the amphitheater variety show had been replaced by the Wallace and Ladmo stage shows, which would entertain crowds at Legend City for the next 20 years.

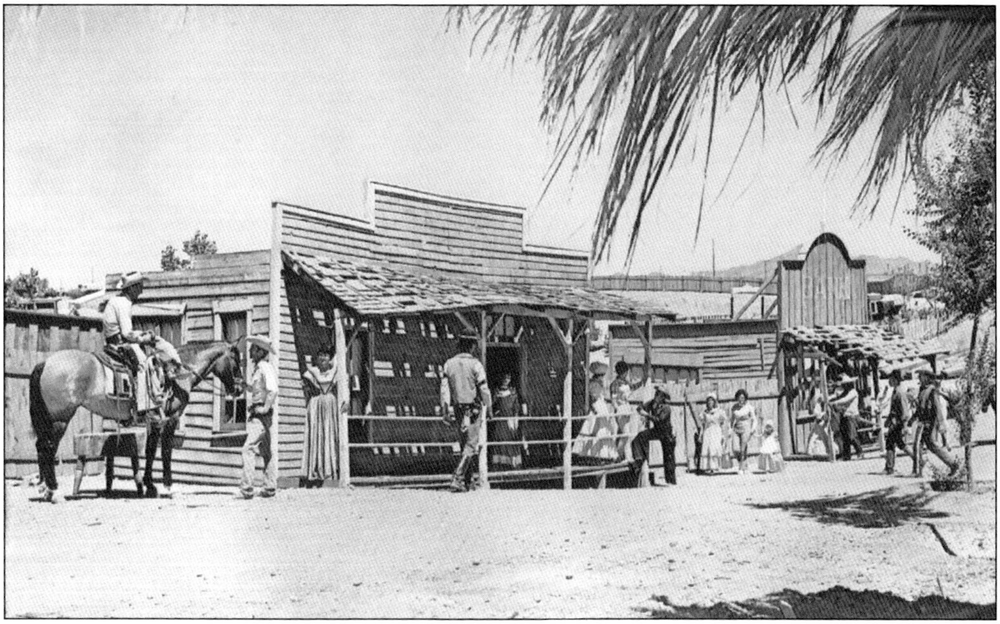

Gunfights and bank robberies were commonplace events in the Boom Town section of Legend City. Also known as the Western section, the area is shown above during an unusual moment of peace and calm. The law in these parts was naturally the stalwart sheriff of Legend City, constantly on call to thwart bank robberies and shoot the outlaws dead. As seen below, the sheriff's office was conveniently located near the Boom Town bank and featured a "Desert Cooler" to hold the bad guys. The Legend City sky ride looms in the background at left.

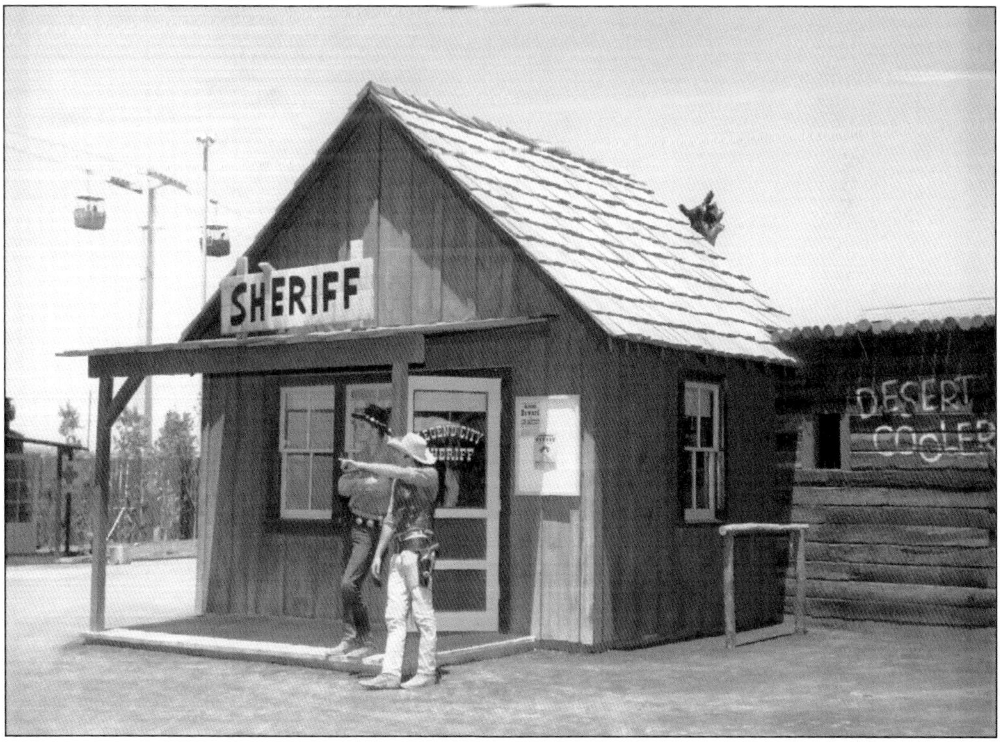

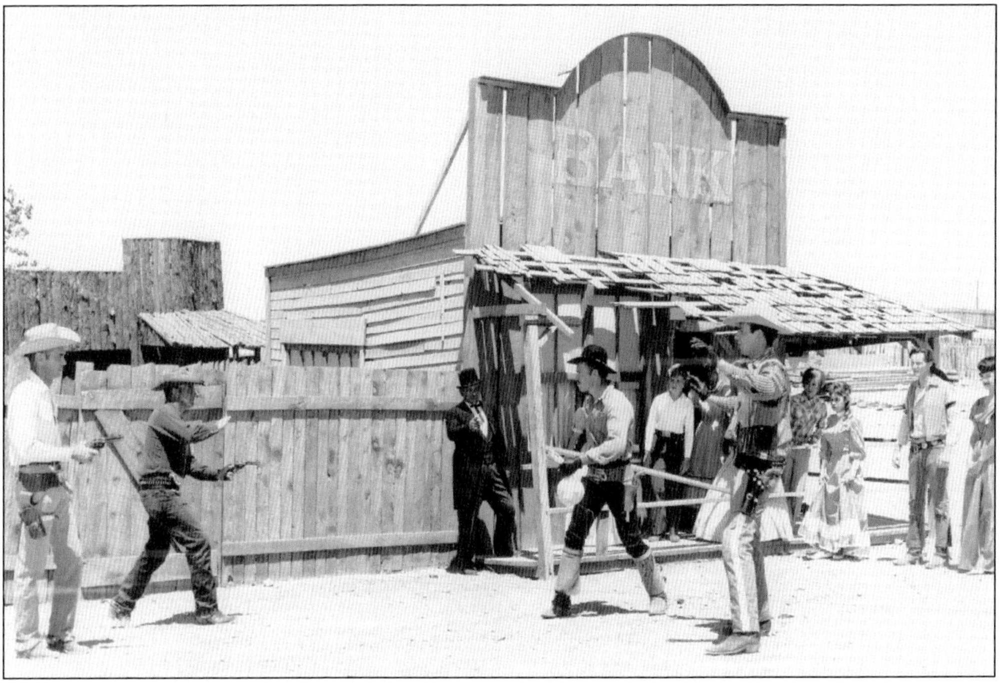

The park employed five stuntmen, most with Hollywood film experience, to liven up the Boom Town section with assorted shoot-outs, bank robberies, attempted train robberies, and attacks on the Indian Village, all of course amazingly unsuccessful. In the above photograph, a crowd gathers in somewhat precarious vicinity to an imminent gunfight between the sheriff and deputy (left) and two desperate bank robbers (right). These things never ended very well for the bank robbers, as shown below. The robberies, gunfights, and other nefarious activities ran continuously throughout the day and into the evening.

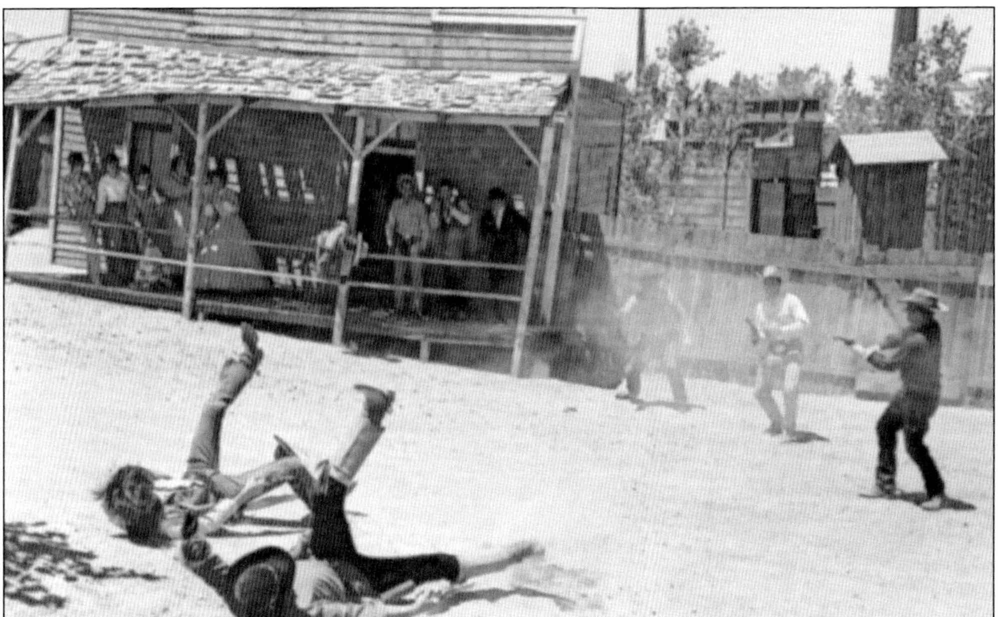

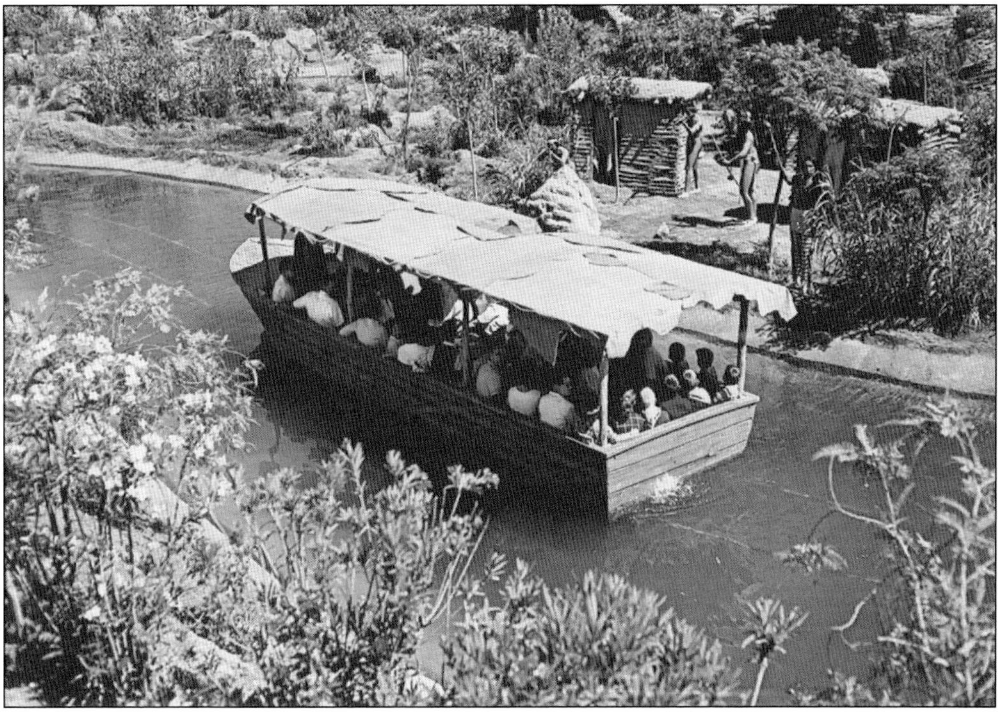

Located near the gateway to the Boom Town section, the River of Legends ride was a centerpiece attraction at Legend City. The boat ride offered visitors scenes of Indian warfare, prehistoric beasts, earthquakes, falling boulders, magical caves, and narrow escapes. The visitors were ultimately safely returned to civilization. Here, a riverboat full of passengers floats peacefully by an Indian village early in the ride.

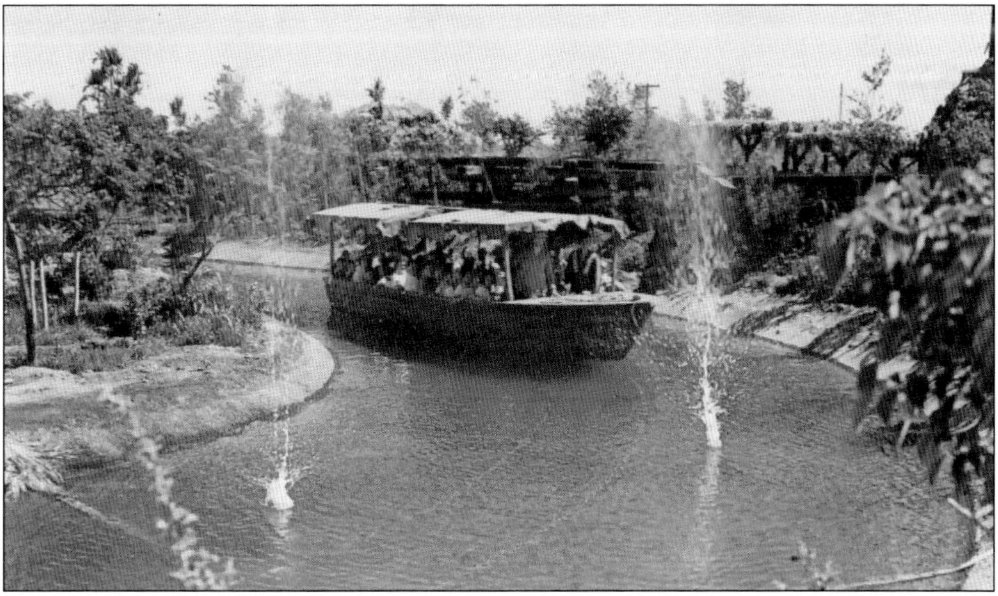

The original river ride showcased a fairly violent gun battle between Indians and Conquistadors. Here, the river scout tries desperately to maneuver his boat as gunfire erupts and perilous cannon fire explodes in the water all around.

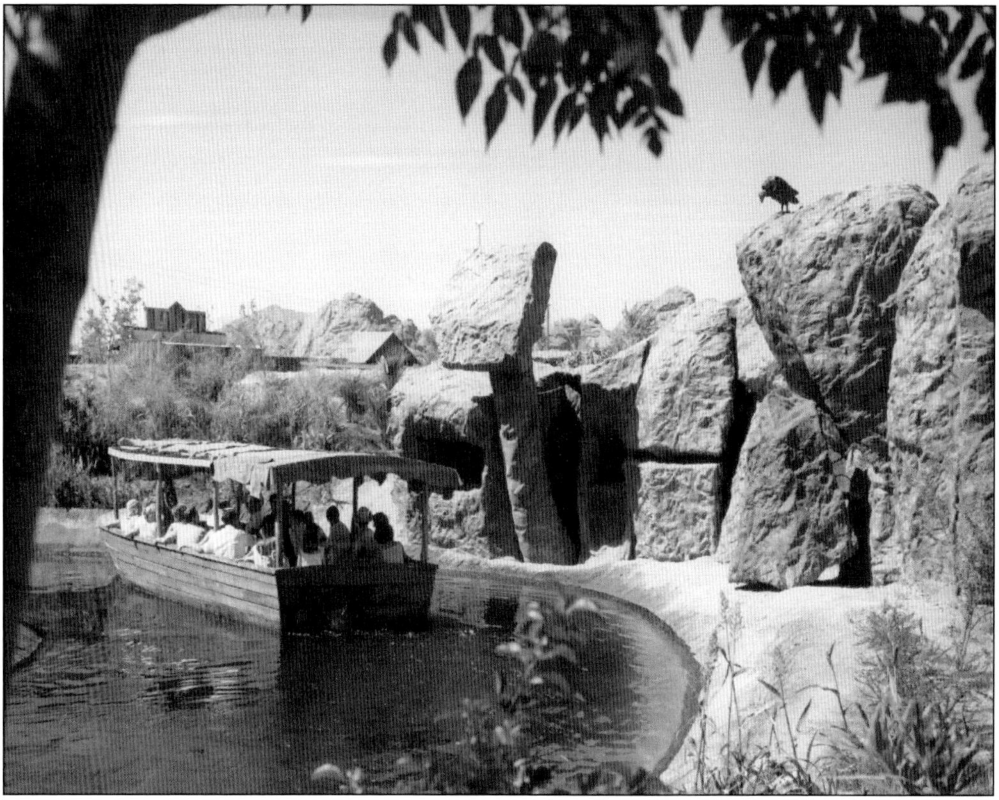

The riverboat approaches a strange canyon rock formation, and a rumbling sound effect warns that all is not well. Earthquake! The walls shake violently, assisted by a loud soundtrack and the river guide's animated delivery over the public address system. A large, precariously perched stone tipples and begins to fall toward the boat, and other stones push out toward the river, as if they are about to give way. At the last second, the boat passes safely by.

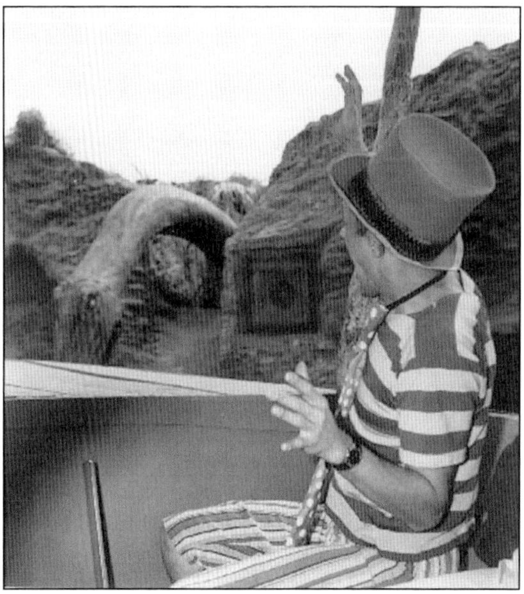

Oddly enough, the river ride earthquake scenario originally featured a fearsome dinosaur head that emerged over the rocks and menaced the passing riverboat. The implication was that the dinosaur's approach was the cause of the earthquake. The maintenance and mechanics of the dinosaur head proved to be problematic, however, and the effect was abandoned within a few years. In this photograph, Ladmo is startled by the appearance of the prehistoric beast. (Courtesy of the Johnny Franklin collection.)

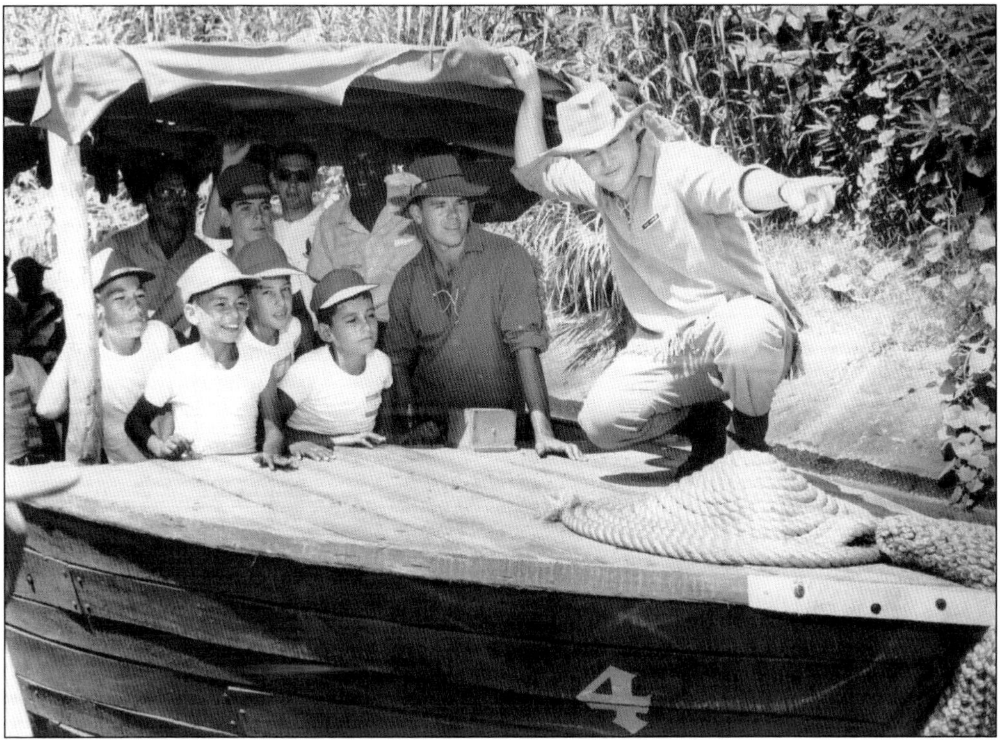

The trusty guides on the River of Legends ride were responsible for performing two essential duties: ensuring the safety of the passengers aboard the riverboat, and delivering a highly emotive narration of the amazing events occurring all around. In this photograph, the river guide alerts the passengers to a mysterious waterfall lying dead ahead.

The riverboat slowly approaches the strange waterfall, which gives way at the last moment to expose the entrance to a dark and foreboding cave. The interior of the haunted cave evolved over the years, with different apparitions and eerie lighting effects employed to achieve varying degrees of spookiness.

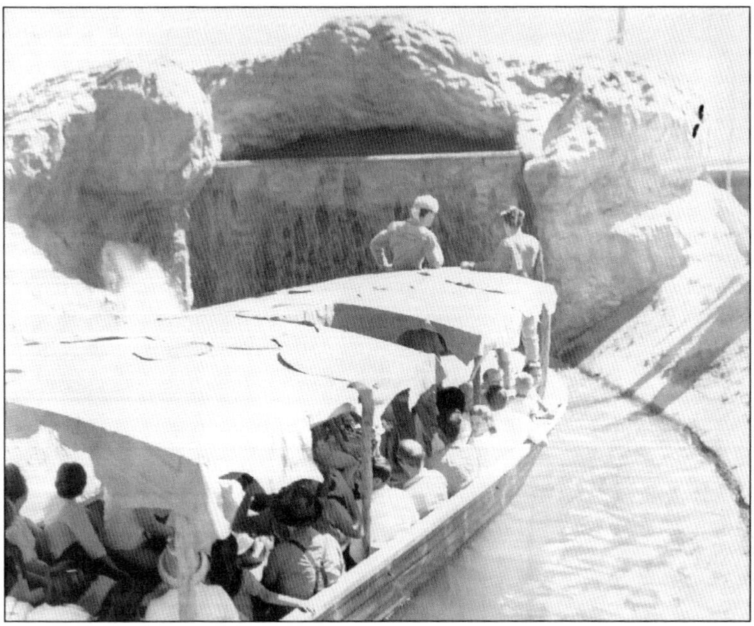

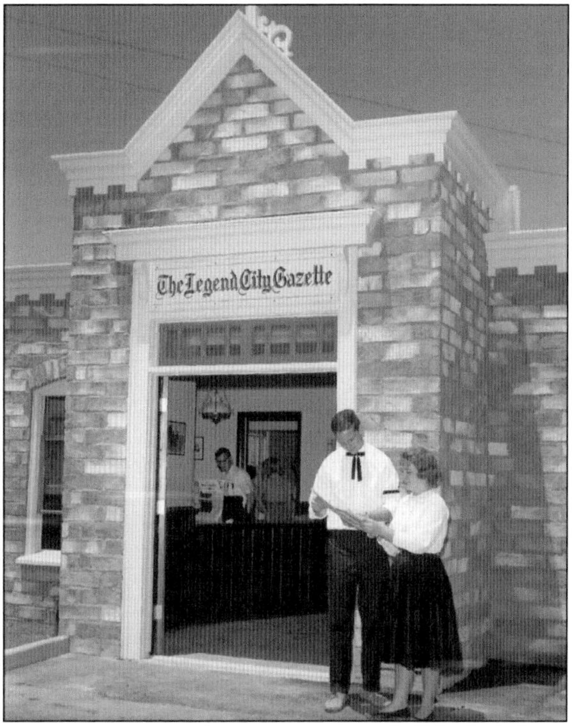

Boom Town had its very own printing facility, an enterprise near and dear to Louis Crandall's heart. The park newspaper was printed and distributed at this location, along with an assortment of other printed souvenirs, such as maps and wanted posters. Louis's brother Don originally ran the Legend City print shop, and, many years later, Louis would open his own historical printing museum in Provo. At left, two print-shop employees stand outside the office, admiring the latest issue of the *Legend City Gazette*. Meanwhile, inside the shop (below), a strangely smiling pair of employees is held at gunpoint by none other than Don Crandall. Note the Chic Albertson map on the front of the counter.

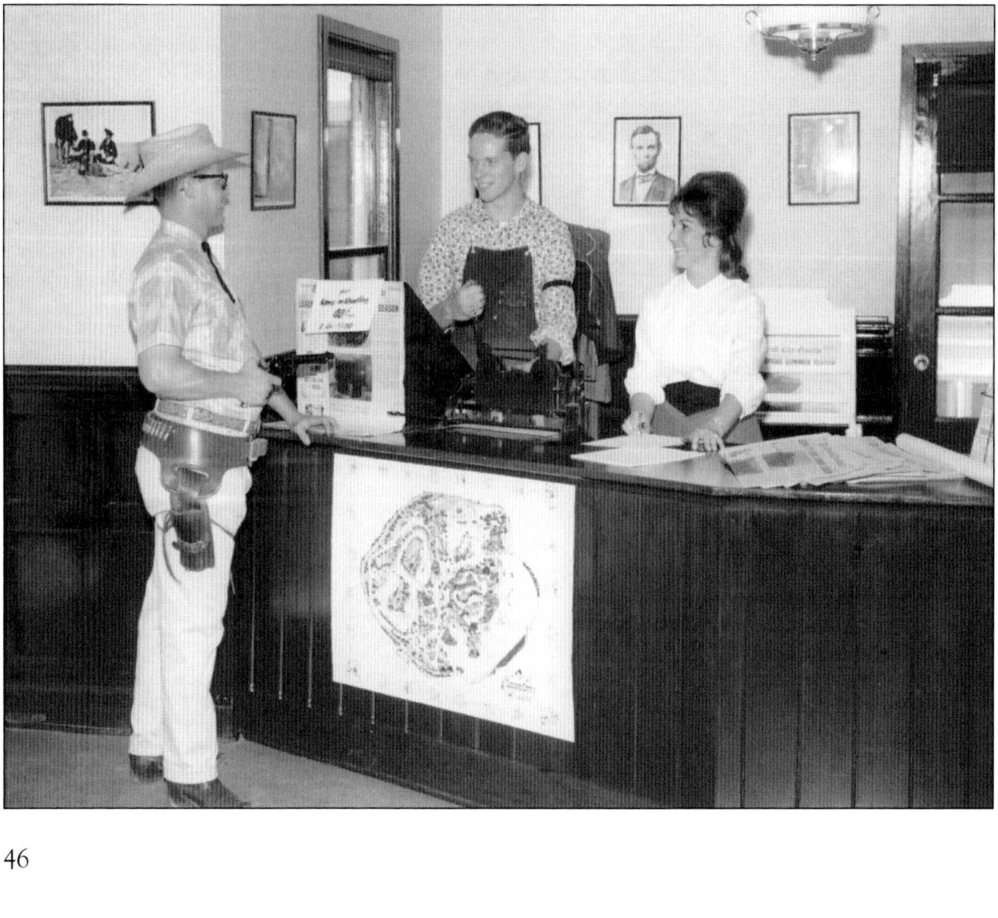

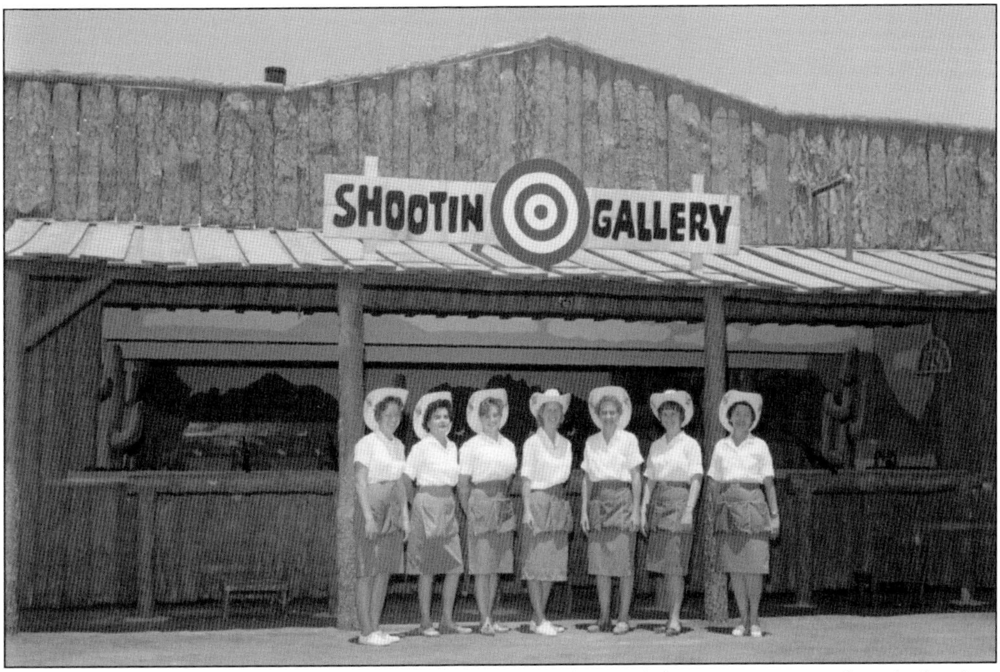

The all-female staff of the Shootin' Gallery poses in front of their amusement during the first season of Legend City. The gallery was located on the cusp of the Boom Town and Ghost Town sections and drew a steady stream of aspiring marksmen. A second, smaller shooting gallery was located on the far west side of the park, near the Modern section.

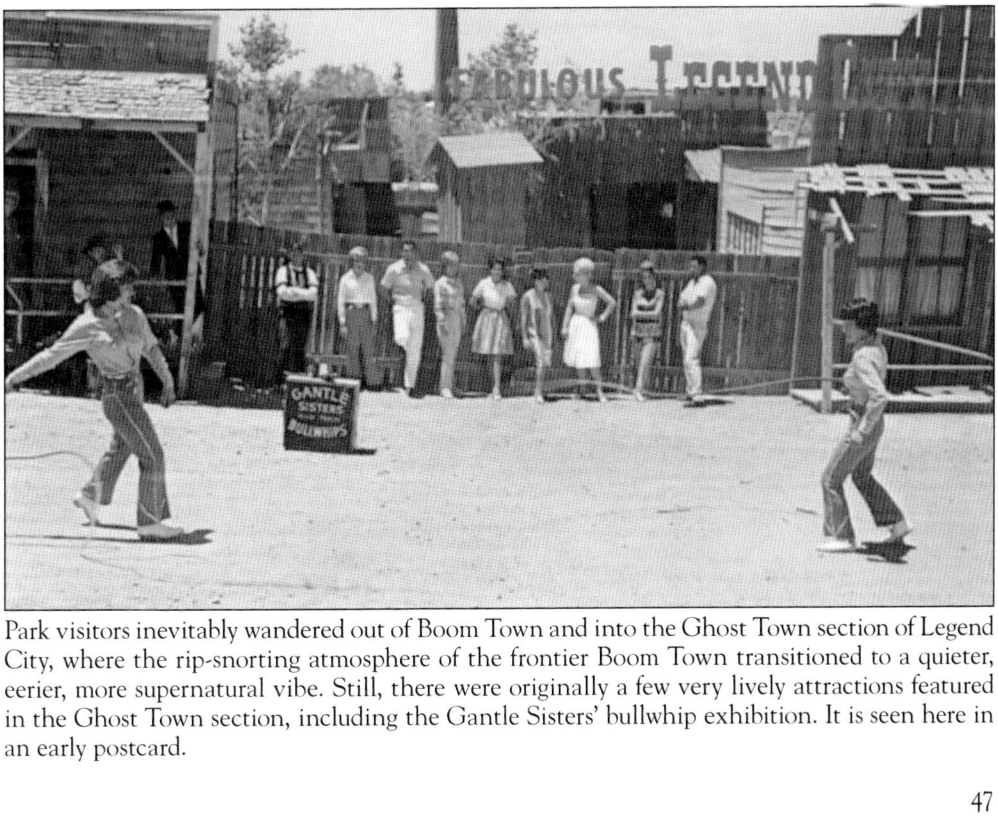

Park visitors inevitably wandered out of Boom Town and into the Ghost Town section of Legend City, where the rip-snorting atmosphere of the frontier Boom Town transitioned to a quieter, eerier, more supernatural vibe. Still, there were originally a few very lively attractions featured in the Ghost Town section, including the Gantle Sisters' bullwhip exhibition. It is seen here in an early postcard.

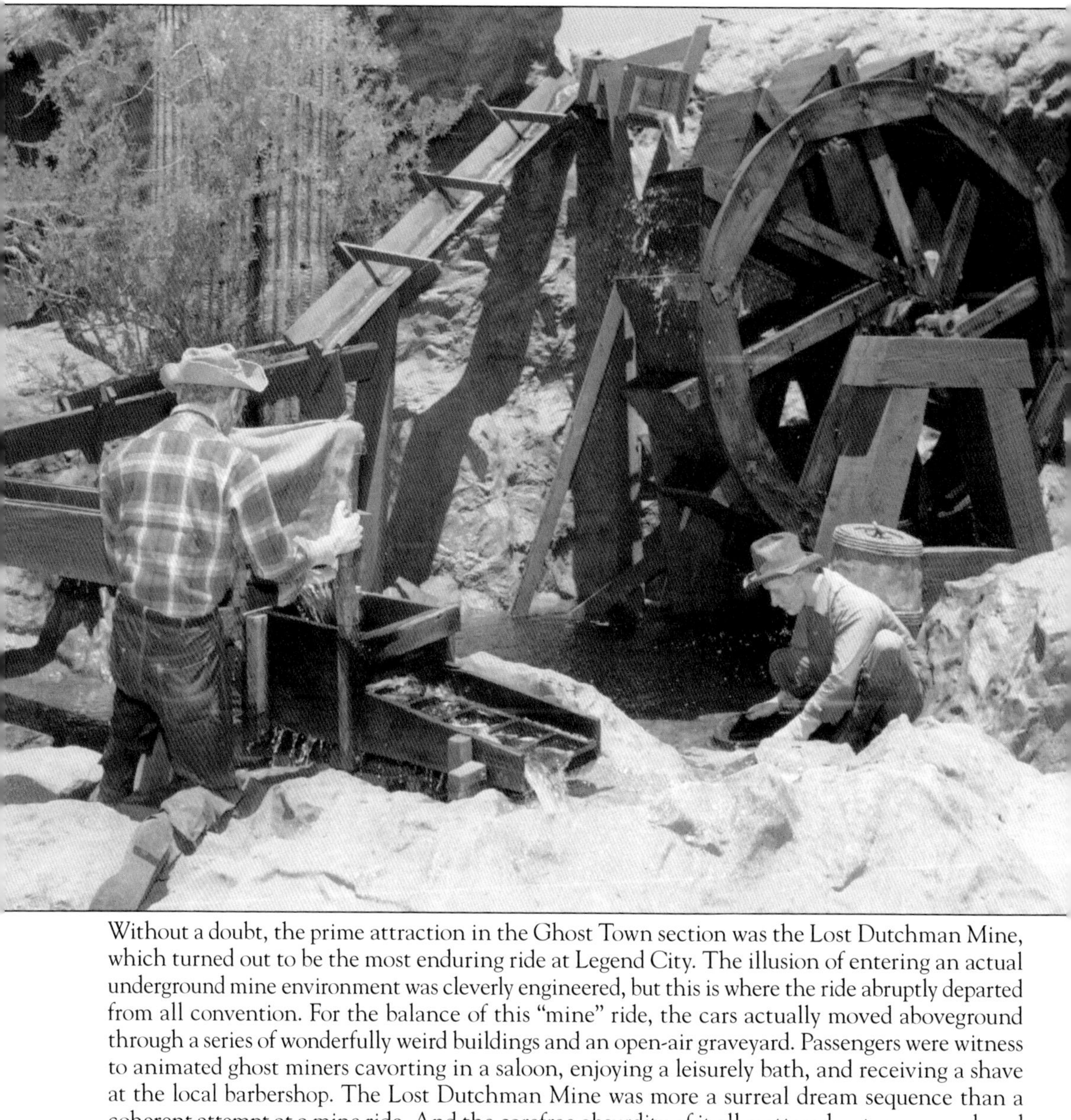

Without a doubt, the prime attraction in the Ghost Town section was the Lost Dutchman Mine, which turned out to be the most enduring ride at Legend City. The illusion of entering an actual underground mine environment was cleverly engineered, but this is where the ride abruptly departed from all convention. For the balance of this "mine" ride, the cars actually moved aboveground through a series of wonderfully weird buildings and an open-air graveyard. Passengers were witness to animated ghost miners cavorting in a saloon, enjoying a leisurely bath, and receiving a shave at the local barbershop. The Lost Dutchman Mine was more a surreal dream sequence than a coherent attempt at a mine ride. And the carefree absurdity of it all mattered not; everyone loved it. The mine ride was the only major attraction at Legend City that lasted for the full 20-year life of the park. While waiting in line for the ride, park visitors listened in on the dialogue of two animated miners (seen here) recounting the amazing tale of the Lost Dutchman.

The haunted mine was infested with animated skeletons. After departing the loading platform and passing through a pair of swinging doors, the mine car approaches a seated skeleton, poised to set off a dynamite charge. The ghostly miner depresses the plunger, the sound of an explosion is heard, and the walls of the mine tremble and shake. The walls now begin to collapse inward, and the ceiling shifts ever lower. Can you survive? The mine car swerves out of danger at the last moment, naturally. (Courtesy of Dick Kraus.)

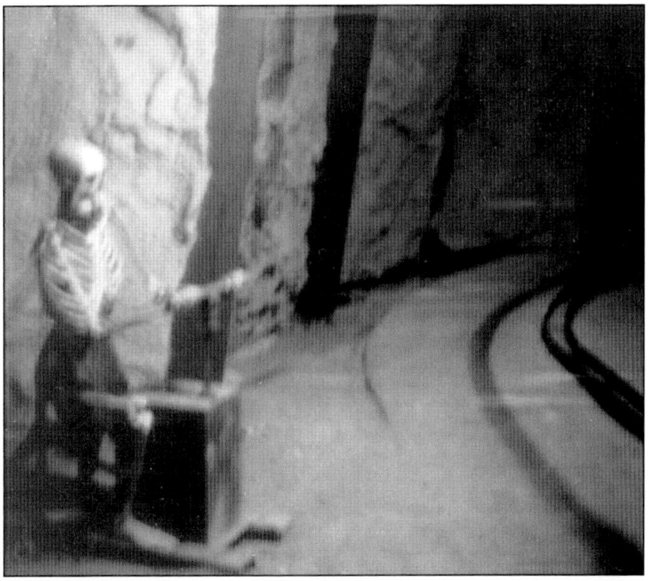

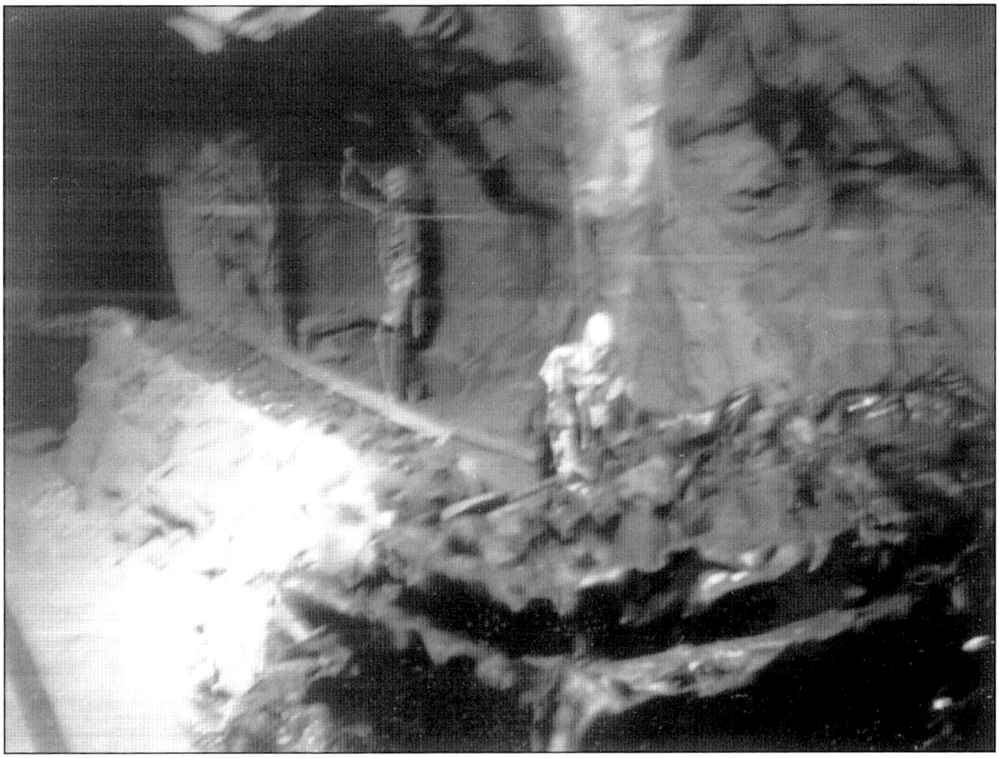

The mining car plunges farther downhill, makes a quick right U-turn, and comes upon two miners hard at work removing ore. One skeleton is using his pickax on the walls, and another scoops ore from the conveyer belt. To the right of the shoveling miner is a huge stalactite, dripping great amounts of water into a "reflecting pool" beneath. This scene, like many others, was illuminated with black light. With the addition of a few drops of Ivory soap, the water would glow an eerie bright white under the black light, with the added benefit that it would keep the recirculating pump lubricated. (Courtesy of Dick Kraus.)

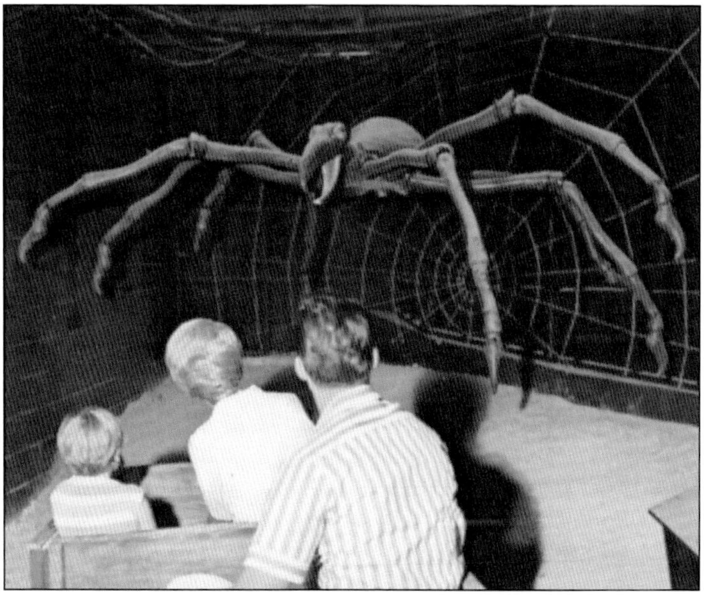

Suddenly, the passengers come face to face with a giant arachnid, touted as the "world's largest carnivorous spider." It is shown here terrorizing an innocent family. Animated with wires to move its legs, the spider guards a vast horde of gold bricks on the ground nearby. The spider was ultimately retired after a number of years, owing to the growing expense of its repair, maintenance, and deployment, a fate similar to the dinosaur head on the river ride.

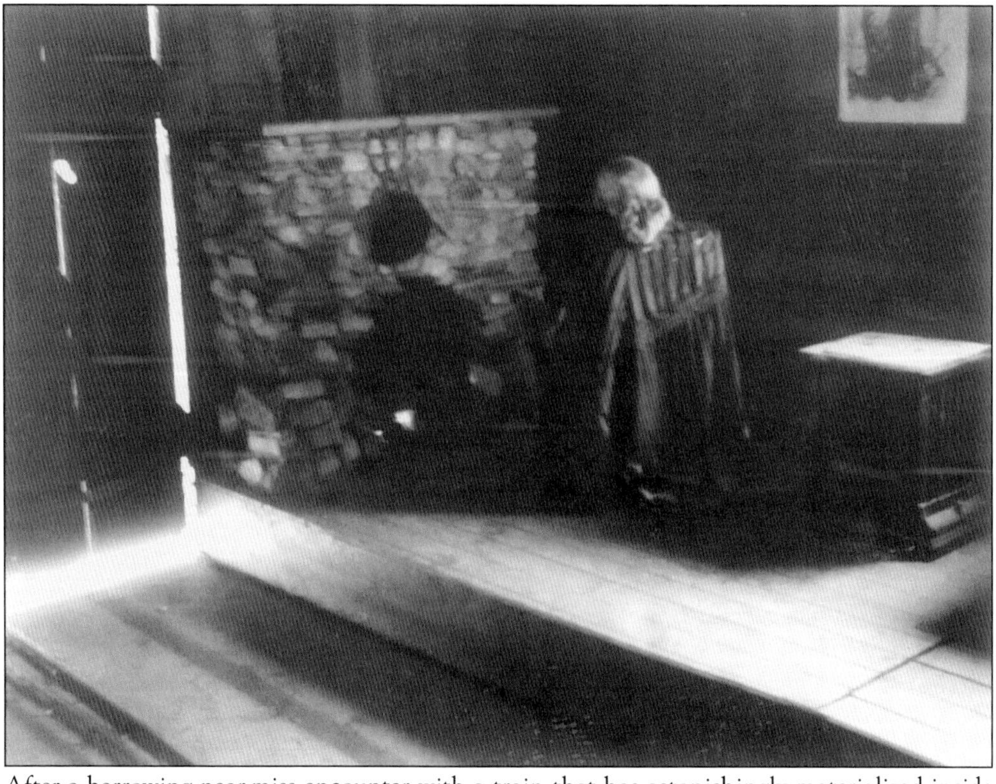

After a harrowing near-miss encounter with a train that has astonishingly materialized inside the underground mine, the ore car lurches to the right, slows, and approaches a seemingly sedate parlor scene. Here, a solitary figure seated in a rocking chair gazes serenely at a fireplace. Suddenly, the chair whips around to reveal the skeleton of an old lady, wispy white hair still attached to her skull. This effect was doubtless inspired by Alfred Hitchcock's *Psycho*, released a few years before Legend City opened. (Courtesy of Dick Kraus.)

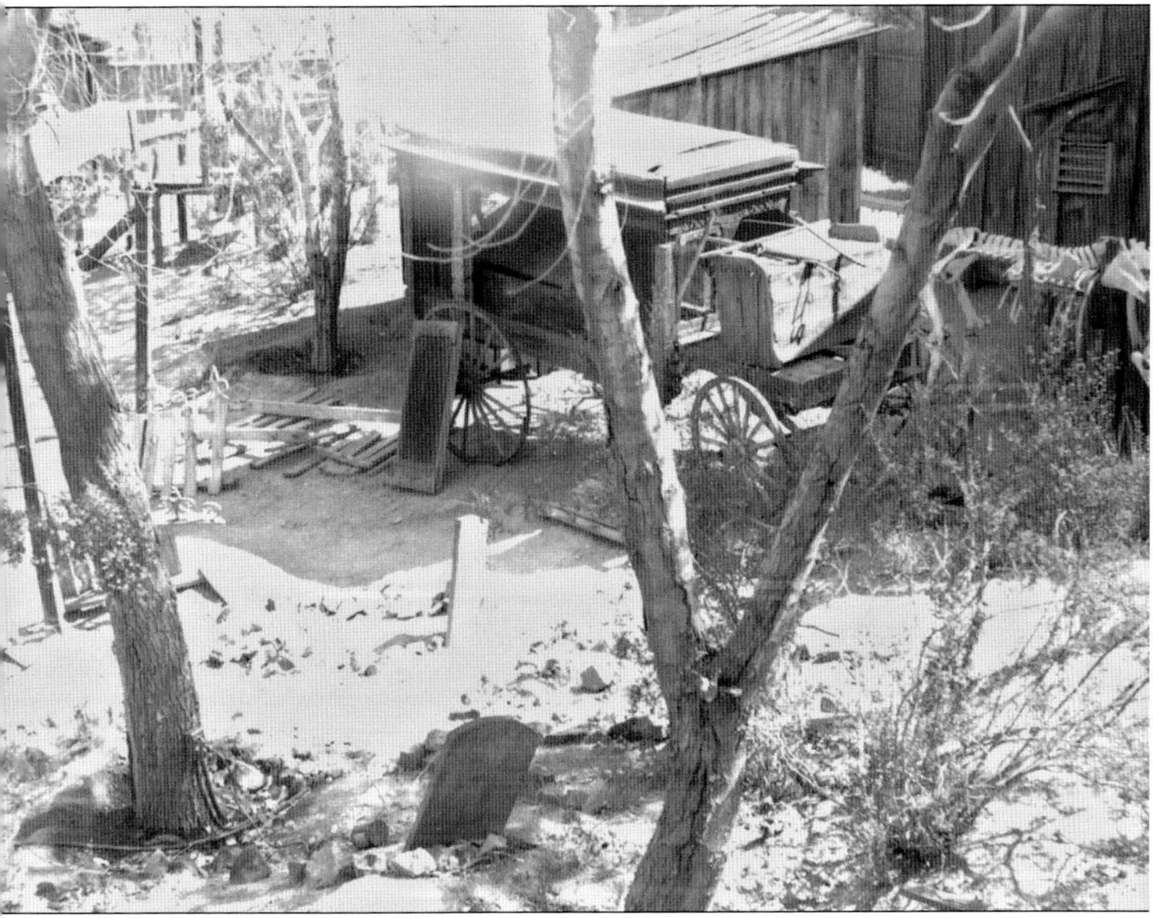

Following the parlor scene, the mine car emerges into the open air and enters a small enclosed graveyard, where passengers immediately notice an old horse-drawn hearse. Inside the hearse rests an ornate coffin, the occupant of which raises the coffin lid about six inches, just enough to expose the skeletal hand and skull inside, and then slams the lid shut. Hitched to the hearse is a skeletal horse, seen here on the far right. Behind the hearse stands a wooden shack, facing away in this photograph. This is an outhouse that will appear again later in the ride, following the encounter with the blacksmith's shop. In the foreground, a crooked wooden headstone casts its shadow upon the ground. Needless to say, the graveyard tableau was especially effective at night. The desolation of the graveyard scene abruptly ends as the mine car suddenly enters another building. (Courtesy of Dick Kraus.)

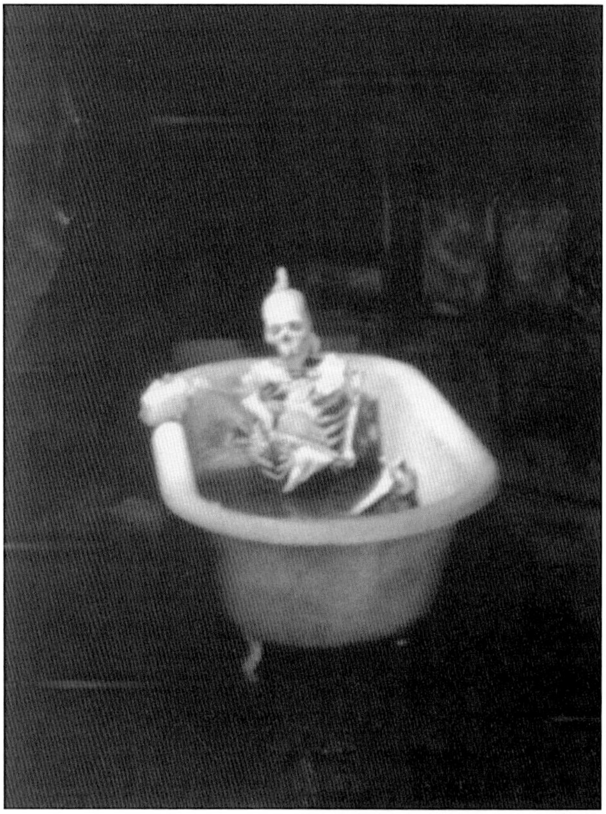

After the disquieting landscape of the graveyard scene, mine-car passengers are treated to some comic relief in the form of a Dutchman skeleton reclining in a bathtub, practicing good personal hygiene. The ghostly miner's right arm is animated to make it appear that he is scrubbing himself with a sponge. Effects man Dick Kraus added a "floating" water faucet to this scene, a clever illusion in which water flows freely from a faucet that appears to hover in mid-air. (Courtesy of Dick Kraus.)

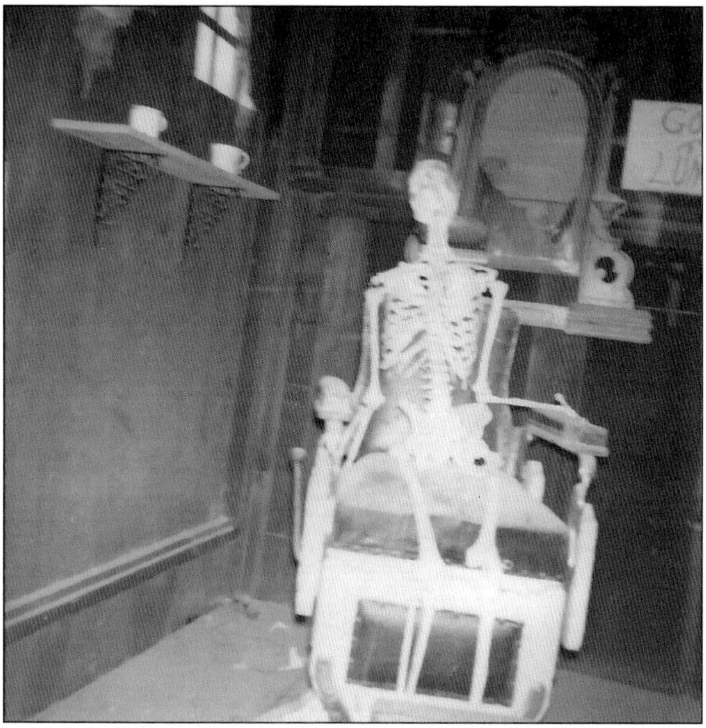

The ghostly barber was animated to stroke a razor on a leather strap attached to the barber chair, and the newspaper-reading "customer" was holding a six-shooter in his lap to assure good service and no funny business with the razor! The barber chair would then sit up from its initial reclining position to reveal the customer. This photograph of the customer was taken in 1965, during a period when the park was closed. According to the sign on the wall at upper right, the barber is out to lunch. (Courtesy of Rob Cook.)

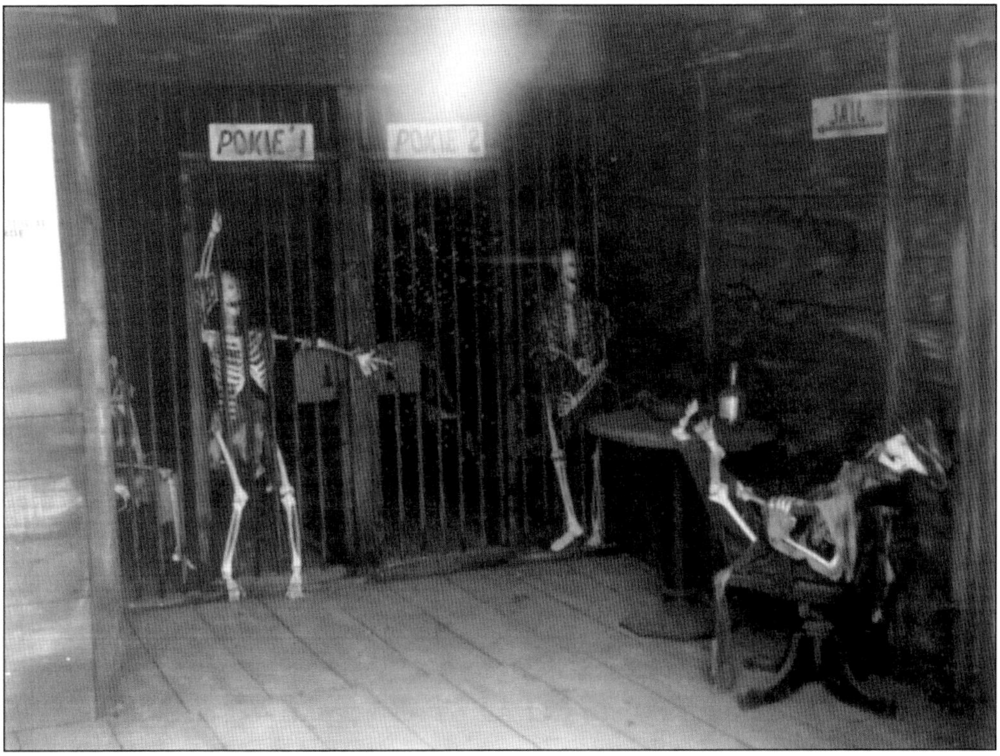

The mine car moves back outside to the graveyard for a short distance of about 12 feet and then returns inside to the darkness, where riders are confronted with the "pokie," or sheriff's office. Asleep in a chair, apparently passed out from the "hootch" on the table, is the sheriff, with the cell keys dangling from his bony foot. In Pokie No. 2, an enterprising detainee uses a broom handle to try to retrieve the keys and make his escape. Meanwhile, over in Pokie No. 1, two inmates observe these developments with great interest. (Courtesy of Dick Kraus.)

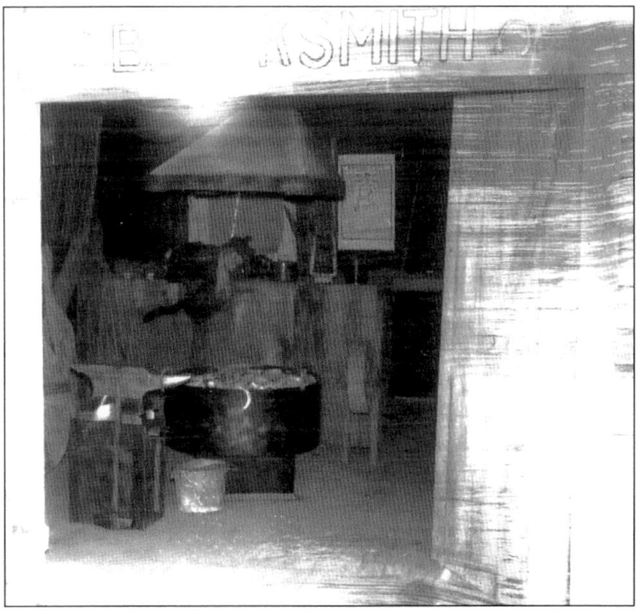

The mine car turns right and returns outside, then heads up an incline. Facing the mine car as it makes this climb is a blacksmith's shop. The center of the shop is dominated by a great forge with an animated fire glowing under rocks and embers. Note the anvil to the left of the forge. This prop was hand-carved from Styrofoam by Dick Kraus and spray-painted blue and silver to resemble the real thing. When this photograph was taken, the blacksmith skeleton figure was missing, having been stolen by souvenir hunters. (Courtesy of Dick Kraus.)

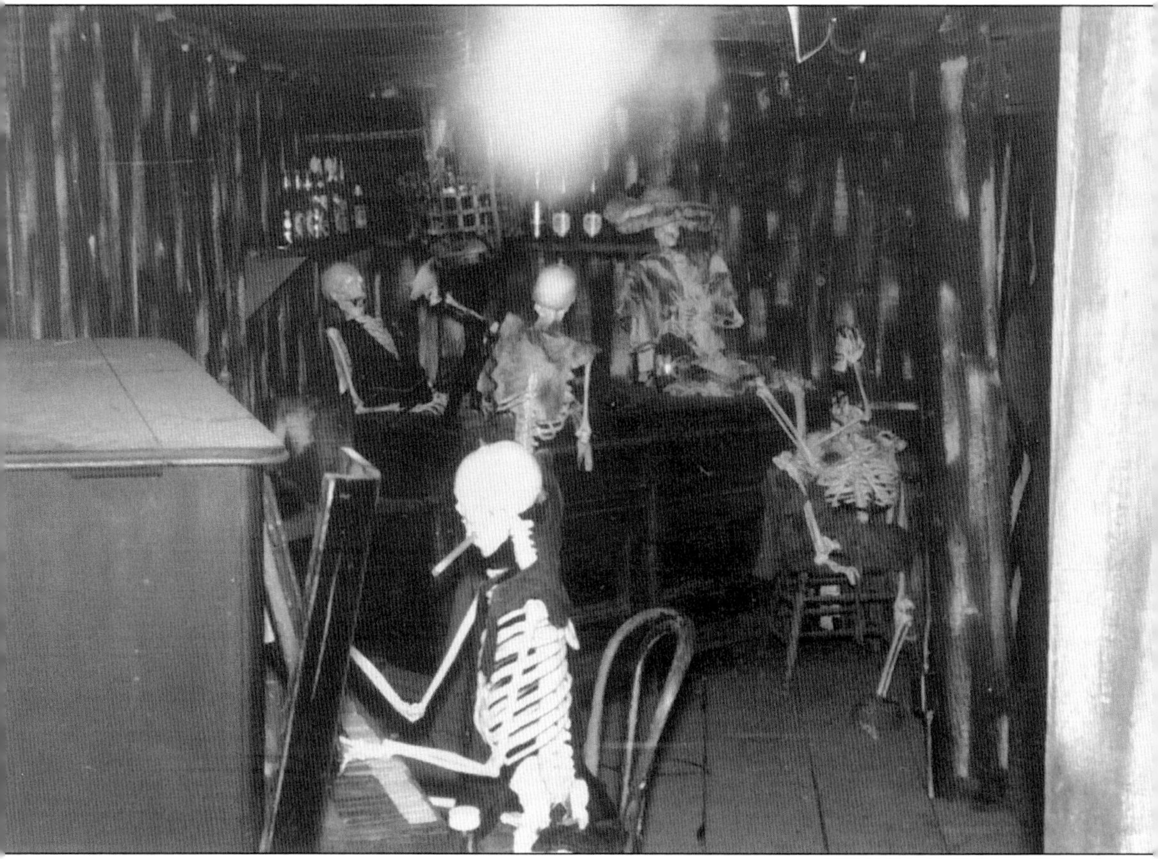

After passing the blacksmith shop, the mine car turns right again and passes by an old-fashioned outhouse standing in the graveyard. The door creaks open a few inches to reveal a skeleton inside, who exclaims, "What is this, Grand Central Station? A feller can't have no privacy around here no more!" The car returns indoors and travels through the Last Chance Saloon, where the ghostly miners go to blow off a little steam after a hard day in the mine. In the foreground sits the cigar-smoking piano player, who is animated to tickle the ivories. Directly behind him is an apparently irate patron who decides to break a bottle over the bartender's head. The bartender, in the black vest, recoils in surprise. Note how his eyes glow eerily. To their right is a female barfly in a festive hat, holding a bottle in her right hand, with her legs dangling off the bar and on top of another inebriated patron. The sounds of honky-tonk music echo as the passengers glide past the debauchery to the final exit and the loading platform, where they will disembark. (Courtesy of Dick Kraus.)

The Lost Dutchman Mine ride workers originally dressed the part. In this photograph from the summer of 1963, a ride attendant pauses in front of the attraction, smoking his pipe and awaiting the next group of eager passengers.

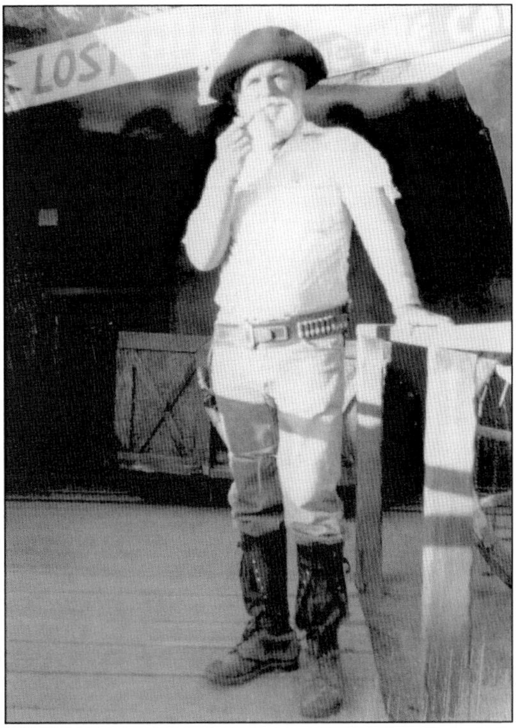

The Spook Magic Shop stood in the Ghost Town section, across from the mine ride and next door to the Dutchman's Shack. The shop sold magic items and an assortment of gag gifts. Here, magic-shop employee Richard Oliver demonstrates a trick for intrigued customers. Note the array of magic novelties in the glass case. (Courtesy of Richard Oliver.)

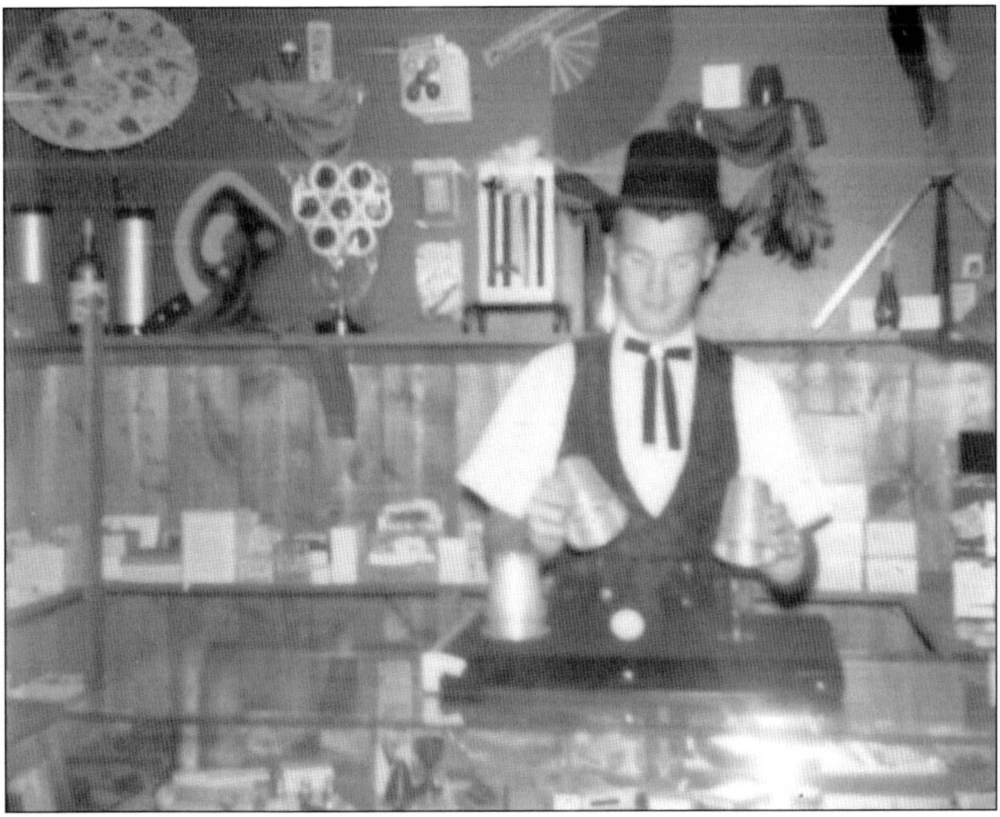

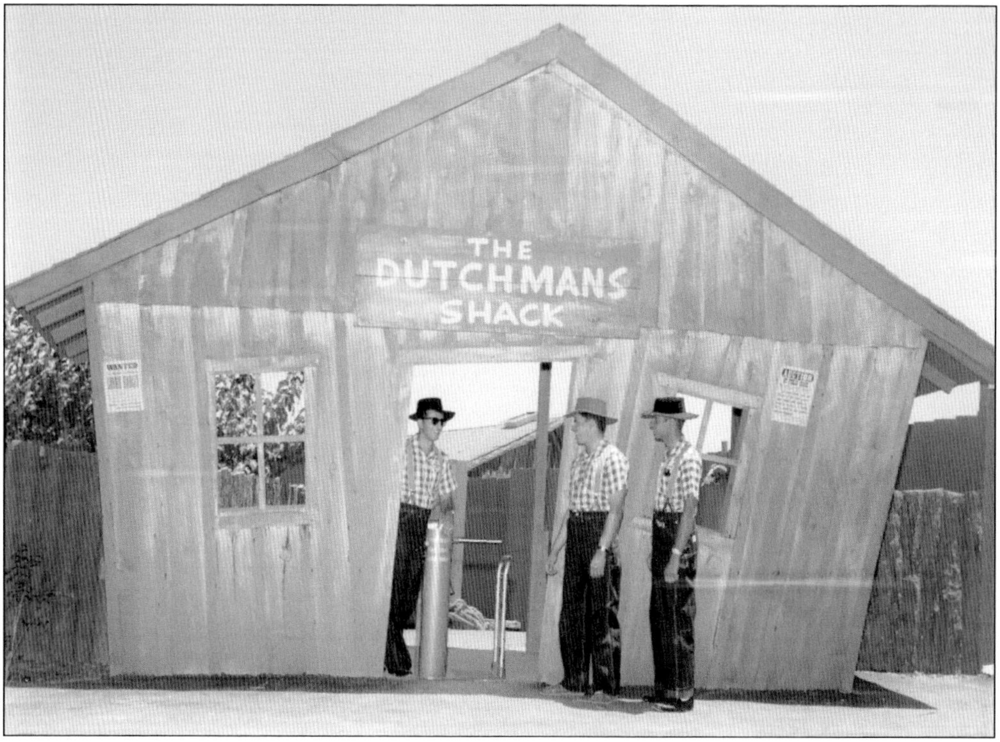

Located directly across from the Lost Dutchman Mine in the Ghost Town section was the popular Legend City tilt house, the Dutchman's Shack. The tilt house was originally to be called "Casa Loco," but the attraction soon became associated with the Lost Dutchman legend due to its proximity to the mine ride. Above, Legend City employees chat in front of the amusement in a posed publicity shot. Below, Ladmo demonstrates the mind-bending illusion created inside the Dutchman's Shack. (Below, courtesy of the Johnny Franklin collection.)

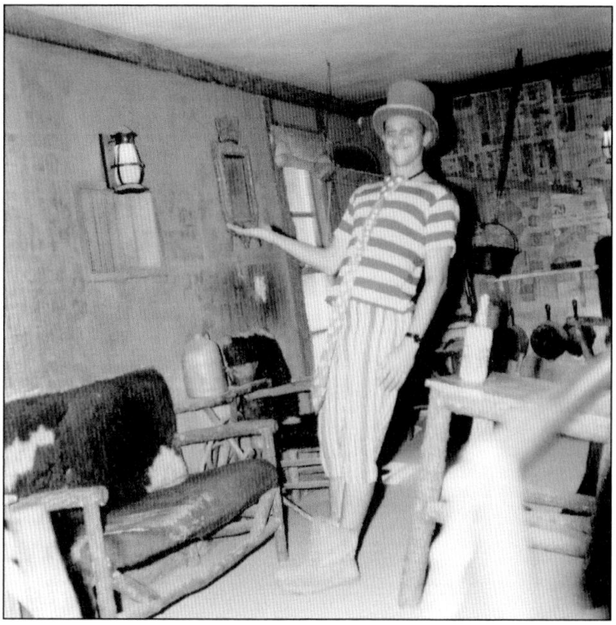

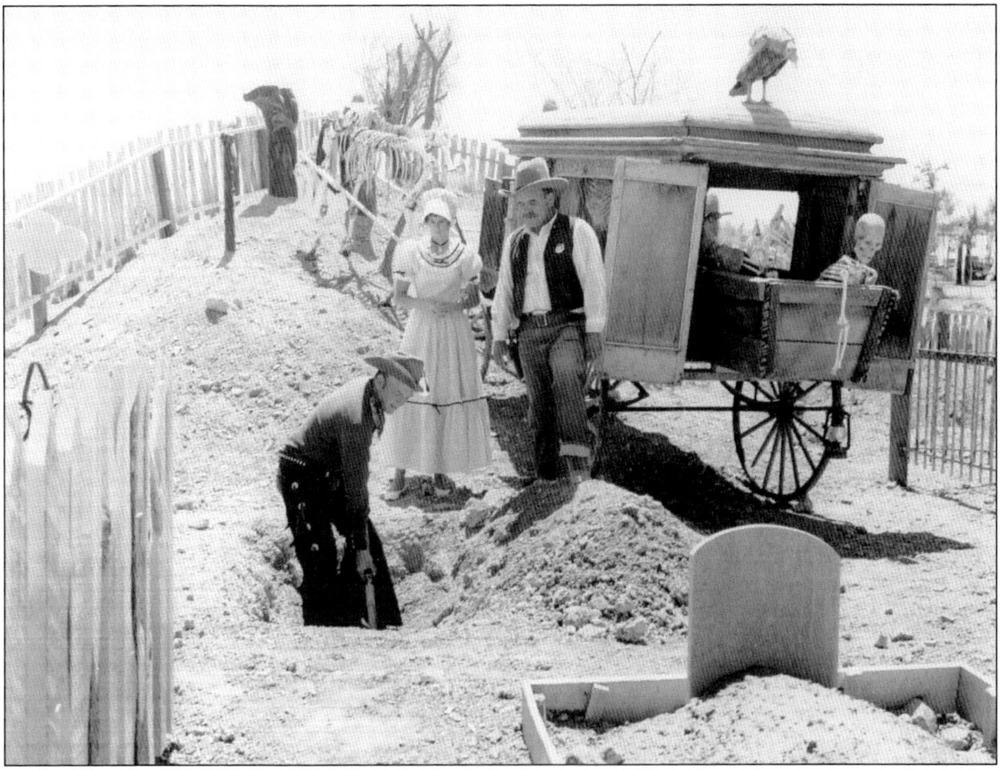

At the far north end of the Ghost Town section lay Boot Hill, the fabled Old West resting place for gunfighters and others who died "with their boots on." In this scene, a bank robber is being obliged to dig his own grave before being strung up. Note the vulture and skeleton at upper right. The hearse and skeletal horse look oddly similar to those found in the graveyard of the mine ride. Crime don't pay, pardner.

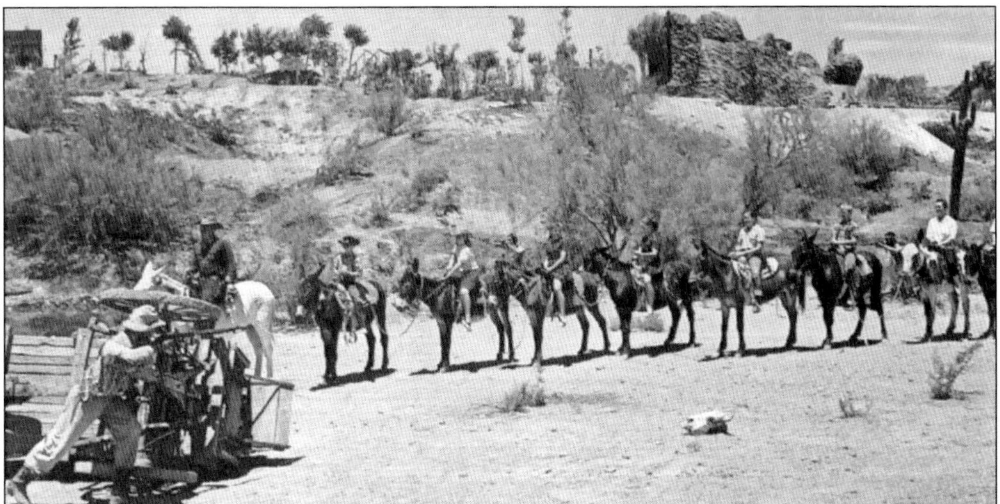

The Burro Ride was situated in a rather desolate area east of the Ghost Town section. The perilous path of the Burro Ride took visitors directly through the line of fire of a party of frontier settlers under Indian attack.

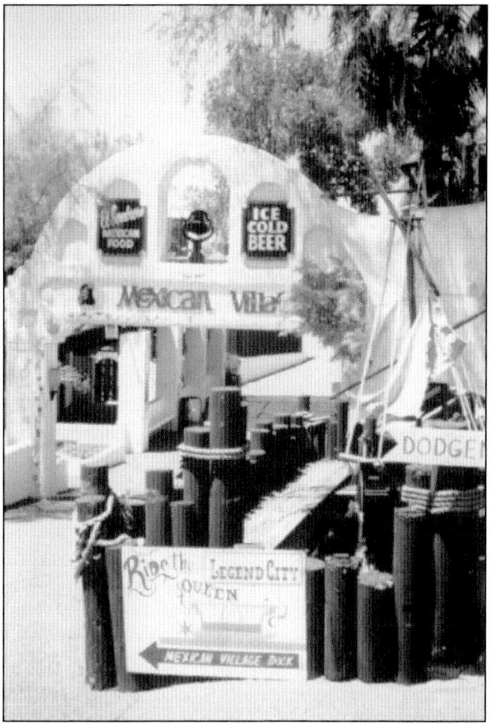

The Mexican Village section of Legend City was located west of Ghost Town, on the eastern edge of the lagoon. The popular Mexican restaurant there drew a steady stream of hungry customers.

The Mexican Village featured two alternating groups of strolling mariachis, the Los Latinos and the Los Ritmos. Performances were also held on a stage set up on a floating platform in the lagoon. Los Latinos member Fernando Quezada was the son of Adolfo Quezada, Mexican consulate in Phoenix.

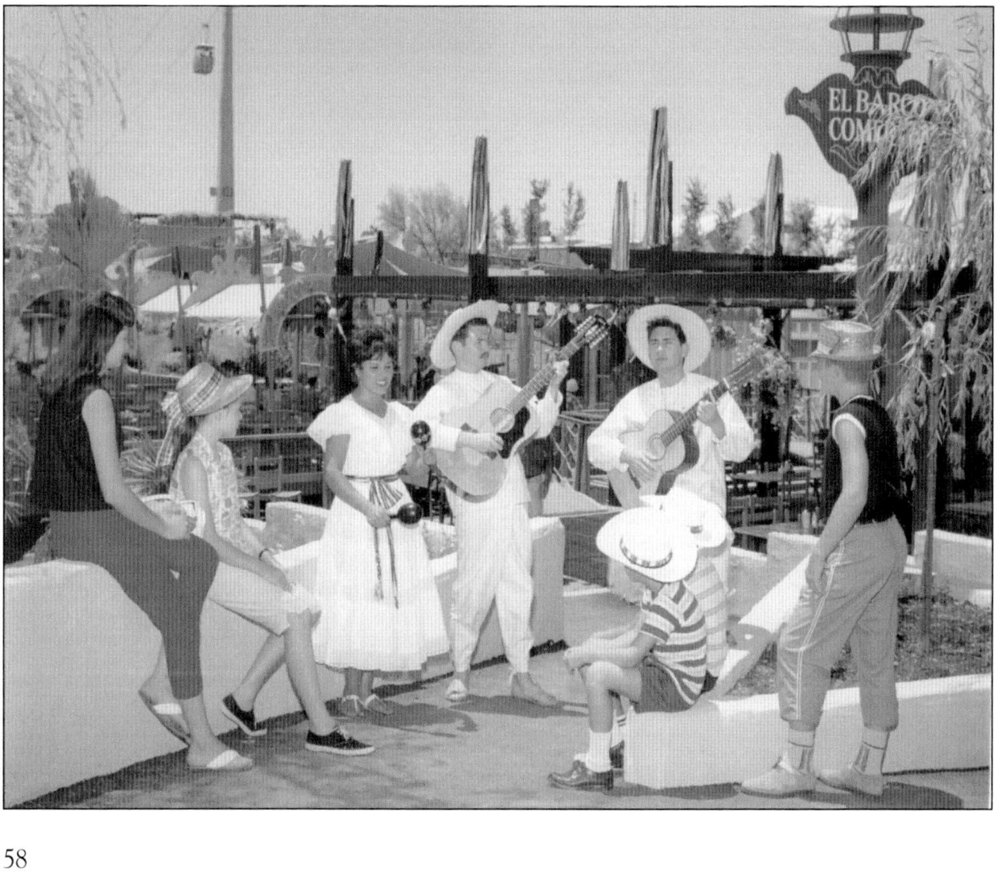

The Gold Camp was established alongside a stream flowing into the lagoon near the Mexican Village. Park visitors could pan for their own genuine gold flakes there, which were then placed in a small souvenir bottle. Here, an old prospector is demonstrating the proper technique for panning the elusive yellow metal.

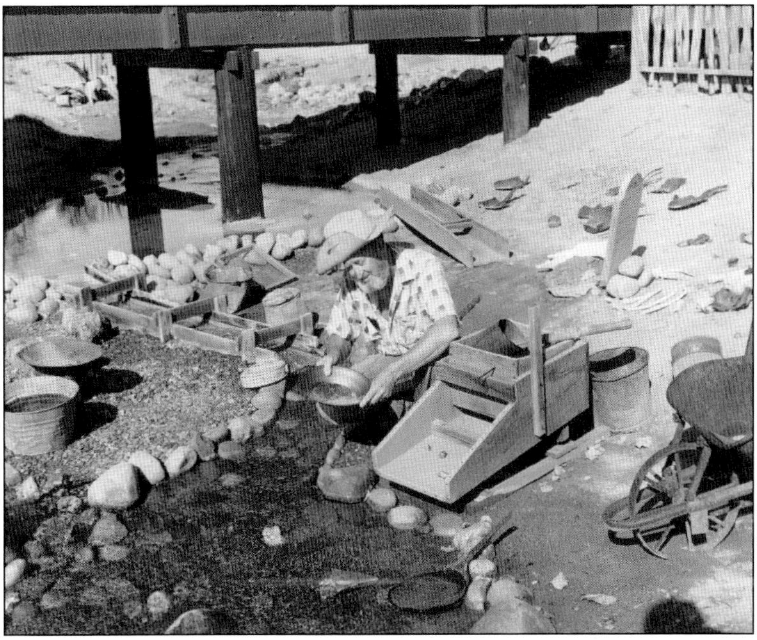

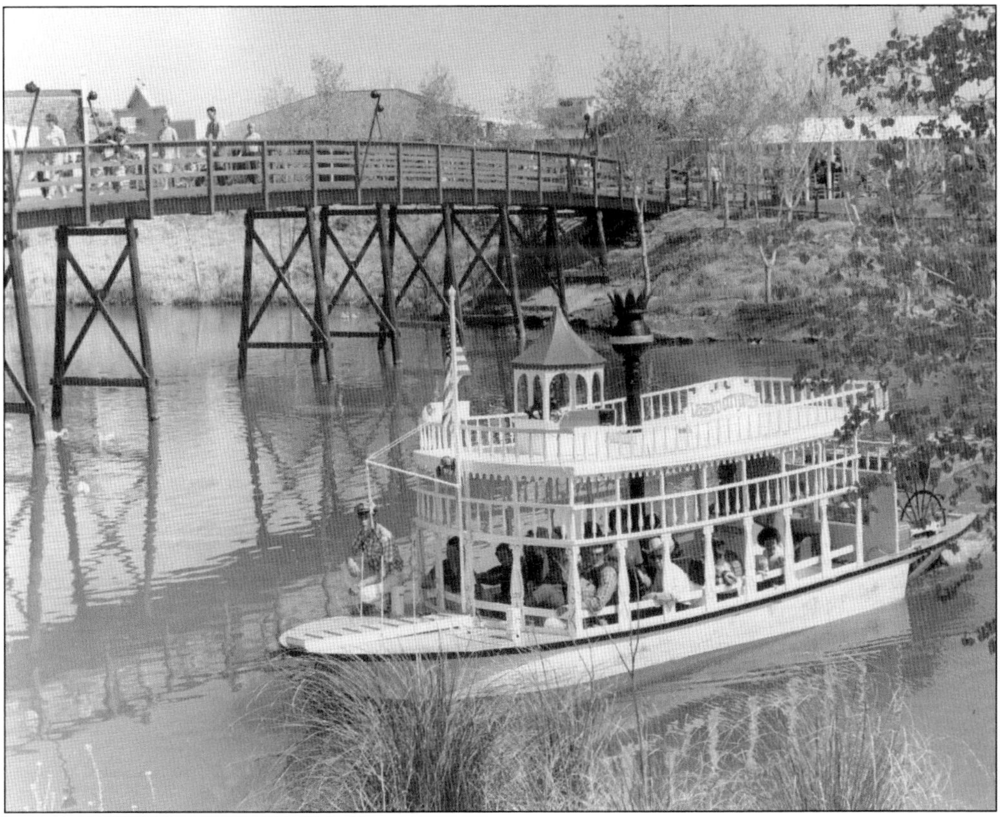

The *Legend City Queen* riverboat was a charming reminder of the Old South. It churned through the park's lagoon. The skipper of the *Queen* and operator of the ride was Robert Shinn, close friend of Louis Crandall.

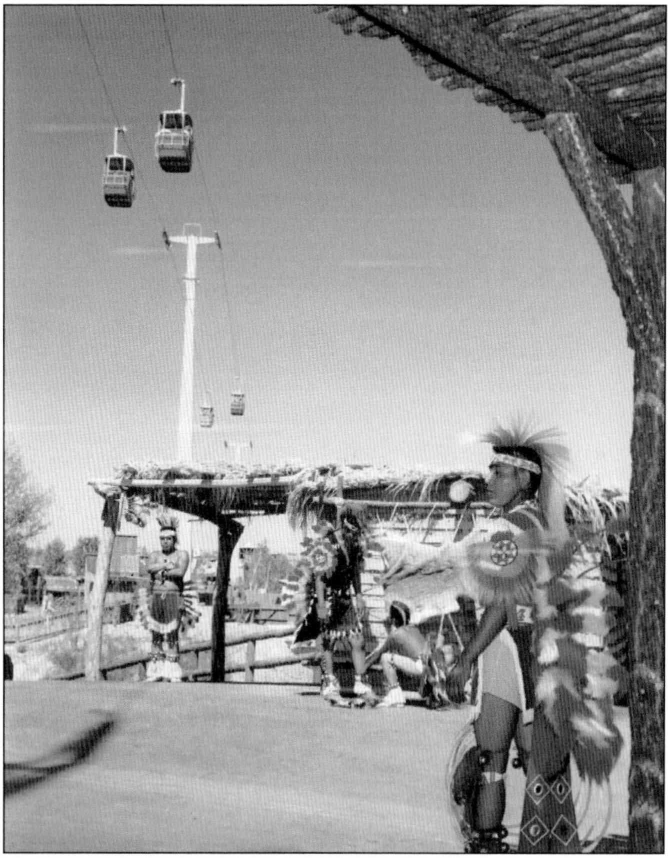

The Indian Village was situated on Indian Island, the northern island of the Legend City lagoon. The entrance to the isle was guarded by a bridge and a fort standing immediately across the lagoon. Dancers from the Maricopa Indian tribe performed each afternoon and evening, recreating the colorful ceremonial dances of various Arizona tribes on a concrete stage at the edge of the island. At left, the dancers prepare for their next performance as the sky ride cars pass overhead. Below, a ceremonial dance is under way on the concrete stage.

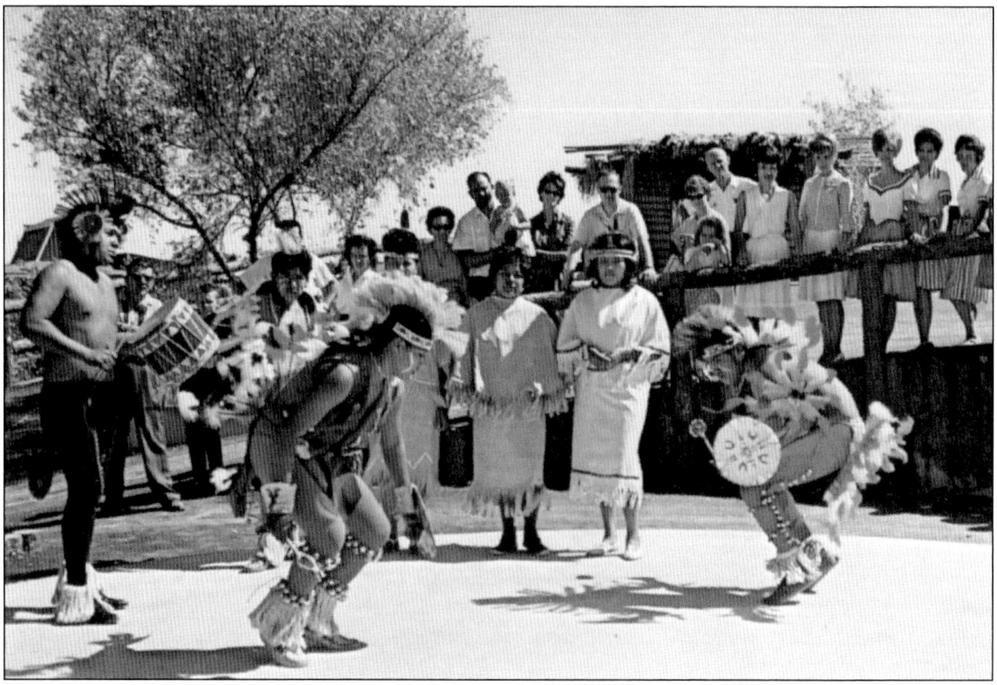

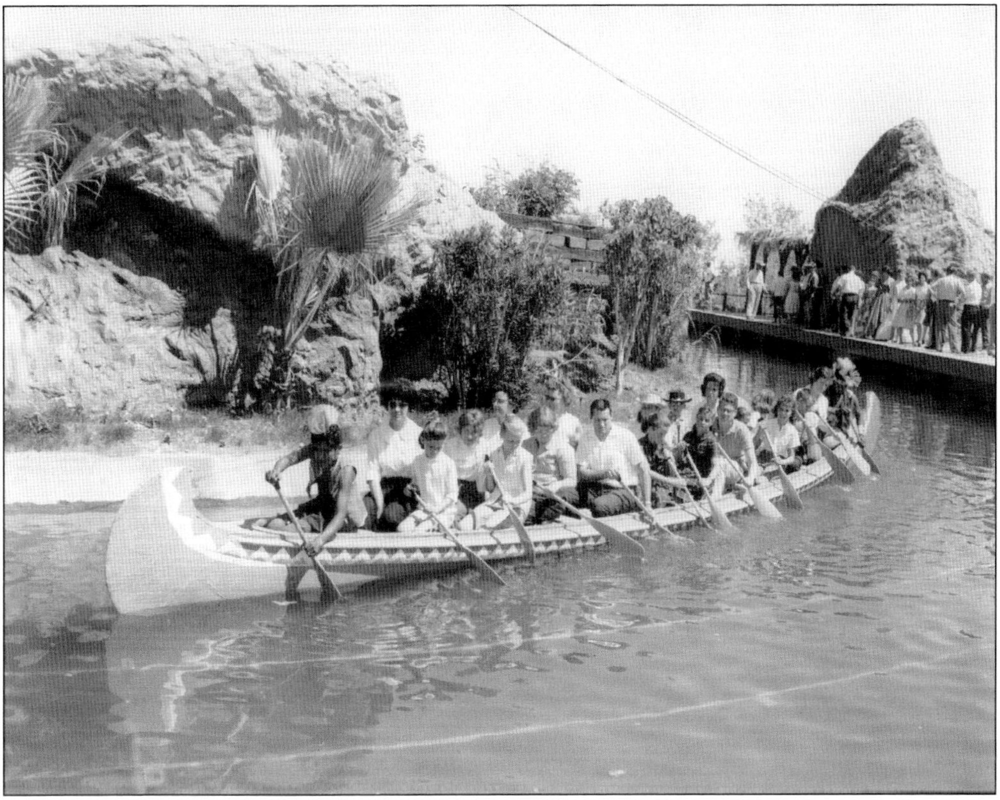

The Indian War Canoe ride was a staple of the Indian Island experience and required the participation of all the passengers for a successful journey around the island. The fiberglass canoes for the ride were acquired from the Freedomland amusement park in New York. Each canoe was 36 feet long and 4 feet wide, and could hold 24 passengers.

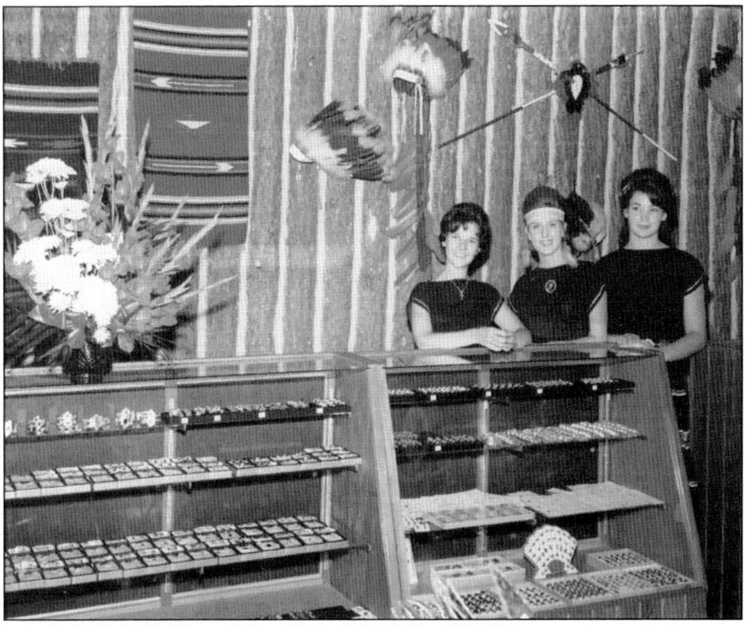

Operated by Jerome Fuller, Jerome's Trading Post on Indian Island offered an excellent selection of merchandise, including Native American jewelry, rugs, headdresses, spears, and arrowheads. Here, the trading-post staff poses for an early publicity photograph.

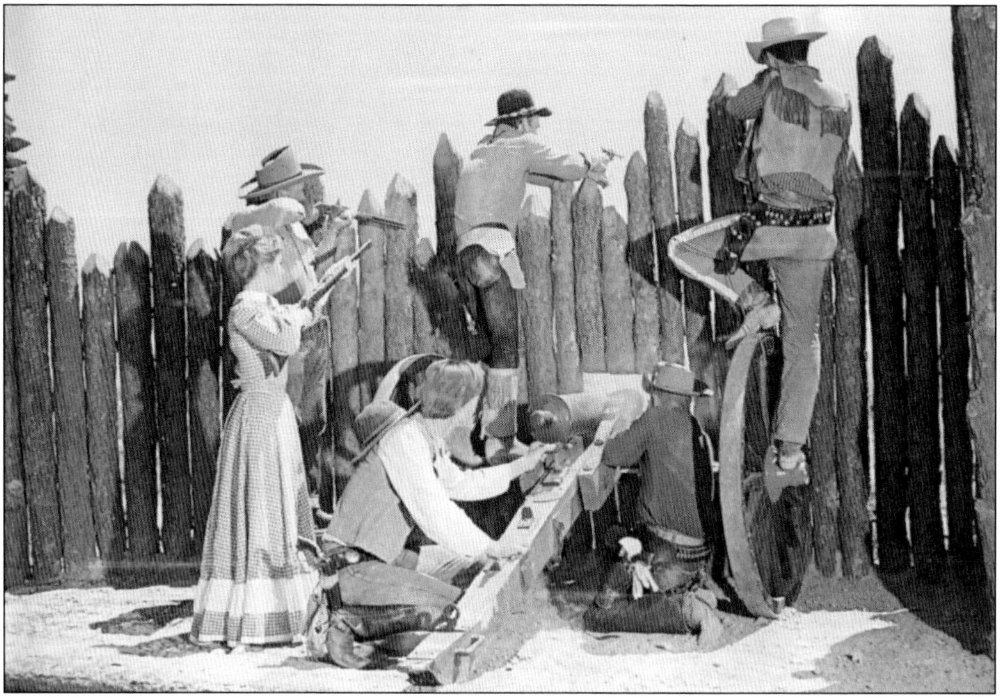

The Legend City Stockade, more popularly known as the Fort, was located across the lagoon from Indian Island, and was originally intended to create opportunities for simulated cowboy and Indian warfare. Above, the entire company and crew of the Fort are at the ramparts, defending against the latest Indian attack. Note the cannon, which exploded in a tragic accident in the summer of 1963, taking the life of one of the original Legend City cowboys. Below, Gerald is placed in the stocks for his latest act of misbehavior. The stocks was a popular spot for visitor photo opportunities. (Below, courtesy of the Johnny Franklin collection.)

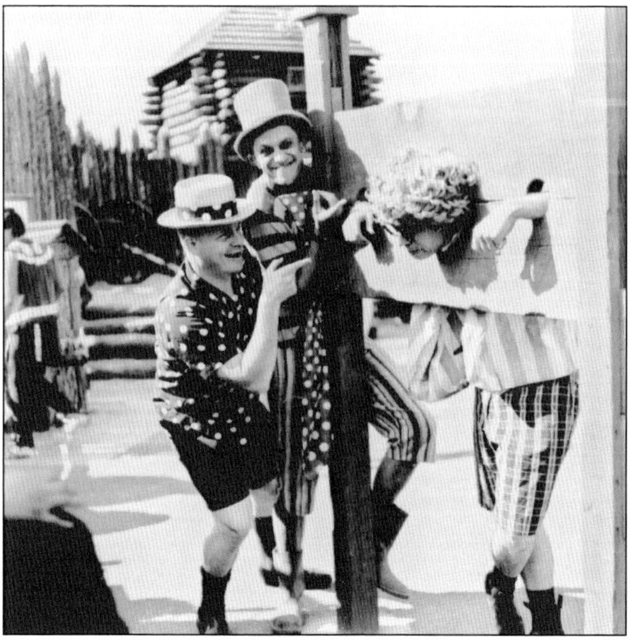

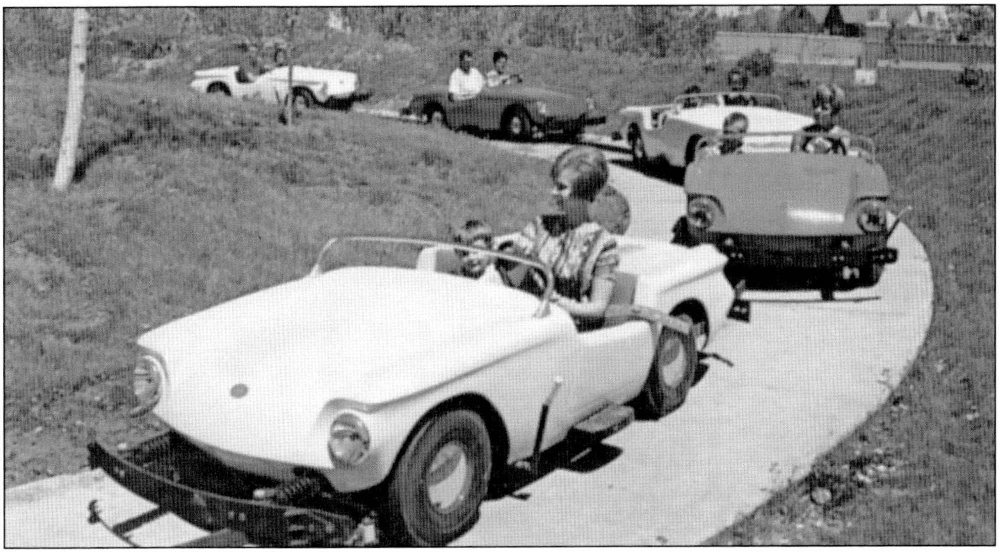

The western end of Legend City was devoted to the Modern section, a notable anachronism in a theme park devoted to Old West Arizona legends. The Modern section was also known as the "Legends of Tomorrow," and was comprised of the Blakely Sports Car ride, the sky ride, and the thrill rides. The sports-car ride was sponsored by the Blakely gas station chain, which had locations throughout Arizona in the 1950s and 1960s. Like the antique cars, the sports cars operated along a winding concrete track and were manufactured by Arrow Development Co.

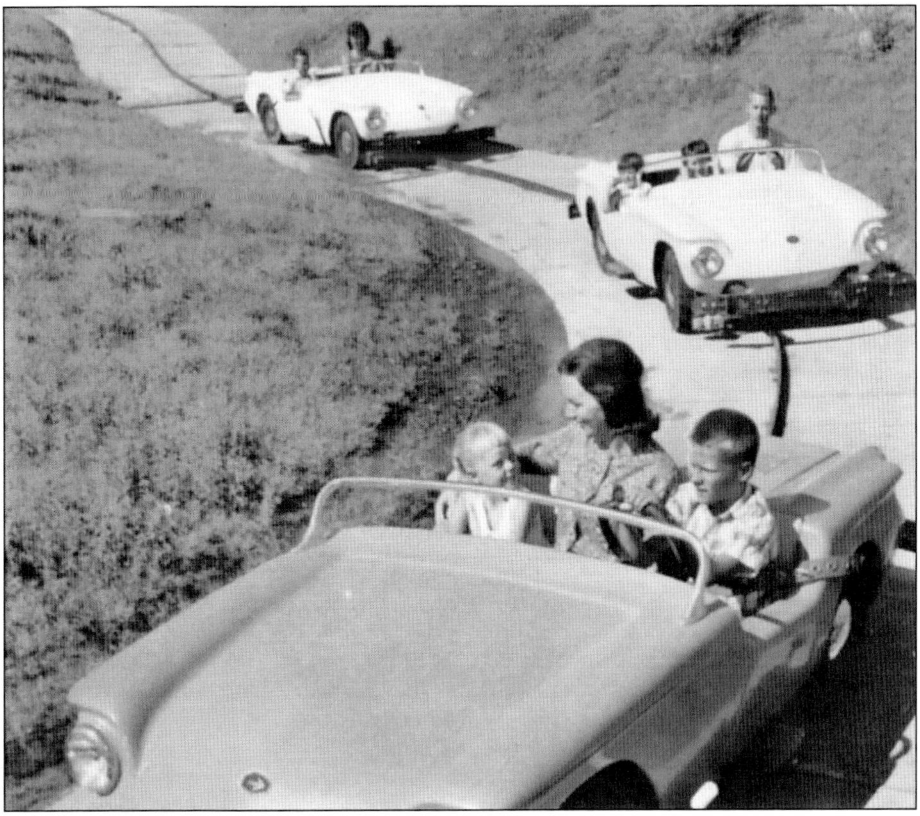

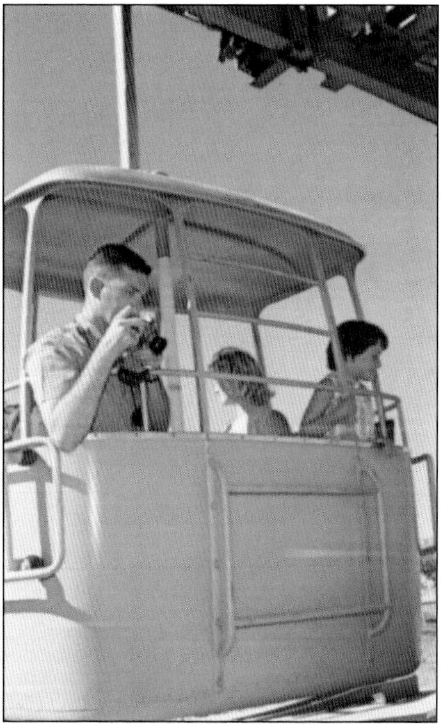

In March 1962, a contract was signed with Skyrides of America of Memphis, Tennessee, for construction of the Legend City sky ride. The ride was built in Switzerland by the Von Roll Manufacturing Company. The terminals of the sky ride were located in the Modern section and the Ghost Town section, on opposite sides of the park. Passengers enjoyed a bird's-eye view of the entire Valley, riding 80 feet above the ground in swinging, gondola-type cable cars. The ride had a capacity of 900 passengers per hour in its 28 cars. The Legend City sky ride was constructed at a cost of $290,000.

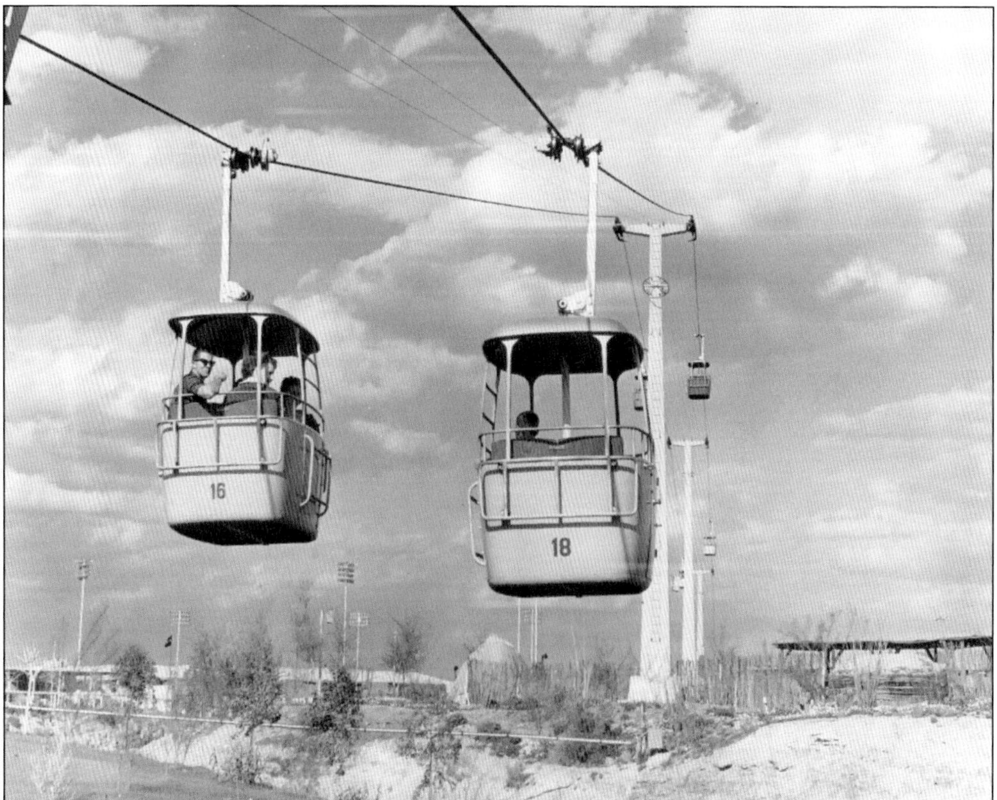

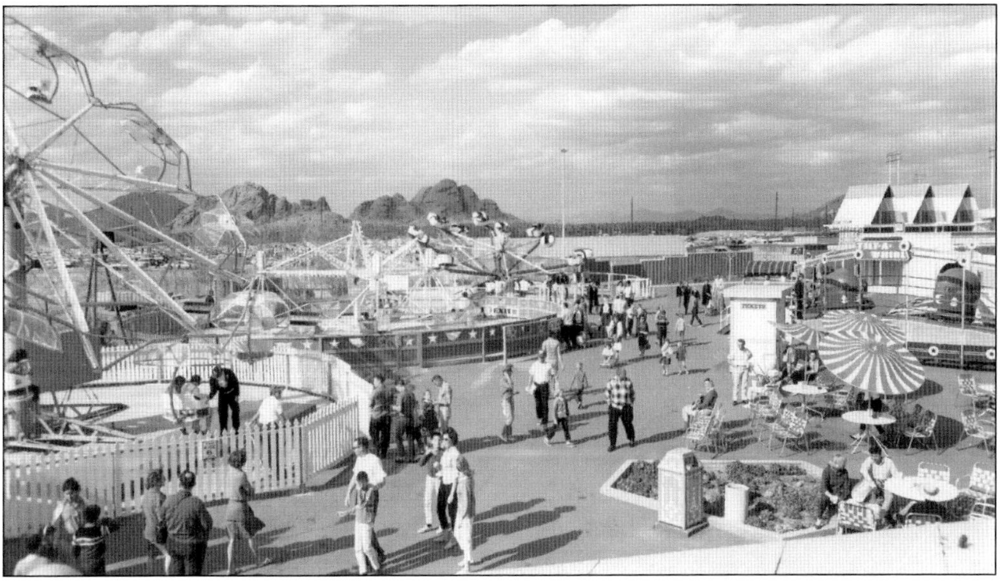

In 1962, Crandall purchased the Warnell Amusement Park in Kansas City, Missouri, using its attractions for the Modern section's thrill-ride area. The purchase included 14 major rides: Octopus, Whale-Ride, Helicopter, Merry-Go-Round, Midget-Racers, Boat Ride, Roller Coaster, Pony Carts, Krazy Kups, Ferris Wheel, Hand-Car Ride, Modern Car Ride, Skyfighter Ride, and a miniature train. Tilt-A-Whirl is in the foreground on the far right side of this photograph, and Pom Pom's Hats is the unusual building behind it with the jagged roof.

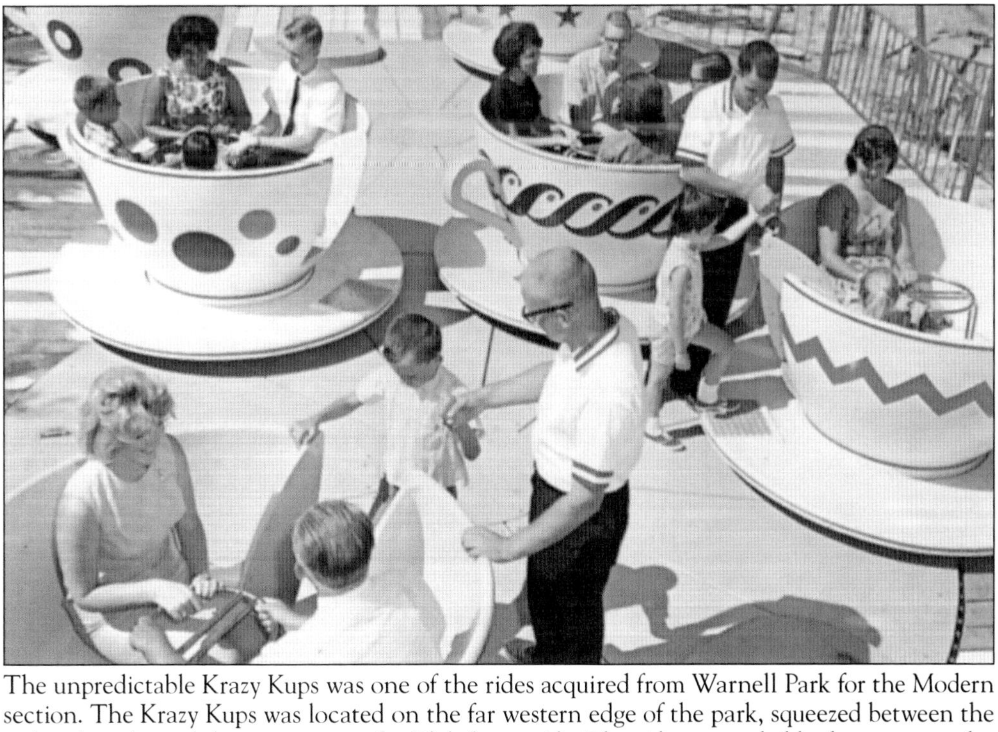

The unpredictable Krazy Kups was one of the rides acquired from Warnell Park for the Modern section. The Krazy Kups was located on the far western edge of the park, squeezed between the railroad tracks and the entrance to the Blakely car ride. The ride was probably the most popular of the thrill-ride attractions.

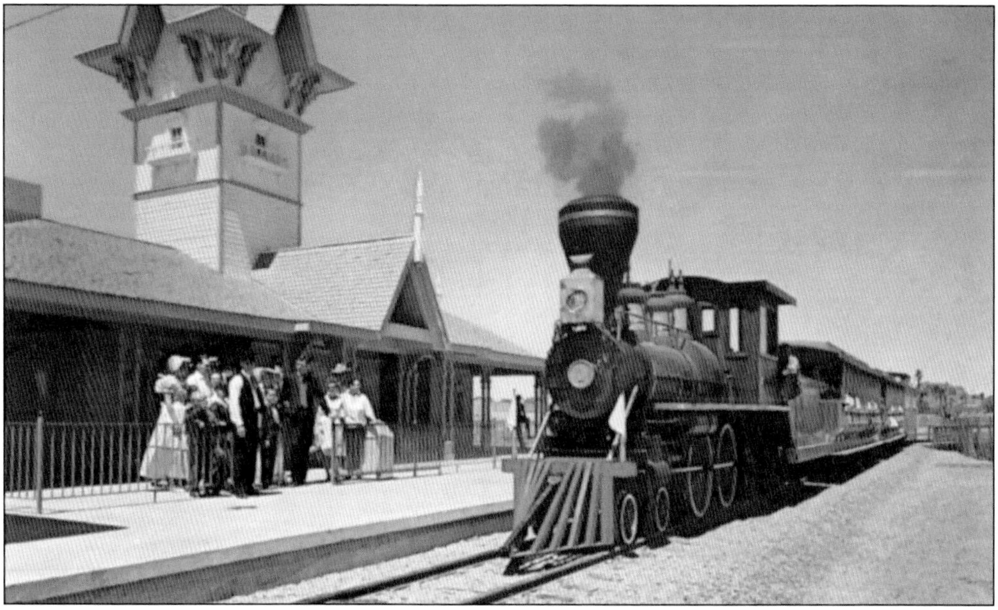

The Legend City Railroad, with its Iron Horse, was an integral part of the park experience. Powered by a replica 1860s steam-engine locomotive, the train ran from the elegant station at the southern edge of the park for a full mile around the periphery of Legend City, giving park guests a grand and thorough survey of their favorite family fun park. Here, a crowd of waiting passengers greets the Iron Horse as it arrives at the Legend City train station.

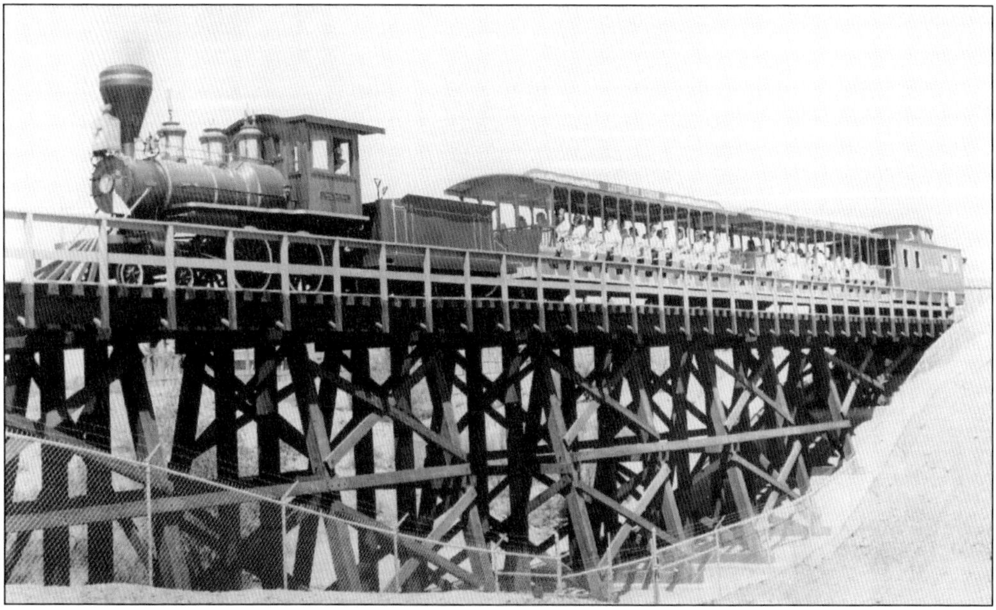

The Legend City train crosses a gulley bridge in this early photograph. The train was built in the shops of Crown Metal Products of Wyano, Pennsylvania, a company that produced miniature train equipment for the amusement park industry from 1959 into the 1980s. The Legend City train consisted of a 36-inch gauge steam locomotive with tender, two coaches, and a caboose. Remarkably, an inept robbery attempt by masked desperados seemed to occur on virtually every train trip around the park.

Unsurprisingly, the Iron Horse quickly became a popular background prop for photo opportunities at Legend City. Here, the Fife and Drum Corps from Sahuaro Elementary School in Phoenix strikes a pose near the mighty locomotive.

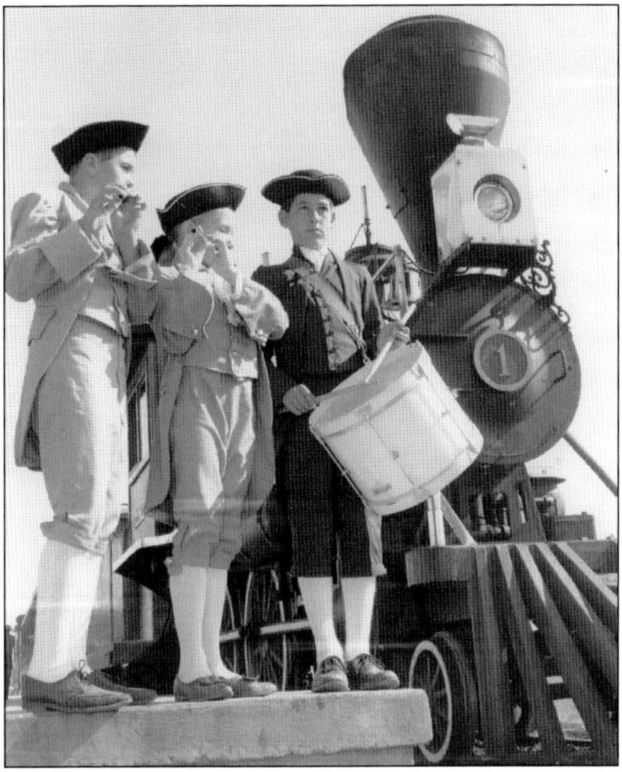

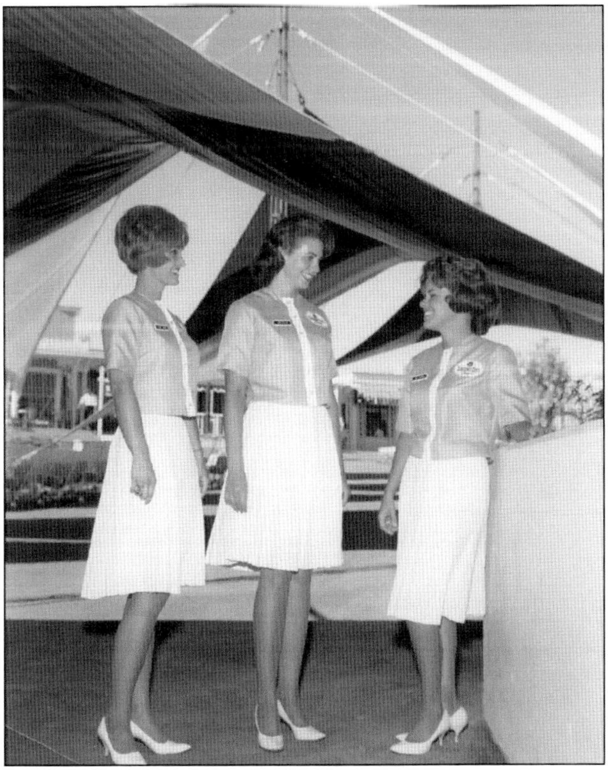

A coterie of lovely Guest Relations ladies was always available to answer questions and address any problems a visitor to the park might have.

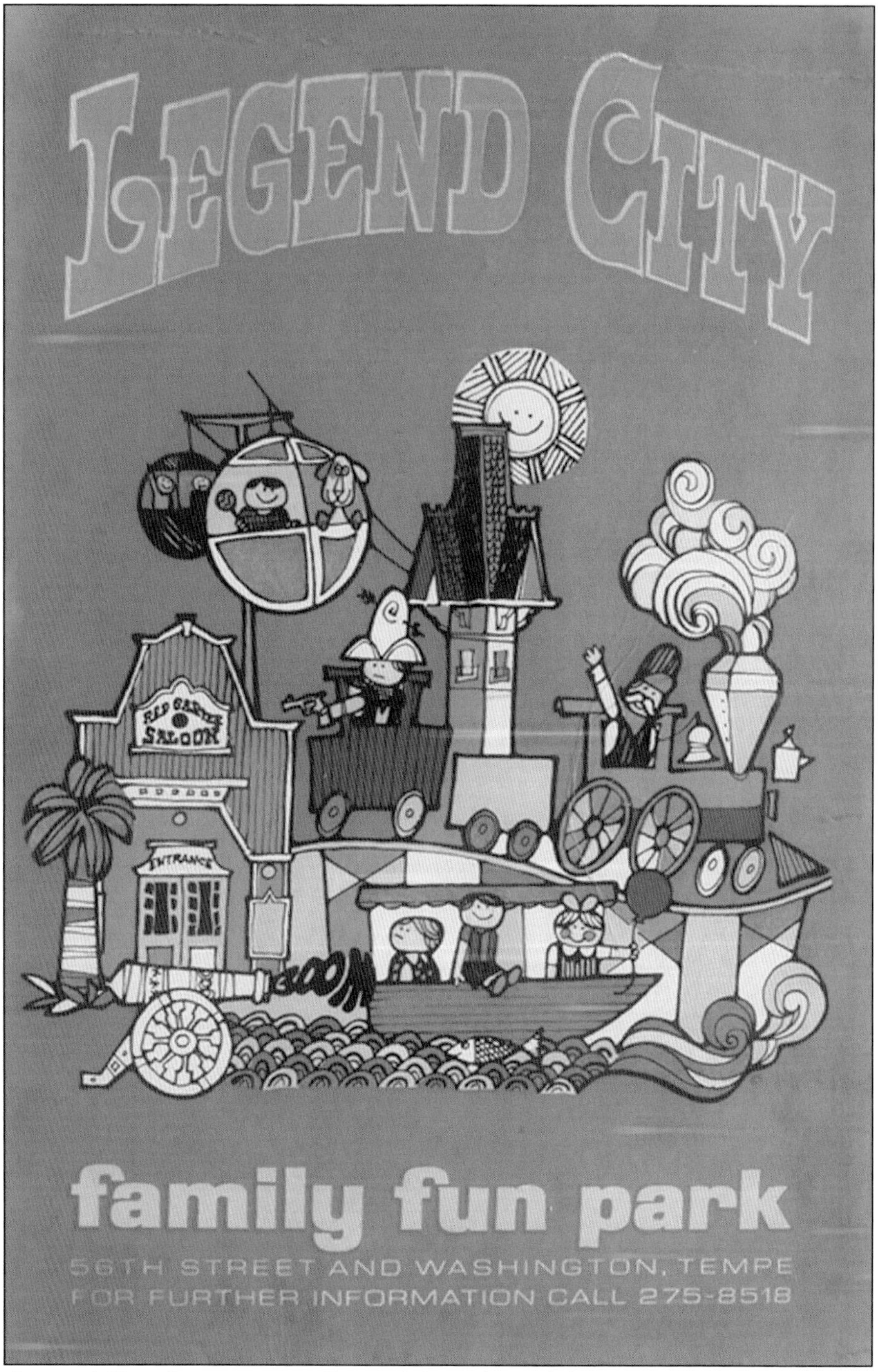

With Leonard Shoen's acquisition of Legend City, the park began a transition from Crandall's 1890s theme park to a more contemporary amusement park. A modern Pop-art 1960s vibe is clearly evident in this advertising poster from 1969. Shoen's original intention was to rename the park Frontier Funland, the same name as his amusement park corporation, but this idea was ultimately discarded, and the Legend City brand was preserved.

Three

BANKRUPTCY AND RENEWAL

Few commercial developments in the history of Phoenix have captured the public imagination as did Louis Crandall's theme park, yet there were financial issues from the outset that crippled the project before it could emerge as a viable, self-sustaining entity.

Following the two wildly successful stock offerings, Legend City Inc. had a kitty of slightly over $3.2 million for expenses. The board of directors saw no need for frugality, and the money went quickly: $750,000 for land, $683,000 for rides and attractions, $365,000 for park buildings, $209,000 for land preparation, and $200,000 for landscaping.

Unanticipated expenses quickly accrued, while gate receipts fell below initial projections. Rides like the antique and modern cars, while extremely popular, broke down frequently and were very expensive to repair. The park sank into increasingly mounting debt. Leadership changes were finally made, and Crandall departed in August 1964 for Provo, Utah. He's been there ever since. "It was the blow of my life when Legend City went under," Crandall remarked years later. "I lost everything I had."

Meanwhile, more stock was sold and further bank loans secured in an attempt to stabilize the business. The park limped through a second season, but its financial health continued to decline, and Legend City went into receivership. A final attempt to right the ship was made in 1965 and 1966 that did meet with relative success; attendance was up and losses were down. But it was not enough. In September 1966, Legend City closed down and entered formal bankruptcy, with outstanding debt of over $1 million.

The once-promising theme park sat dark and dormant for over two years before U-Haul entrepreneur Leonard S. "Sam" Shoen rode to the rescue in 1969. Shoen sank millions into Legend City, including the purchase of amusement rides from Pacific Ocean Park in Santa Monica. By the time the park finally reopened in May 1969, few of the original Legend City amusements were still in place. However, the park was finally on relatively firm financial footing.

Legend City was saved, but one consequence of these changes was the dilution of Crandall's original vision. The theme park was rapidly morphing into a mere amusement-ride park, the very thing Crandall wished to avoid.

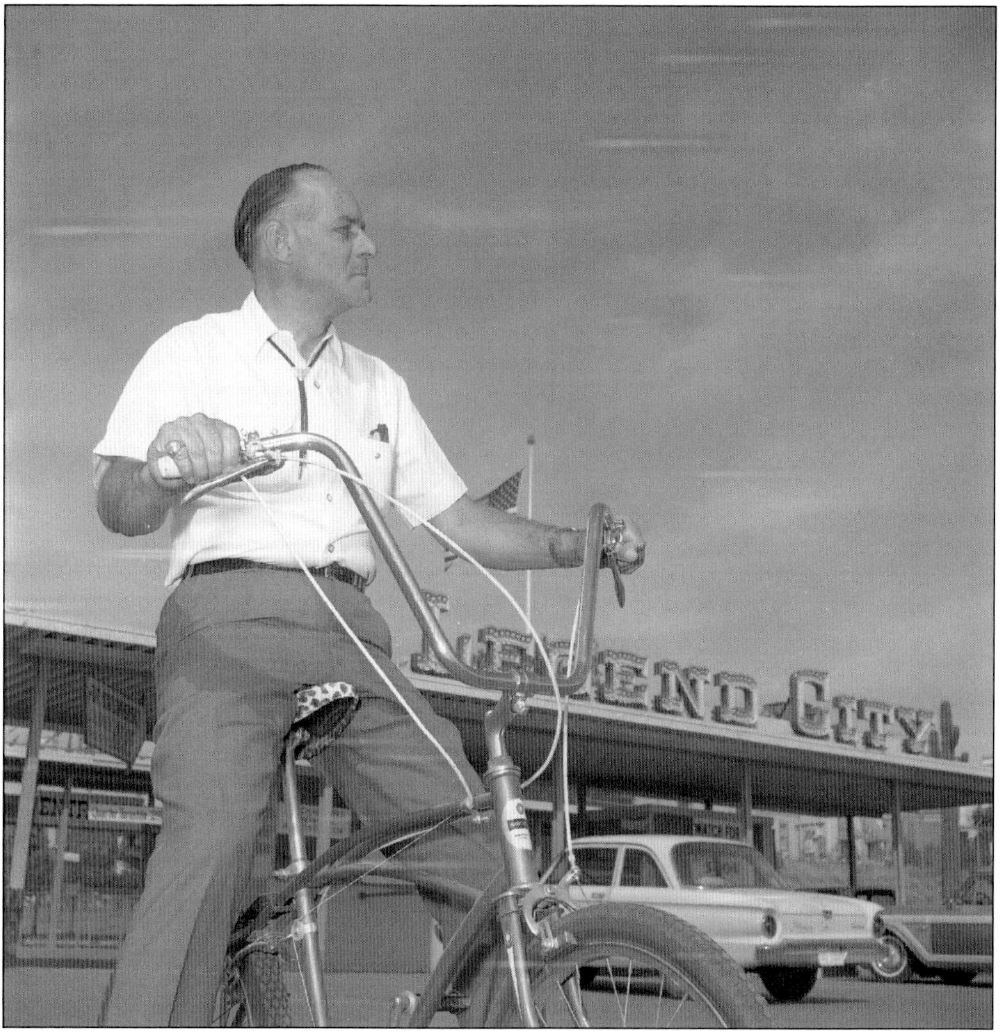

After just two seasons, Legend City was in a dire financial position. In the spring of 1965, Legend City stockholders banded together in a spirited attempt to save the park and thereby their substantial investments. Regular meetings were held at the park, and marketing strategies were carefully devised. Some stockholders even pitched in to help prepare the park for its reopening on May 1, painting buildings, repairing the sound system, and manning the front office. Resolute stockholders used whatever transportation was available to reach the meetings that spring, as shown here. Another two summer seasons were eked out before the whole operation was shut down in the face of bankruptcy in September 1966. Legend City stock then became, henceforth and forevermore, absolutely valueless. (Courtesy of *Arizona Contractor and Community* magazine.)

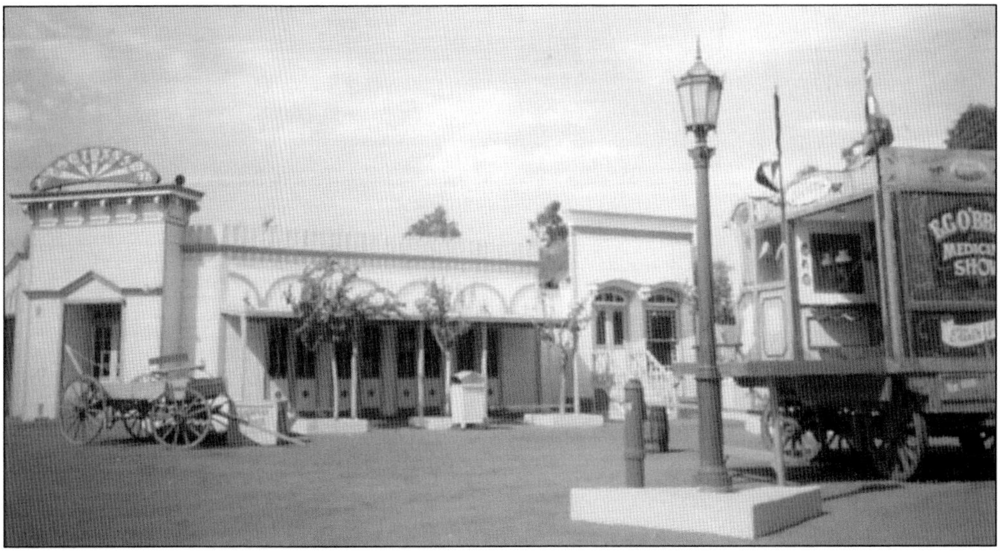

Many changes were made to get Legend City up and running after two years of dormancy. The Penny Arcade building, seen here, went through a steady evolution during this period, as arcade game fashions changed. By the time this photograph was taken in the early 1970s, the building's sign read "Fascination," the name of a popular arcade game. Note the medicine show wagon at right.

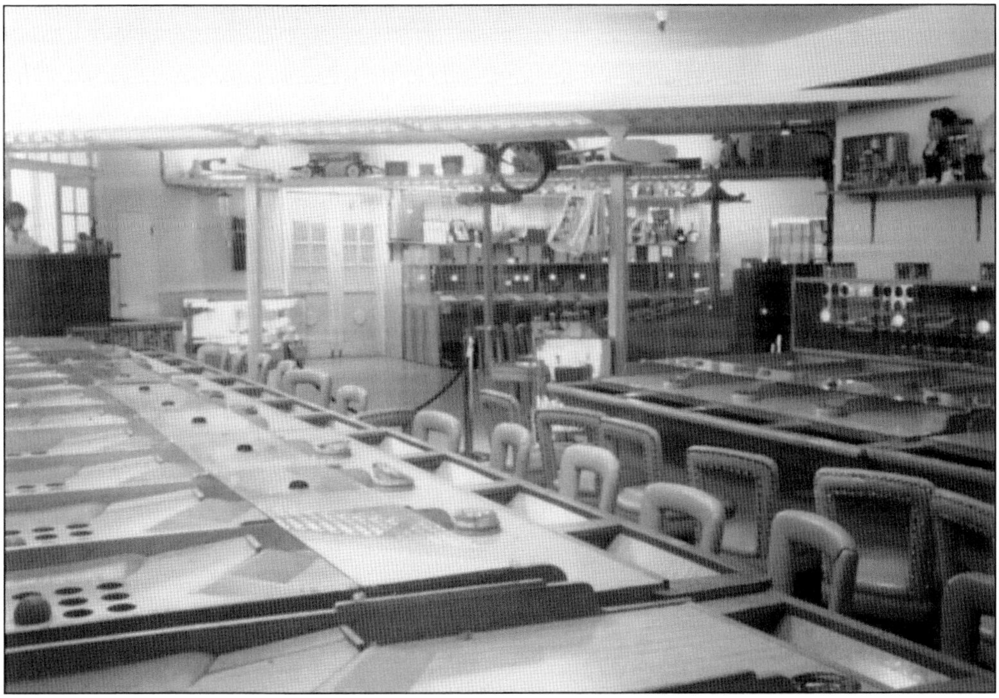

This photograph offers a glimpse of the interior of the arcade, which is dominated by the wooden Fascination game tables. The game involved rolling a rubber ball along the table toward holes at the other end and attempting to make five in a row in a horizontal row or vertical column, much like bingo. An announcer sits at far left, presiding over the games and awarding prizes to the winners.

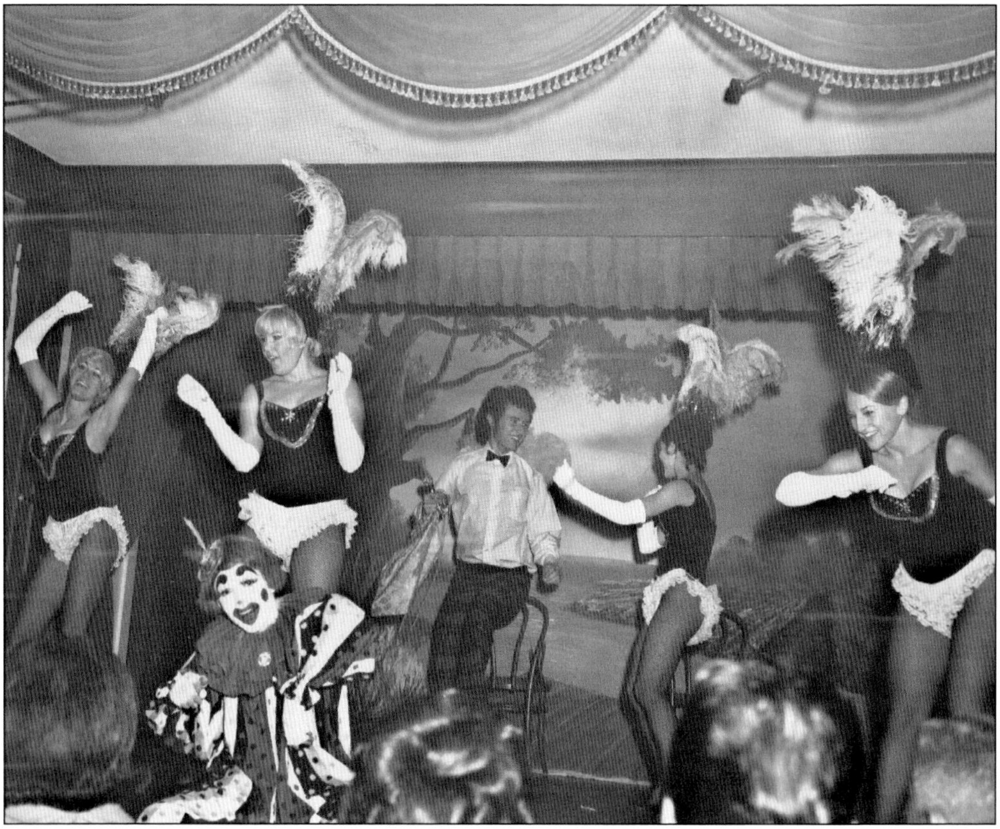

The Golden Palace Saloon was rechristened the Red Garter Saloon when Legend City reopened, and if anything, the shows onstage became more raucous than ever. These two photographs document a "Red Garter Revue" performance in the summer of 1969. The free live show featured singer Kip Miller (with microphone), four dancing girls, a band, and a clown. (Courtesy of Kip Miller.)

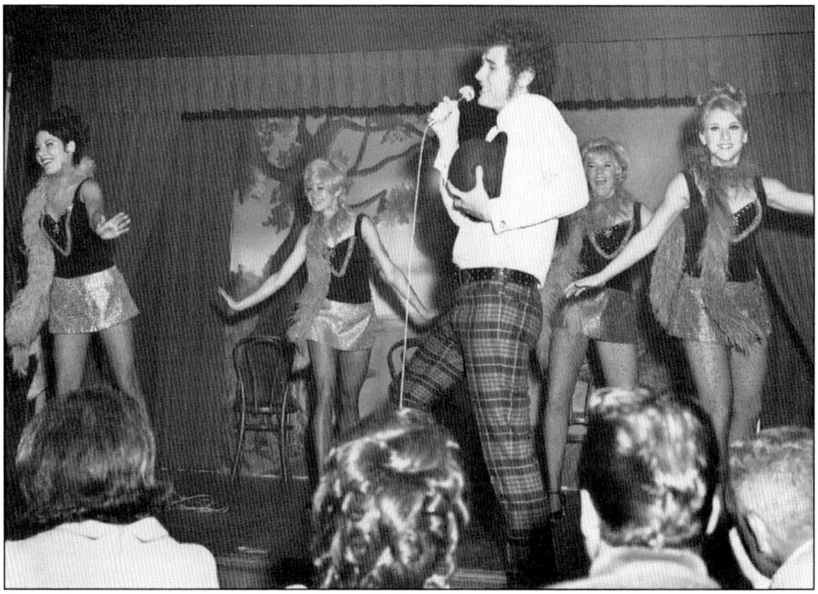

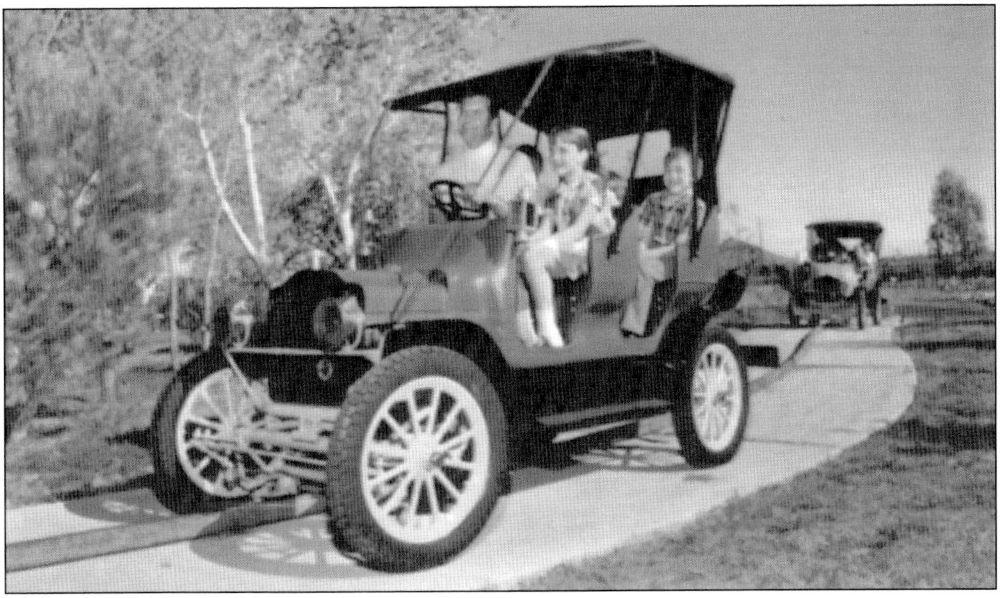

The popularity of the Antique Car Ride was completely unaffected by the park's closure and two-and-a-half-year hiatus. The long lines for the ride resumed as soon as the park reopened, as did the chronic mechanical problems and difficulties procuring car parts. All the cars got a fresh coat of paint before the reopening of the park.

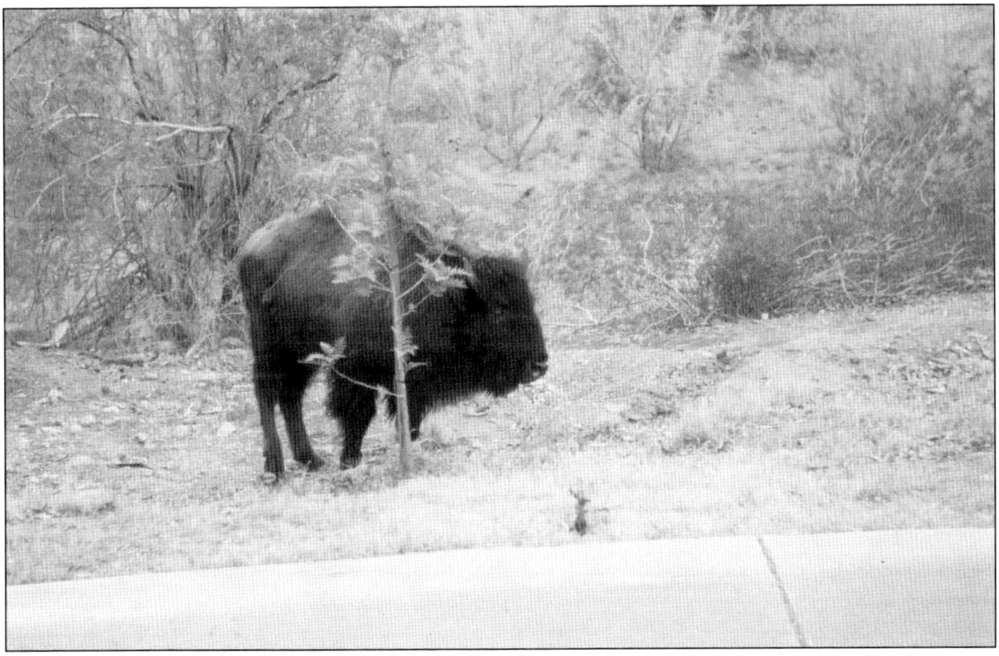

Legend City acquired two live bison in the early 1970s to lend authenticity to the Cochise's Stronghold river ride. This interesting experiment proved fairly disastrous, as the bison insisted on wandering all over the park, as bison are wont to do, causing significant chaos and destruction in their wake. In this photograph, one of the creatures is paying an unauthorized visit to the Antique Car Ride. One of the animals died not long after arriving at the park, and the other ultimately had to be dispatched by park staff. (Courtesy of David Doyle.)

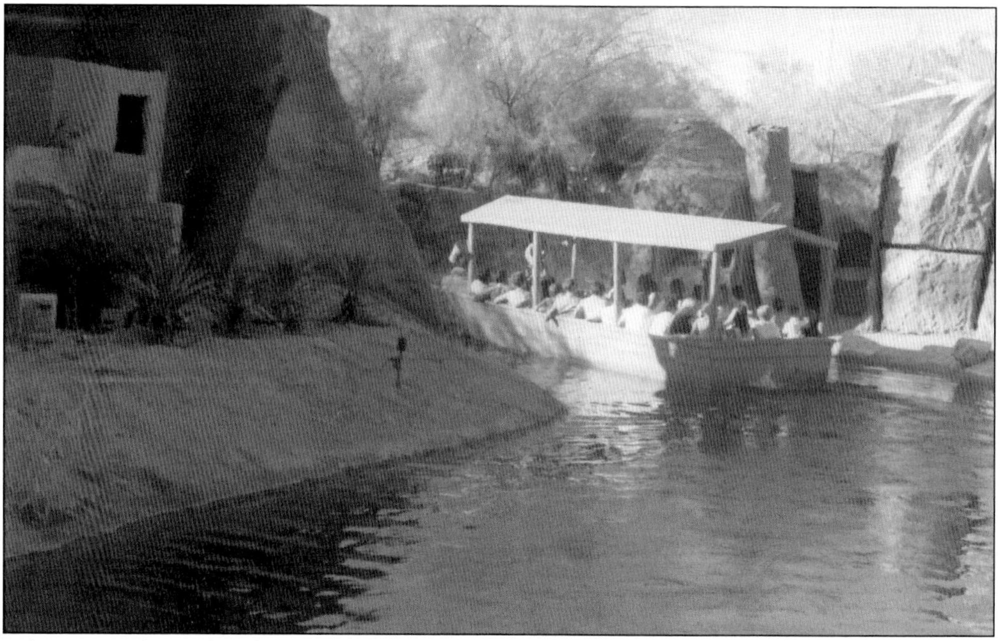

When Legend City finally reopened in 1969, the scripts for the mine ride and river ride, arguably the two most important attractions at the park, had been lost. The scenarios were revised by Jonathan Abel, and when Dick Kraus returned to Legend City for a second tour of duty in the early 1970s, he visually documented the updated attractions. The river ride (above), now known as Cochise's Stronghold, became loosely associated with actual place names in Southeastern Arizona such as the San Simon River, Fort Bowie, and Apache Pass. The fact that the San Simon was not navigable and Fort Bowie never had a port seemed minor details at the time. This photograph comes from John Muessle, who was the park president under Shoen and directed the city's extensive refurbishing. (Courtesy of John Muessle.)

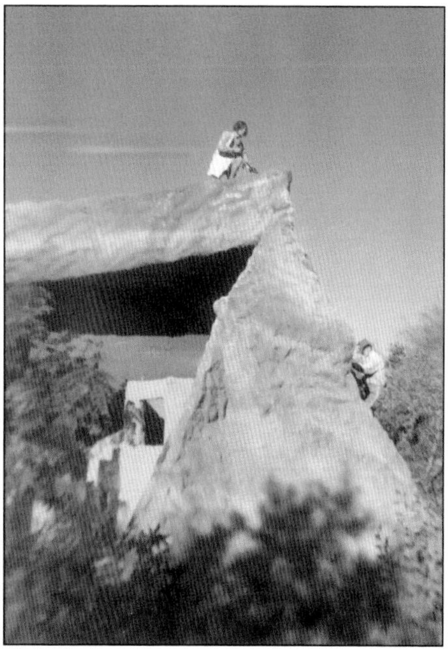

After repeated warnings of dire peril from the river guide, the journey down the San Simon River began with a glimpse of the San Simon Indian cliff dwellings, which were almost certainly inspired by the Montezuma Castle ruins in the Verde Valley. Passengers then noticed a brave soldier attempting to climb the steep rock formation. At the top of the cliff, an Indian brave is taking a knife to the climber's rope in an attempt to drop the soldier into the raging river below. (Courtesy of Dick Kraus.)

The Indian Village scene remained largely unchanged from the River of Legends days. Here, an Indian maiden (center) stirs a pot, her arm animated for the stirring action. In the foreground, another maiden looks over a string of beads that were probably obtained from the Trading Post upriver. (Courtesy of Dick Kraus.)

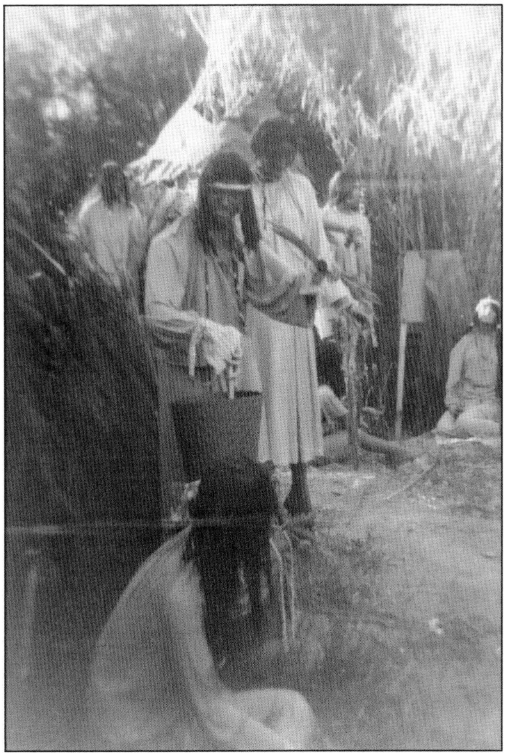

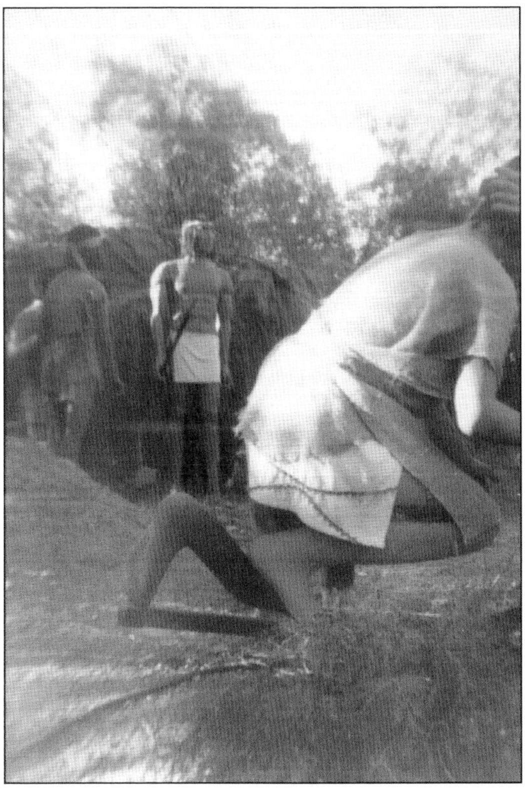

The warrior in the center of this photograph raises his spear-wielding arm to passengers as they ride by. Note the kneeling Indian in the foreground. He is actually one of a pair of Indian children who are wrestling; the hand of the second child appears on the first child's head. The steel beam used to anchor and counterbalance the mannequins into position is clearly visible. (Courtesy of Dick Kraus.)

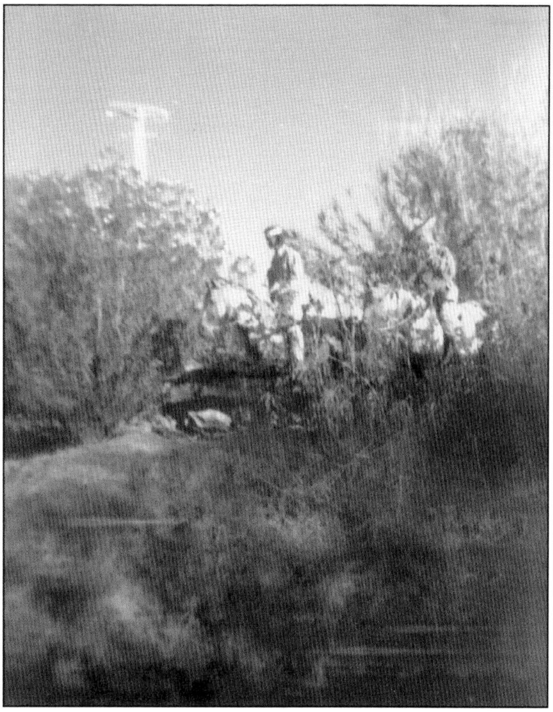

Suddenly, the river guide spots the fearsome Cochise himself. Sitting high on a hill atop his trusty steed, Cochise has joined forces with Mangus Colorados, who aims his gun directly at the approaching riverboat. A support pylon for the sky ride is visible to the left of Cochise. (Courtesy of Dick Kraus.)

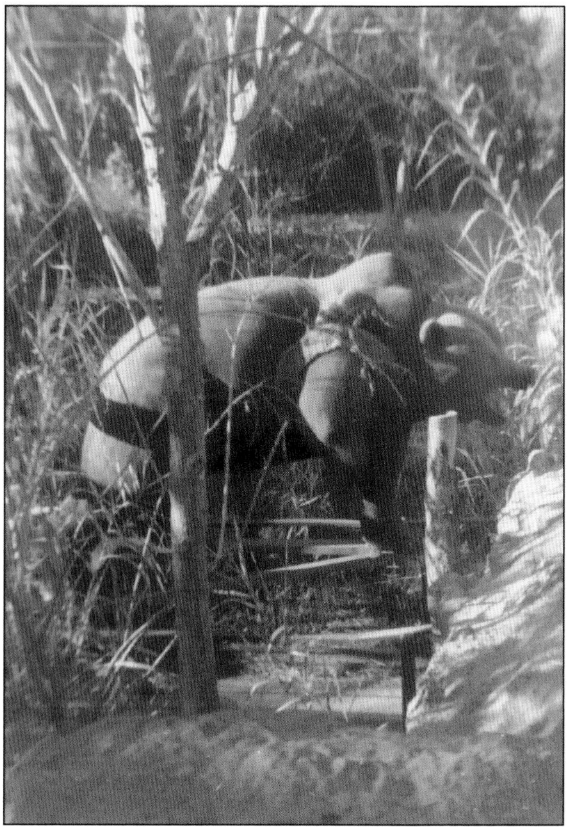

The riverboat passengers and their guide were traversing wild country. Ferocious animals were likely to be encountered at any moment; sure enough, a ravenous black bear suddenly appears. The bear stood on a motorized track, and when triggered by the movement of the boat, it would suddenly roar forward. The various animal props made for the river ride were constructed from fiberglass and manufactured in a small shop in Alpine, California. (Courtesy of Dick Kraus.)

Loud moaning diverts the boat passengers' attention to the unfortunate Sgt. Mitchell, lying nearby with more than a few poisoned arrows protruding from his body. As the boat sails past the mortally wounded sergeant, he warns the river guide in no uncertain terms to turn back and avoid Apache Pass. Seconds later, the boat and passengers are in the midst of outright warfare, with the Indians on one side of the riverbank, firing across the river at the soldiers on the opposing bank. Mannequins of teenage boys were used for these scenarios since they were the correct size from the perspective of the boat's passing onlookers. Full-sized male mannequins would have appeared gigantic. Because teen boy mannequins were hard to come by, some of the figures were actually female mannequins, with their faces redone by attaching beards and mustaches. (Courtesy of Dick Kraus.)

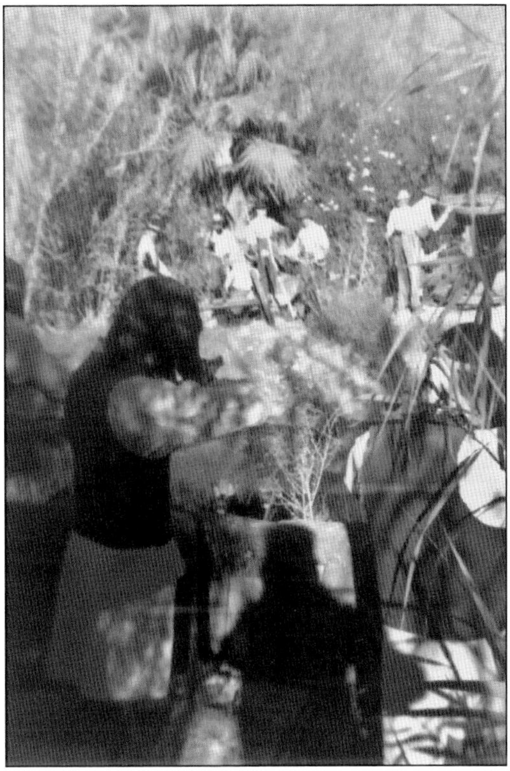

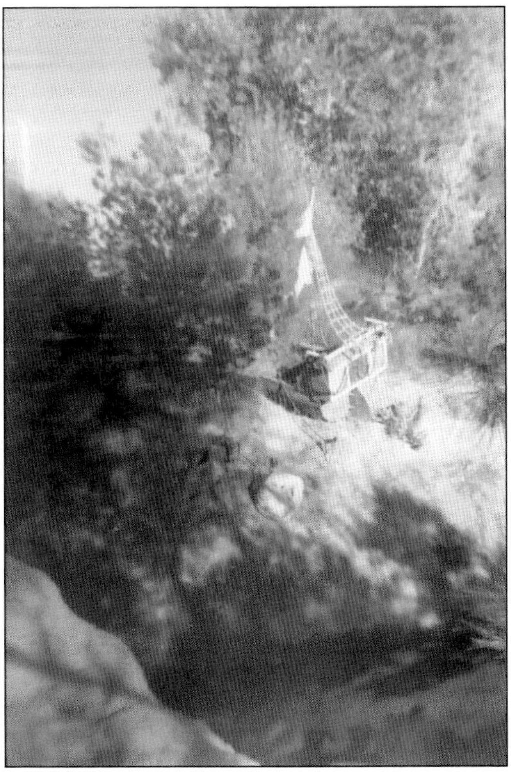

Apparently not everyone on the river ride comes through unscathed. The boat now encounters a shipwreck of earlier explorers and their deserted campsite. Dick Kraus fabricated the wreck with scraps and leftovers from various parts of the park. After the boat passes the shipwreck, the riverboat guide announces that Fort Bowie should be coming into view momentarily. Relief changes to concern as the boat approaches what appears to be a wall of solid rock, and then a waterfall comes into view. The riverboat slowly enters the cave portion of the ride. (Courtesy of Dick Kraus.)

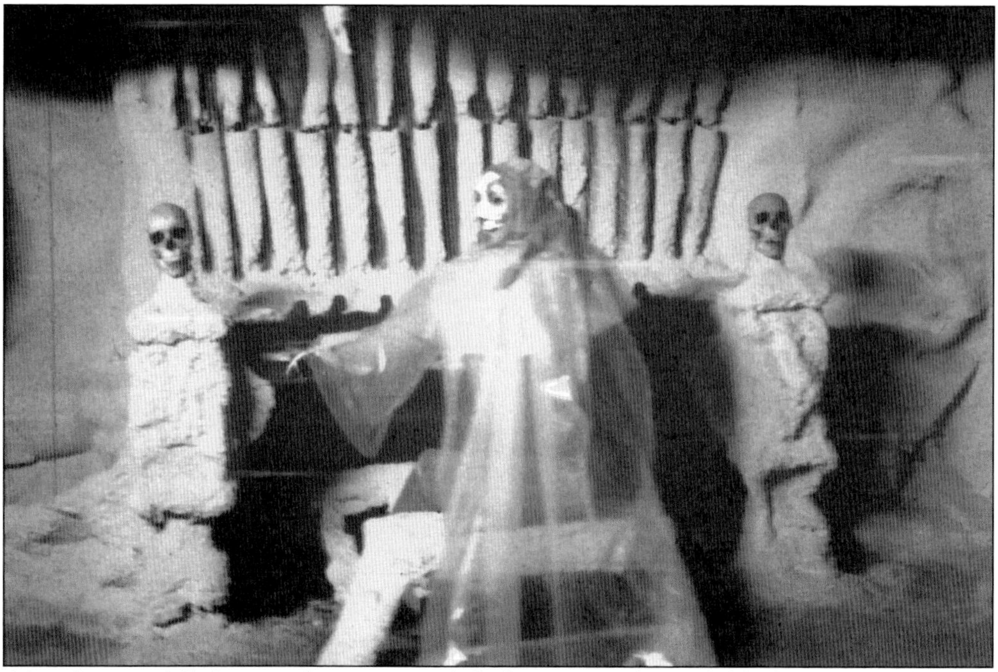

After the waterfall, the cave doors open and the boat enters the pitch-black interior of the cave. Soon, the passengers see fireflies, an illuminated treasure chest, and then a ghostly skeleton playing a stone-carved organ (shown here). The specter's skull was cleverly designed to create the illusion of looking over its right shoulder as the boat approached, and then over its left shoulder as the boat moved away. Dick Kraus created this illusion by splitting the skull into a "V" shape and placing it with the rear of the skull facing the water. Thus, the illusion of the skull watching passengers coming and going was achieved without any moving parts involved. (Courtesy of David Doyle.)

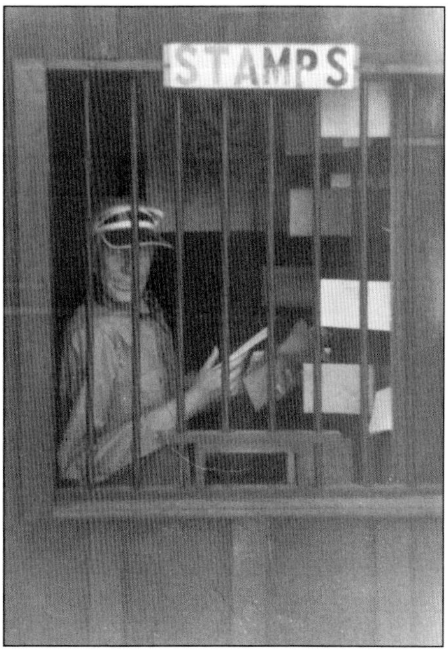

As the boat approaches the end of the ride at Fort Bowie, it passes a postman sorting the daily mail, freshly delivered from one of the riverboats. He begins to place a piece of mail in the appropriate box, catches a glimpse of the riverboat, and then drops his "sorting" arm down a bit. He watches the passing riverboat for a moment before resuming his work. (Courtesy of Dick Kraus.)

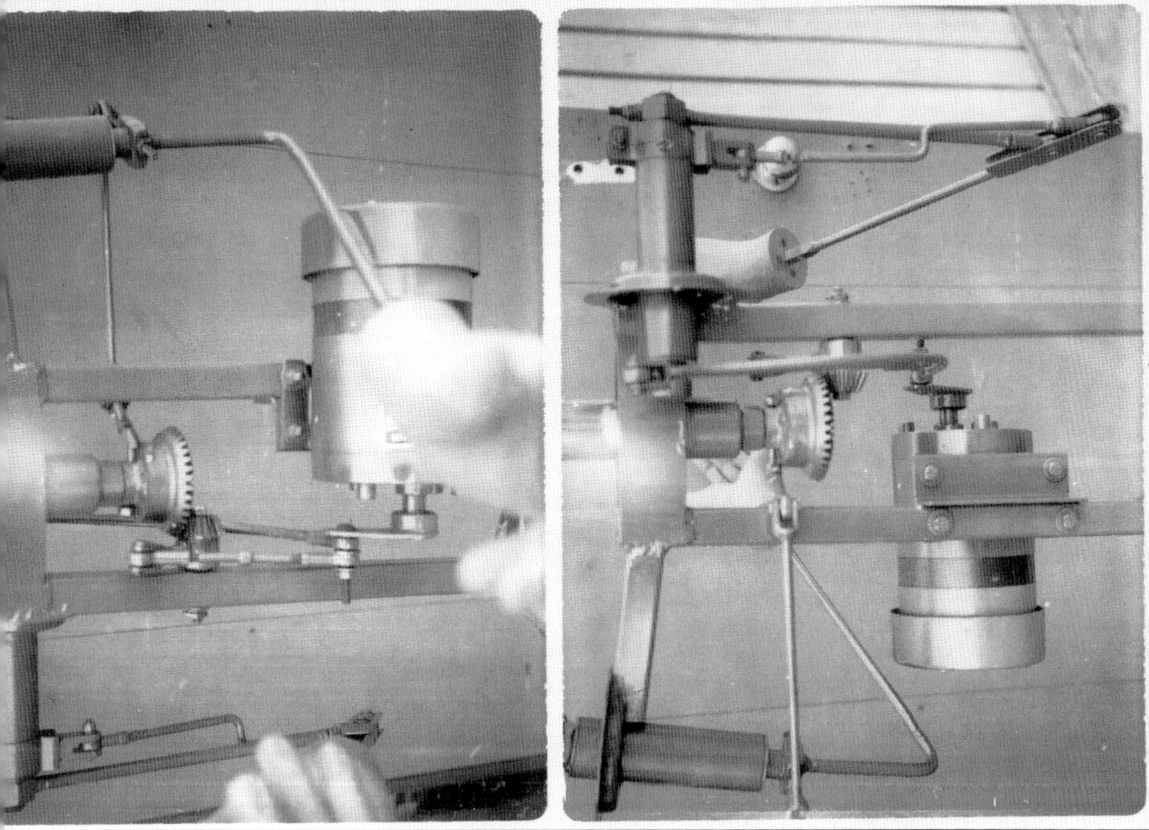

These photographs reveal the gear mechanism that Dick Kraus devised for animating the river ride postman. Kraus built the mechanism entirely out of old parts he found around the park. The only component that was new was the motor to run the contraption. In the left photograph, note the hand that points toward the viewer. At the very bottom of that photograph are the fingertips of the postman's other hand. The photograph on the right is a reverse angle, with both hands visible. (Courtesy of Dick Kraus.)

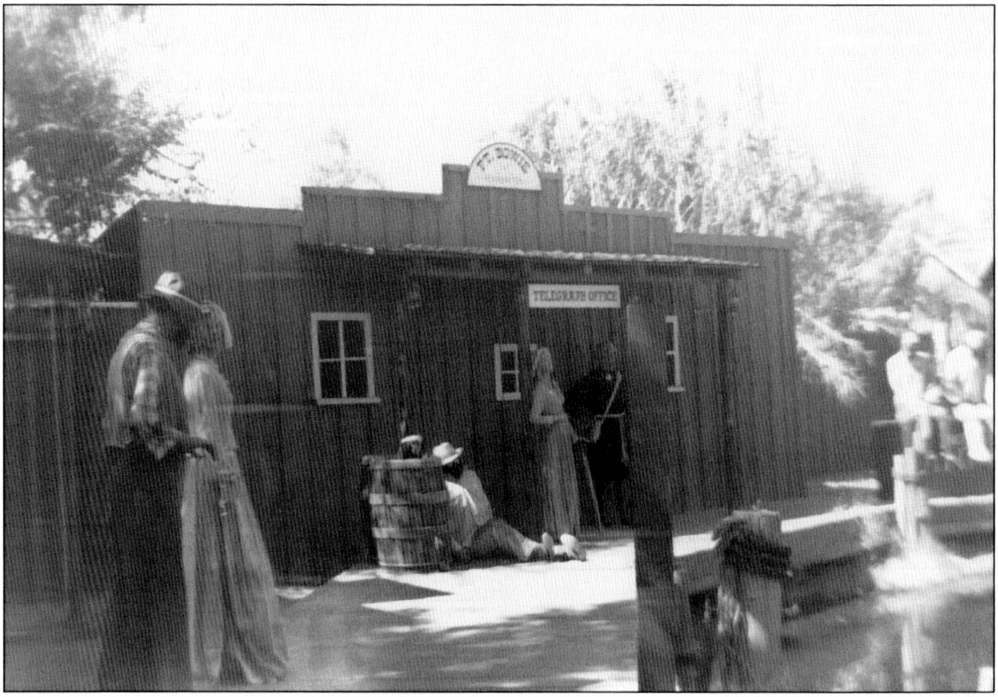

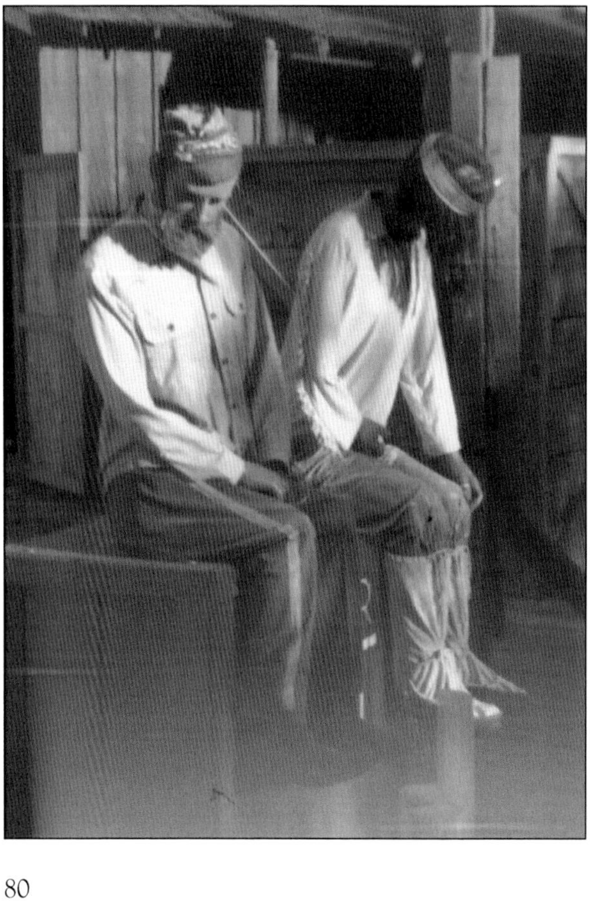

After exiting the haunted cave, the riverboat finally enters the safety of the port at Fort Bowie. Civilization at last! Here we see the Fort Bowie Headquarters and Trading Post with Telegraph Office. A variety of interesting characters mills about the pier, waiting for the next riverboat to dock and bring supplies, mail, visitors, and, most importantly, army reinforcements. (Courtesy of Dick Kraus.)

The two fellows sitting on the red crate, one a soldier and the other an Indian, are thoroughly inebriated. Animated by Dick Kraus, they rock to and fro, singing a drinking song. The words "Danger—TNT" are painted on the crate, introducing a distinct note of danger to the otherwise humorous tableau. (Courtesy of Dick Kraus.)

Waiting patiently at the dock are a well-to-do married couple, probably a landowner and his wife. Their married status is evident because they both wear rings, she on the third finger of her left hand, and he on the second finger, since his third finger is missing! The gentleman is smoking an extraordinarily large cigar, befitting his affluent status. (Courtesy of Dick Kraus.)

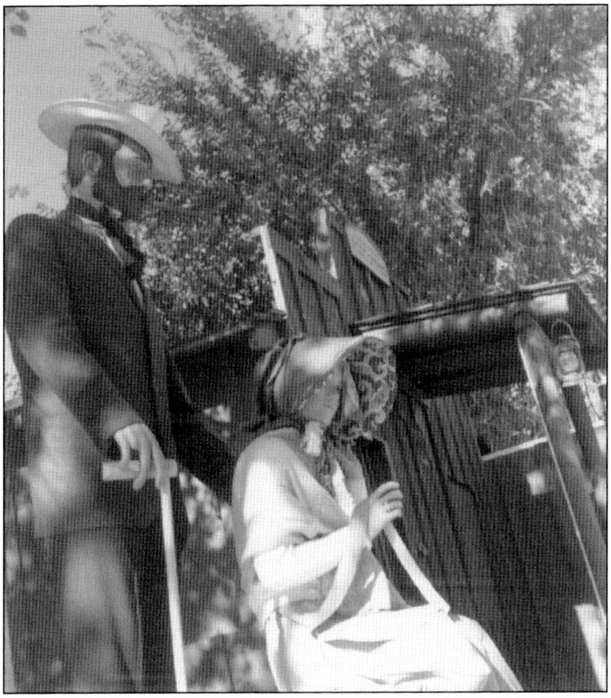

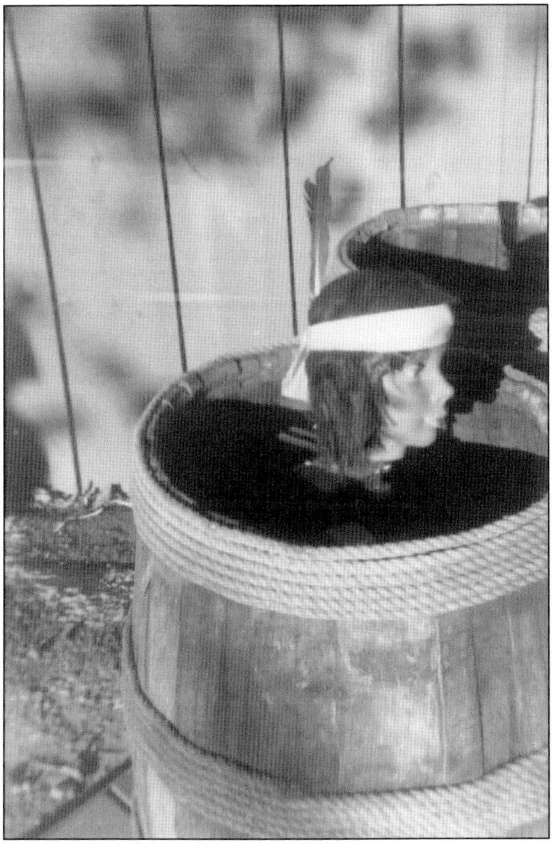

As the passengers arrive at the Trading Post and prepare to disembark the riverboat, they are greeted by a playful Indian child hiding in a barrel in front of the Telegraph Office. From the boat, only the child's head is visible, and onlookers naturally assume his body occupies the inside of the barrel. However, closer examination reveals the child's head is attached to a motorized mount that turns to follow the boat as it passes by. Here is another example of a female mannequin altered to resemble a child. The shape of the nose gives it away. (Courtesy of Dick Kraus.)

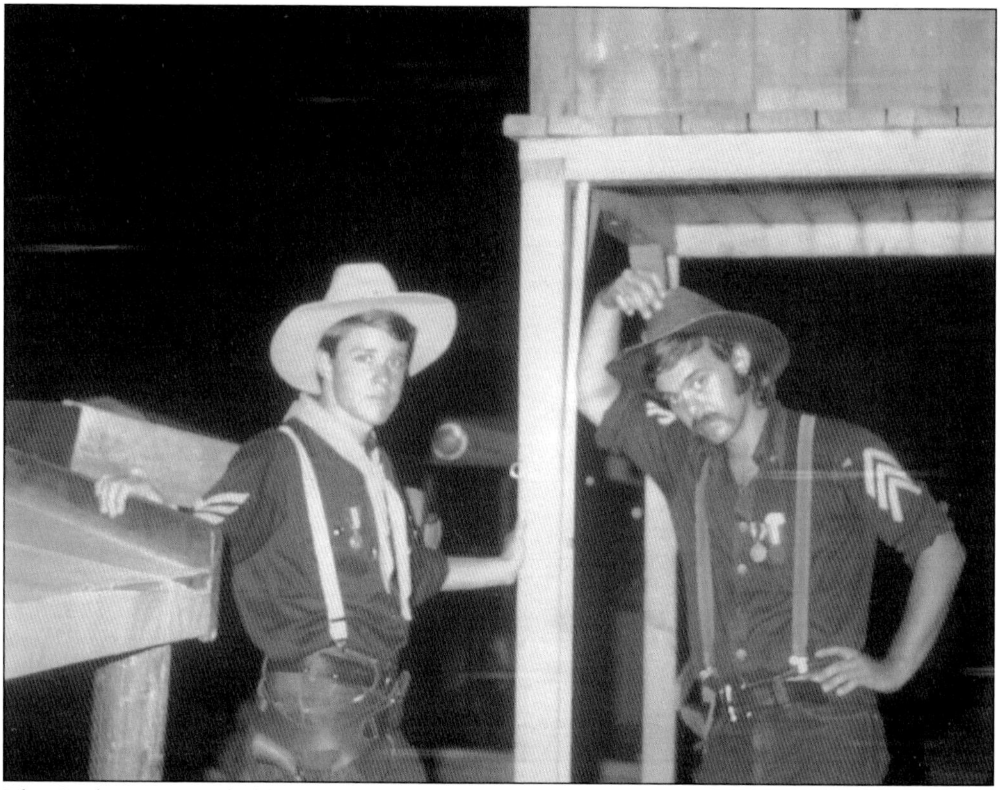

The Cochise's Stronghold river guides delivered a wonderfully corny shtick as they ferried their charges down the "roaring, raging and treacherous 'Have You Not' San Simon River," as they fondly referred to the perilous waterway. Before departing down the river, the guides half-heartedly attempted to talk their passengers out of attempting the journey. When this failed, they ominously informed everyone that their birth certificates had just expired! Sgt. Dave DuPree (left) and Sgt. Rick Brown, shown here, were the intrepid river guides in 1970. (Courtesy of Wendy Wasson.)

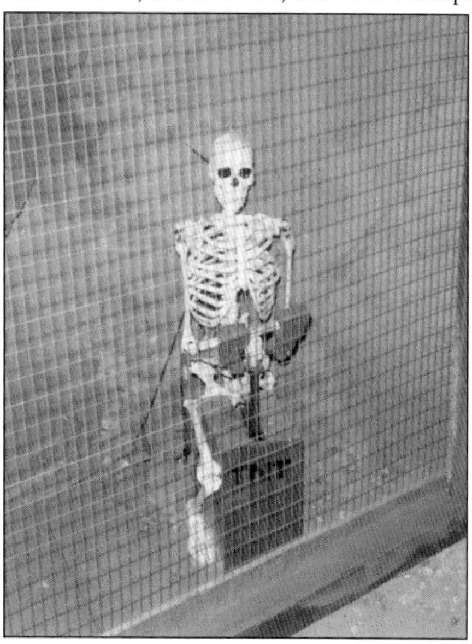

From the very beginning, the Lost Dutchman Mine ride was a popular target for vandals and thieves, and this unfortunate phenomenon led the new management to install security screens around many of the scenes. This measure succeeded in slowing down the illicit activity, but it also detracted from the ride and was not entirely effective in stopping the destruction. The screen mesh is clearly visible in this view of the dynamite-blasting skeleton near the beginning of the ride. (Courtesy of Dick Kraus.)

This photograph shows the Dutchman Mine shaft following the initial mine "explosion." At the end of this tunnel was a waterfall streaming down the back wall. The water ran along the sides of the shaft at floor level. The small track in the center of the floor guided the mine cars, and the black lines on either side were left by the rubber back wheels of the cars. Around the corner to the right, passengers will encounter the pair of skeletal miners at work with their conveyor belt. (Courtesy of Dick Kraus.)

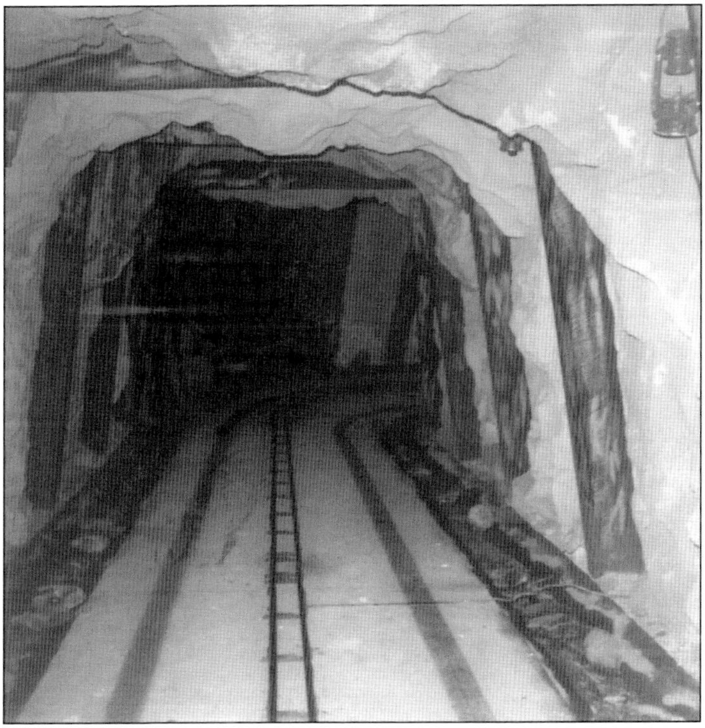

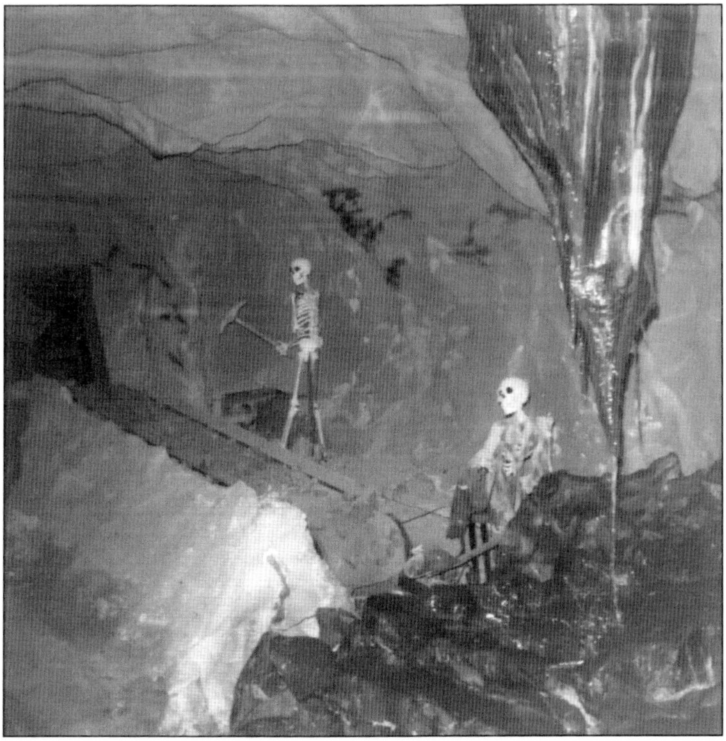

The two ghostly miners at work were framed by the large stalactite, reflecting pool, and the cleverly devised conveyor belt. Gold ore was glued onto an endless loop of fabric resembling a belt, and, with the small retaining wall concealing the mechanism, a convincing portrayal was produced. The water for the reflecting pool was on a recirculating pump separate from the preceding waterfall. (Courtesy of Dick Kraus.)

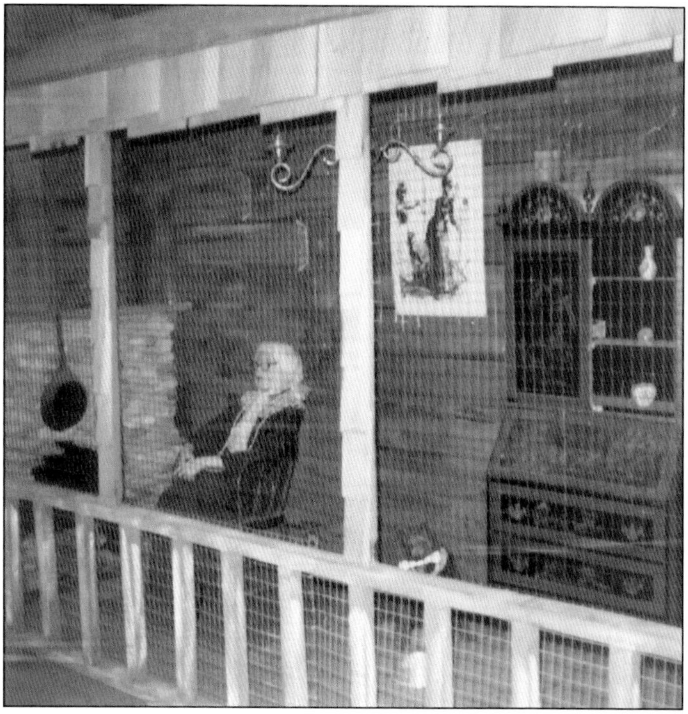

By the early 1970s, the mine ride parlor tableau had been extensively upgraded. An entirely new background was created and illuminated, and the old lady's skeleton was replaced by a female mannequin. The scene also now features an antique cabinet with china pieces, a newly added light fixture, and an antique advertising poster. In front of the cabinet, partially obscured by the security screen, sits a small dog holding a bare bone in his teeth. Kraus animated his tail to wag playfully as the passengers rode by. (Courtesy of Dick Kraus.)

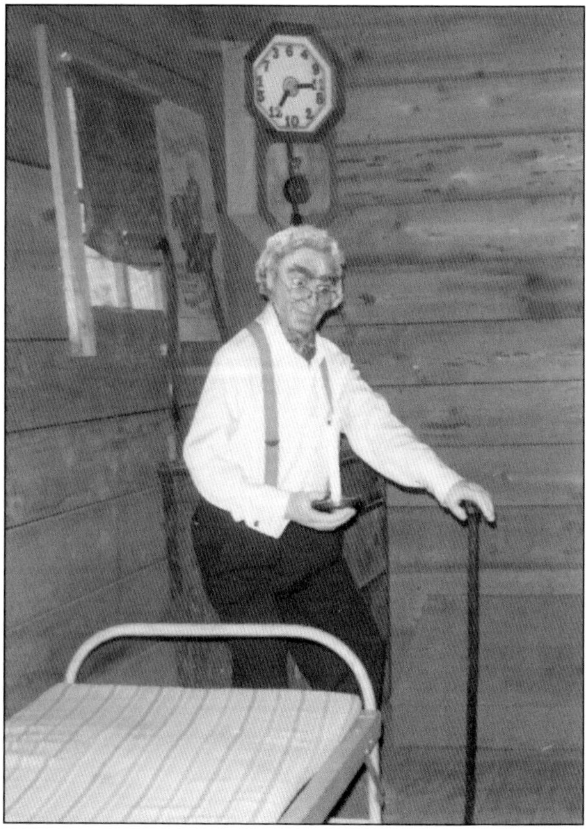

Directly across from the old lady and her pooch now stands an elderly miner with his candle, cane, and clock. Contrary to popular belief, this figure was not intended to be the Lost Dutchman, but was inserted simply to address concerns that there was not enough to see in this portion of the ride. Here is yet another example of a female mannequin repurposed to serve as a male figure. Dick Kraus handmade the miner's cane, the lit candle, and the unusual clock on the wall. Close examination reveals that the clock face numbers are jumbled entirely out of sequence. (Courtesy of Dick Kraus.)

The revised barbershop scenario was called "Black Bart's," a reference to the giant mural on the back wall depicting Black Bart in the barber's chair. In this photograph, the results of vandalism are apparent. The figures now sport clothing and shoes to cover the broken and missing skeleton pieces. The barber has grown a mustache, and the customer's need for a shave and a haircut has become exceptionally pronounced. (Courtesy of Dick Kraus.)

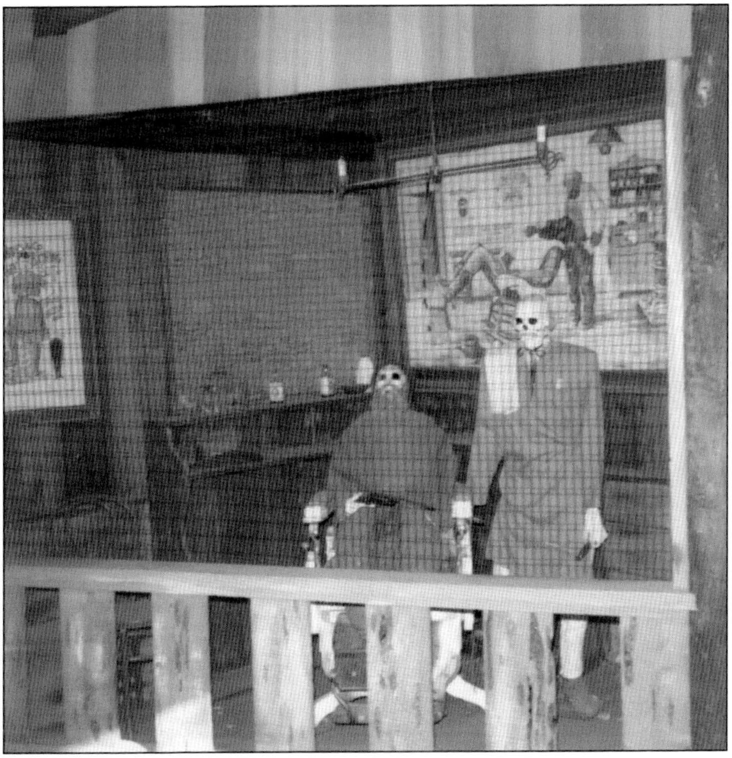

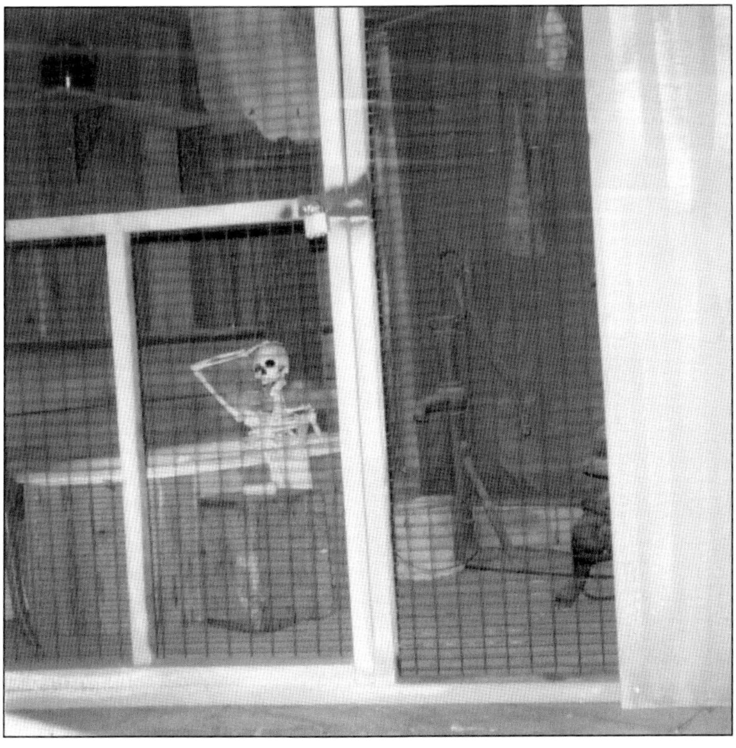

In the new bathtub scene, the tub is now enclosed and the miner is rubbing his head. A hand pump and bucket for water appear right of center, and a Franklin potbellied stove stands at the far right side of the scene. A towel drapes over the edge of the tub, and the bather appears to be quite relaxed as he smokes a corncob pipe. His pants hang on the wall behind him. Sadly, the padlock on the security screen is clearly visible. (Courtesy of Dick Kraus.)

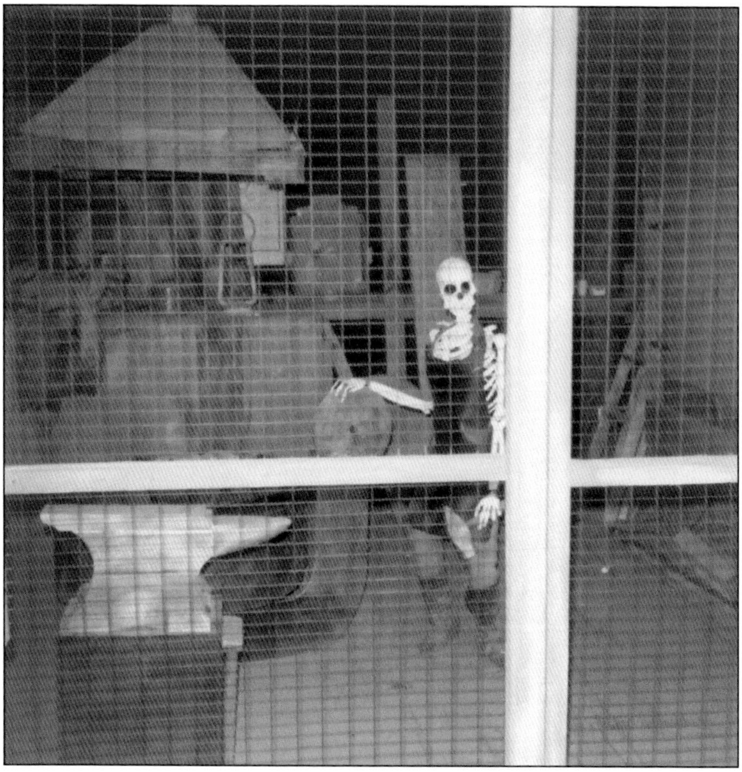

The blacksmith skeleton has been returned to his shop, and is now wearing a proper apron and holding a sledgehammer while working at the grinding wheel. The anvil still stands in front of the forge, which is glowing with hot embers, although it is now obscured by the security screen. (Courtesy of Dick Kraus.)

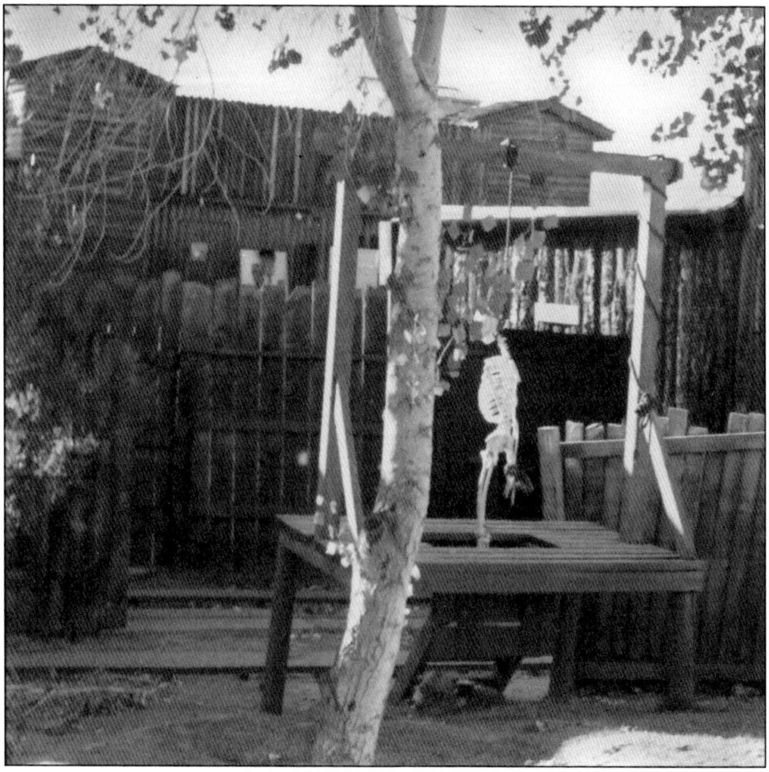

Meanwhile, out in the graveyard, the mine car moves past a gallows and an unfortunate Dutchman ghost at the end of his rope. This was a new addition to the graveyard tableau. Note the fort looming in the background. (Courtesy of John Muessle.)

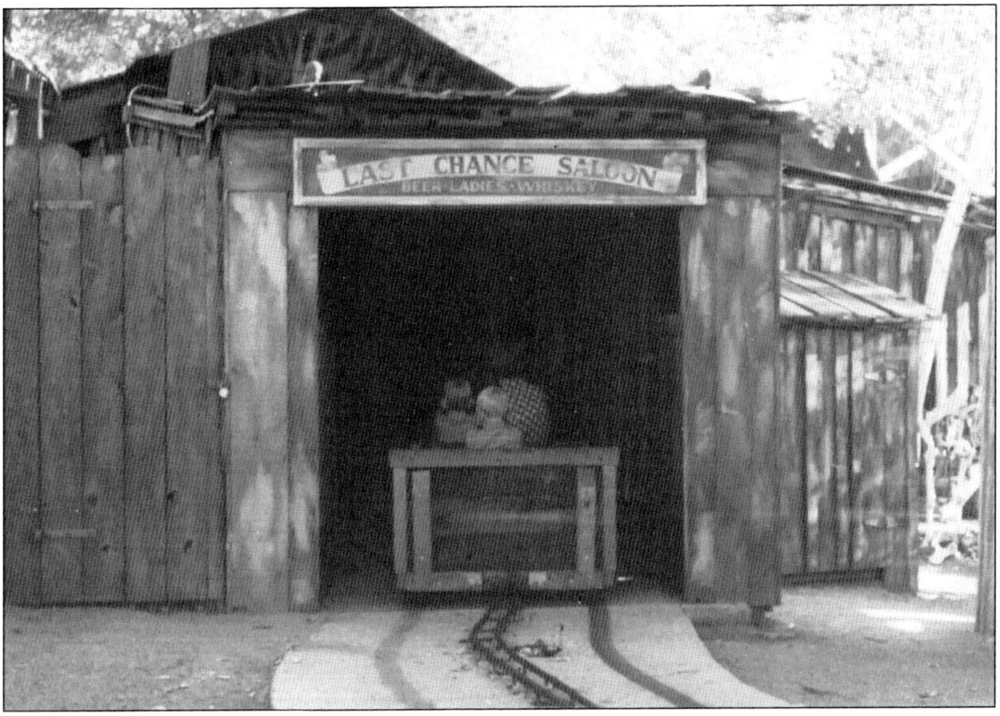

Leaving behind the somber graveyard, a mine car disappears into the gloom of the final building of the Lost Dutchman Mine ride, and the climactic saloon scene. (Courtesy of John Muessle.)

The Dutchman saloon scene had been extensively modified by the time this photograph was taken in 1972. The bartender is now alone at the bar, waiting to pour another drink. The saloon cutie gazes out at the passing mine car, looking quite alluring in her finest outfit. Strangely, the hand of the saloon girl is not skeletal, but rather a mannequin hand. On the left edge of the photograph is another Franklin stove, and directly above it, perched in the upper left corner, hangs a startling anachronism: a mirrored disco ball. (Courtesy of Dick Kraus.)

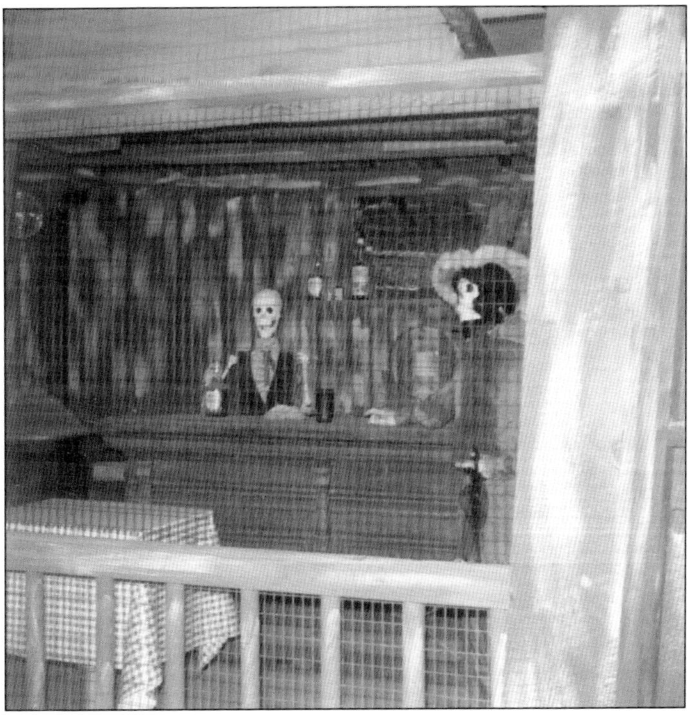

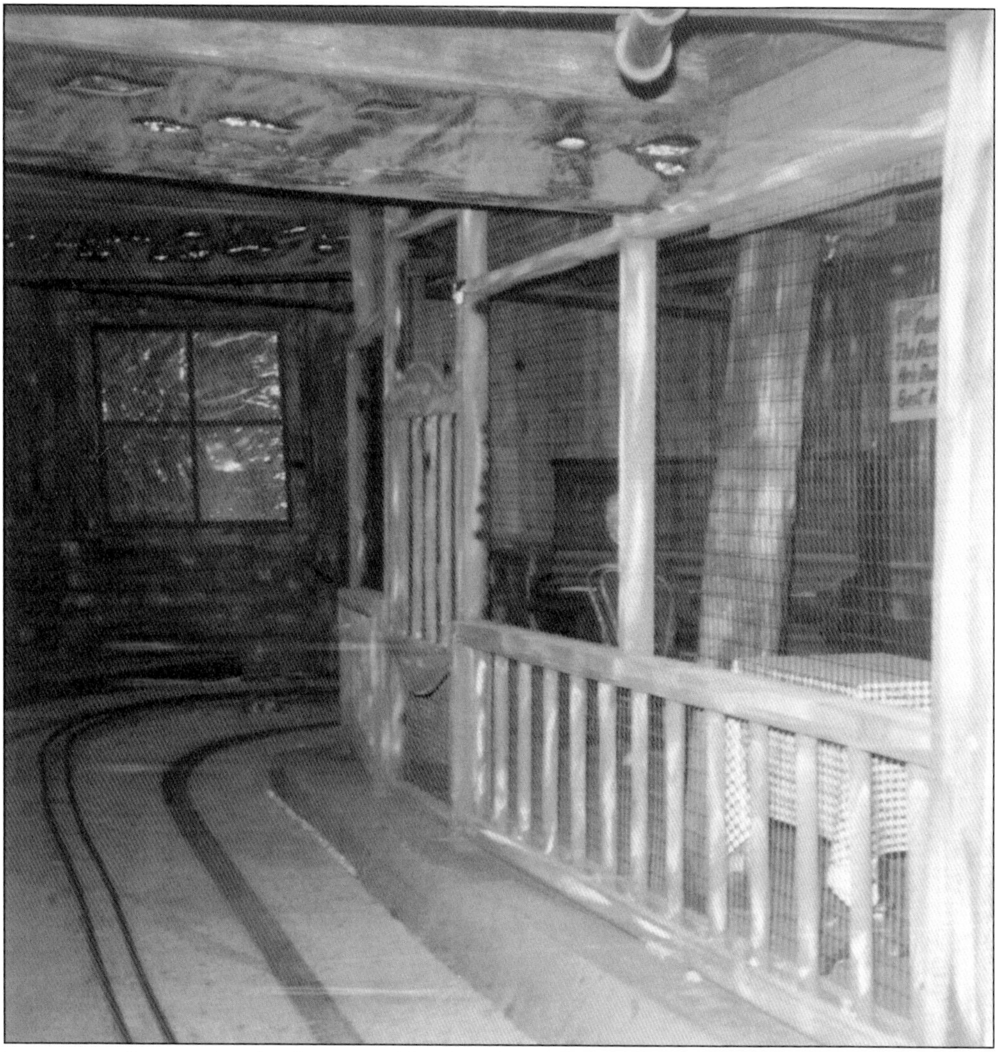

Passengers glimpse their final vision of the Lost Dutchman's Mine before the mine car exits back into the park. The piano player now sits on the far left side of the barroom, and is clothed due to vandalism. On the wall, a sign reads "Please don't shoot the piano player! He's doing the best he can!" Behind the top edge of the piano emanates an ominous red glow. The piano appears to be aflame, and in fact, the whole saloon seems to be on the verge of imminent immolation. The supporting beams above are glowing with embers, and the window directly facing the mine car reveals flames licking at the outside of the glass panes. The panes were actually translucent plastic stretched over the window frames. A floodlight projected a combination of red, yellow, orange, and blue light through a revolving color gel holder. A floor-mounted fan gently blew strips of reflective plastic upward behind the windows, creating the illusion of real flames licking at the window "glass." (Courtesy of Dick Kraus.)

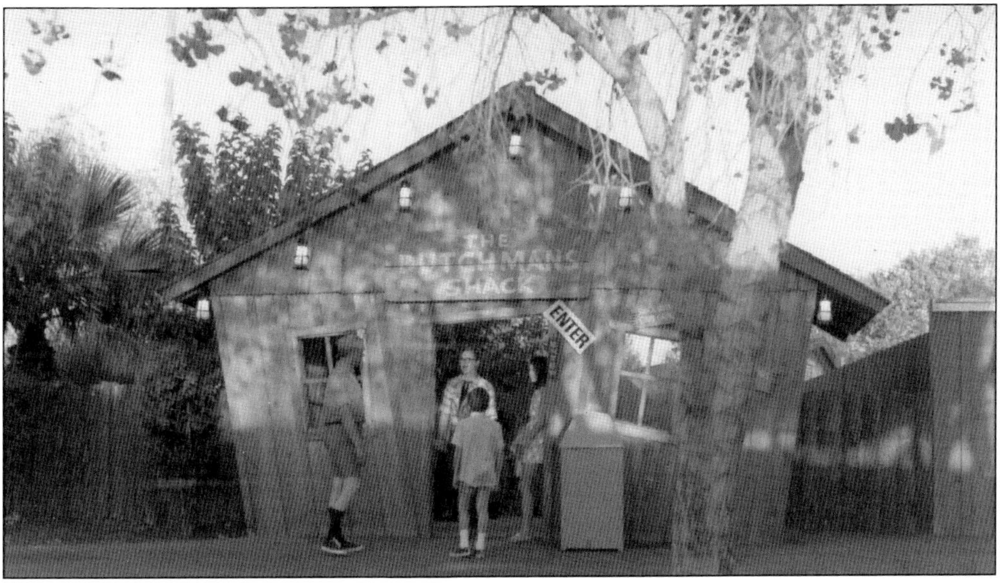

The Dutchman's Shack tilt house continued to be a popular Legend City draw throughout the 1970s, vindicating Louis Crandall's insistence on including the attraction in his original vision of the park. The above photograph shows the exterior of the attraction as it appeared during the Shoen era. Below, a group of youngsters enjoys the bizarre effects of the interior of the tilt house during the same period, around 1969. (Courtesy of *Arizona Contractor and Community* magazine.)

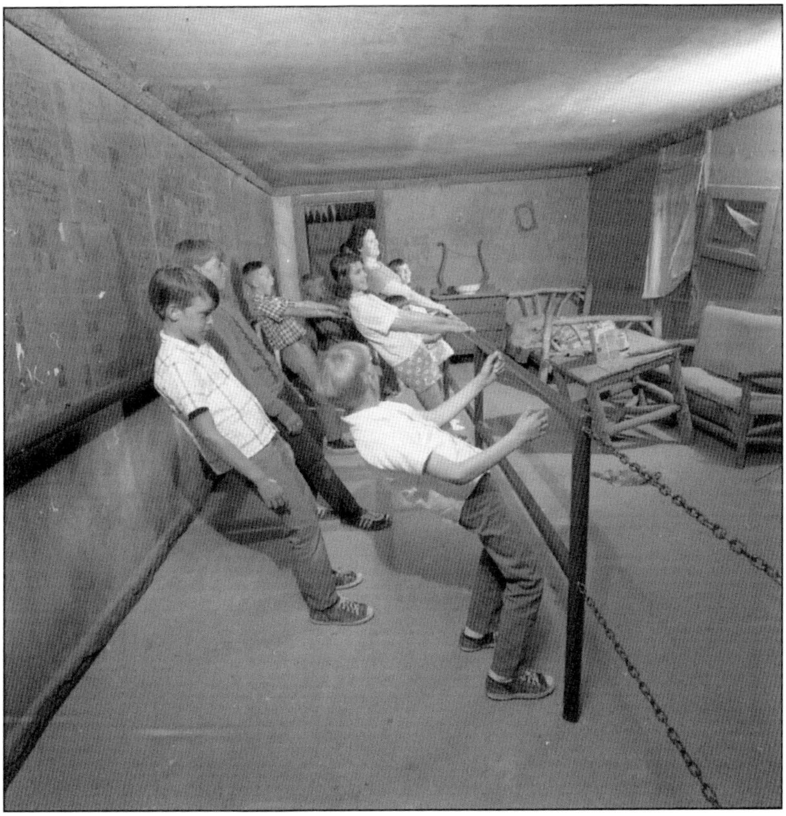

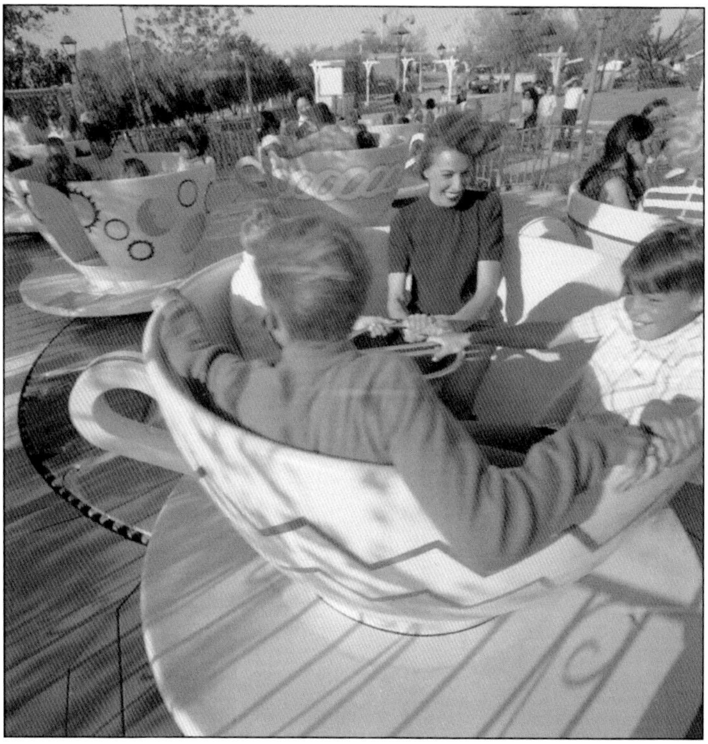

The emphasis shifted decisively to amusement-park rides in the new Legend City. Shown here are examples of both the old and the new. At left, park visitors continue to experience the simple joys of the Krazy Kups. Among the amusement rides that Shoen acquired for Legend City was the Monster Mouse (below), purchased for $10,000 at Pacific Ocean Park's auction in 1968. Renamed the Gila Monster, the ride was later moved to make room for the flume ride, and then its original name was restored. (Left, courtesy of *Arizona Contractor and Community* magazine; below, courtesy of John Muessle.)

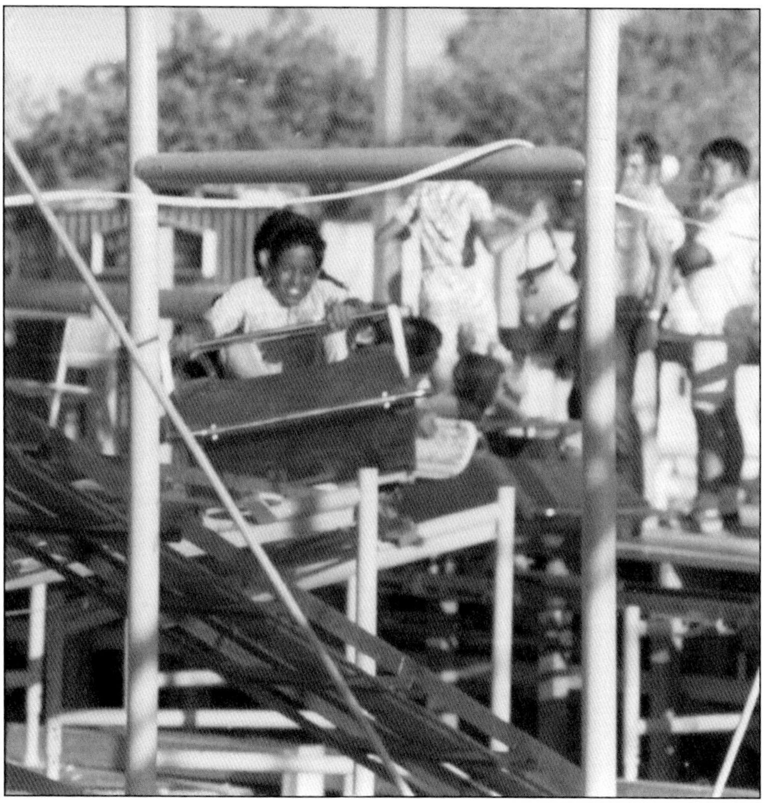

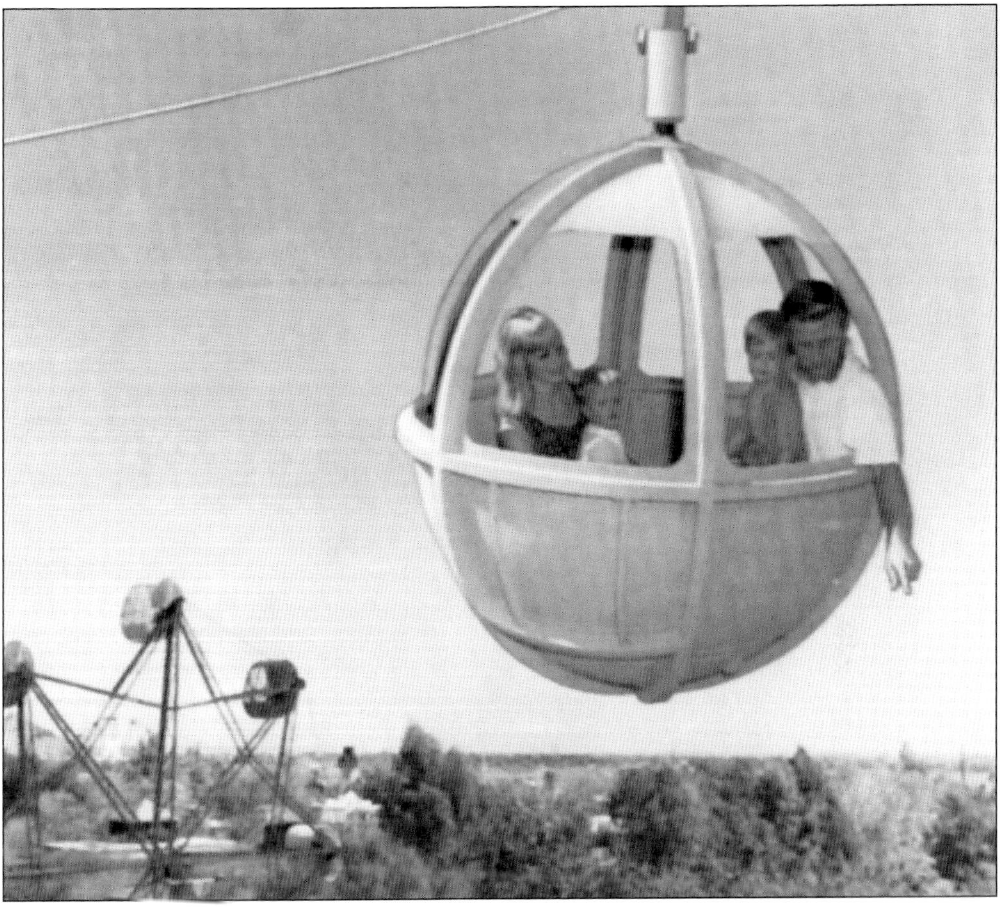

The Legend City sky ride underwent a major overhaul when Frontier Funland Inc. took over the park. The old gondola-style cars were changed out for space-age orbs, and the attraction was renamed the Satellite Ride. Park visitors would eventually discover that this ride provided one of Legend City's best respites from the daytime heat, as a gusty breeze often buffeted the cars gliding up to 120 feet above the park grounds.

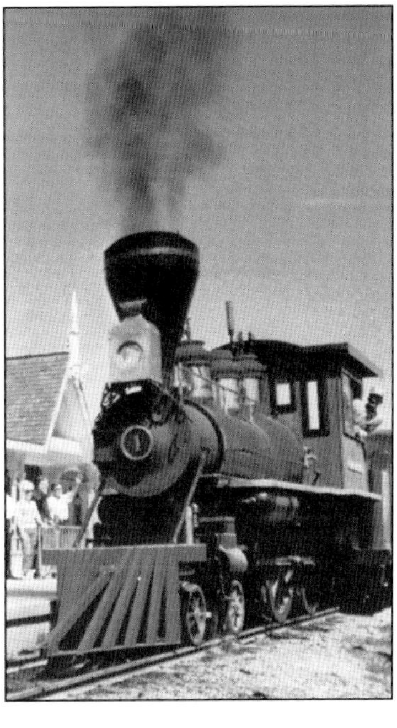

The Legend City train presented some problems when it was returned to service. The engine was coal-fired, but a design flaw emerged with the control valve rods. Excessive heat was required to create and maintain a good head of steam. This problem was solved by shortening and then welding back two of the rods. Another issue involved ineffective air brakes, which prompted the operators to stop the train exactly as it was done in the old days, by putting it in reverse and giving it a little throttle. The Iron Horse is seen here as it appeared shortly after the park's reopening.

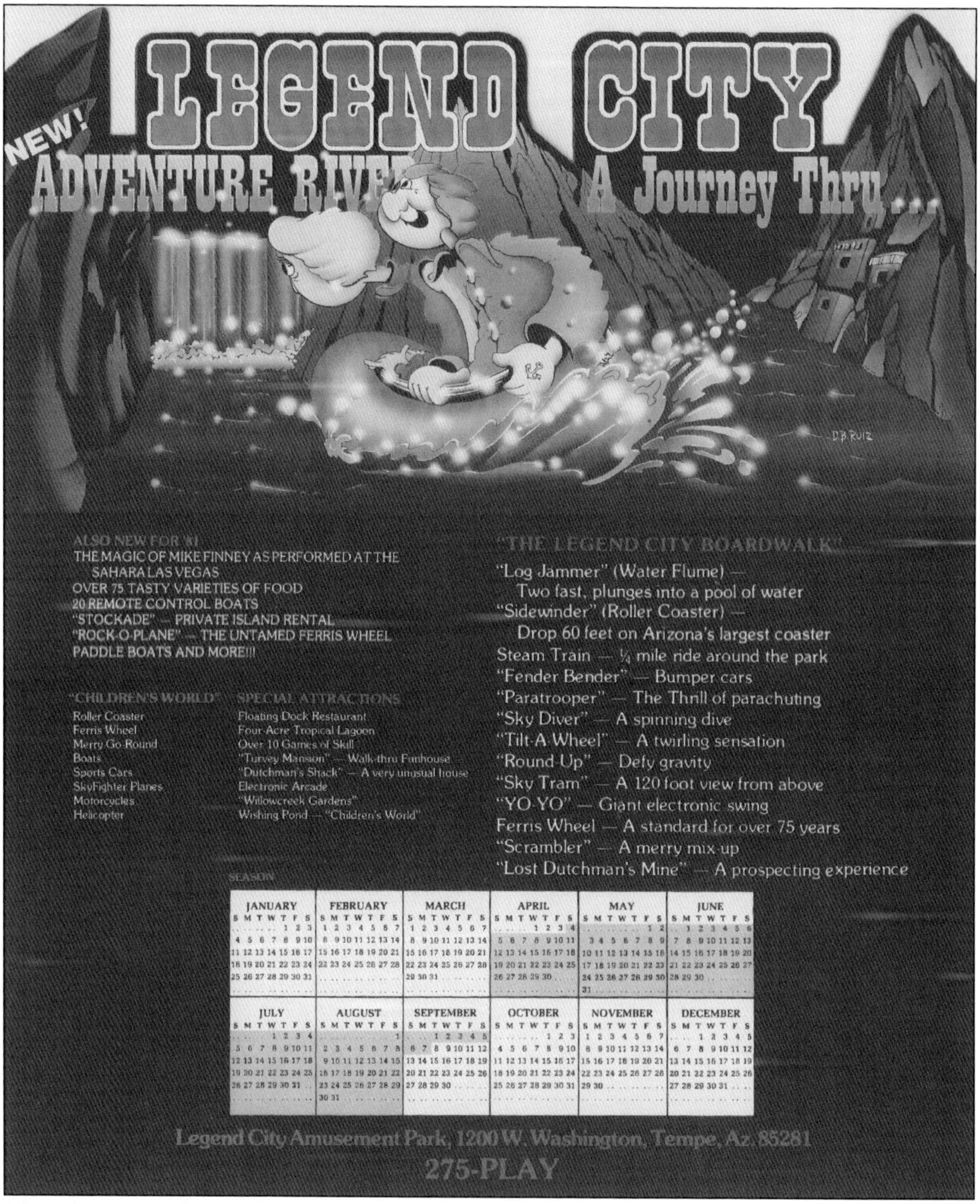

This advertising placard from the 1981 season provides detailed documentation regarding the state of Legend City in its final few years of operation. Note the increasing emphasis on amusement and carnival-style rides and attractions. The river ride has been renamed Adventure River and now features smaller, inflatable boats. The old Indian Island and Stockade facilities are available for rental by local companies. The only truly original park attractions in evidence are the Dutchman's Shack and Lost Dutchman's Mine ride. Interestingly, the 1981 season ran from early April through the Labor Day weekend, skipping the cooler months entirely. (Courtesy of Jim Madden.)

Four

The Twilight Years

Legend City's transformation to a carnival-ride park escalated through the 1970s with two more ownership changes. After four years of mixed success with the park, Sam Shoen lost interest in the business and sold Legend City in March 1973 to Continental Recreation Inc., a subsidiary of a Japanese amusement park ride manufacturer. The venture was not a successful one for Continental. Inadequate attendance forced the park to close yet again, in December 1974.

The park resumed operations in June 1976, thanks to the efforts of the Capell family, traveling carnival operators originally based in Coolidge. William Capell had managed Legend City during its time in receivership, and he was keen to try his hand at ownership. The Capells purchased the park rides and buildings and secured a management contract from the Japanese owners, enabling them to lease the property and reopen the park. In early 1977, the Capell family firm, Dot Amusement Corp., purchased the land outright, completing their acquisition of Legend City. "I am almost 46 and never owned and operated a park before," Capell said at the time. "I thought I'd like to do it."

The Capells had grand plans for Legend City, and, to their credit, they delivered to some extent, bringing in a variety of entertainment acts and a world-class roller coaster in addition to an array of carnival-style rides. They maintained the park for eight years, longer than any other owners.

Legend City at last began to generate substantial revenue, with the Capells grossing over $1 million a year at times during their tenure. But by the late 1970s, while the park was becoming increasingly dilapidated, the real estate beneath it was becoming increasingly valuable. This reality would seal the fate of Arizona's family fun park.

The Salt River Project had long coveted the park's land as a potential site for its new corporate headquarters, and in 1982, SRP acquired the property. Legend City closed for the last time on Sunday night, September 4, 1983. A two-day auction was held the following spring, and the demolition of the park followed shortly thereafter. Just two short decades after its glorious and optimistic grand opening, Legend City was no more.

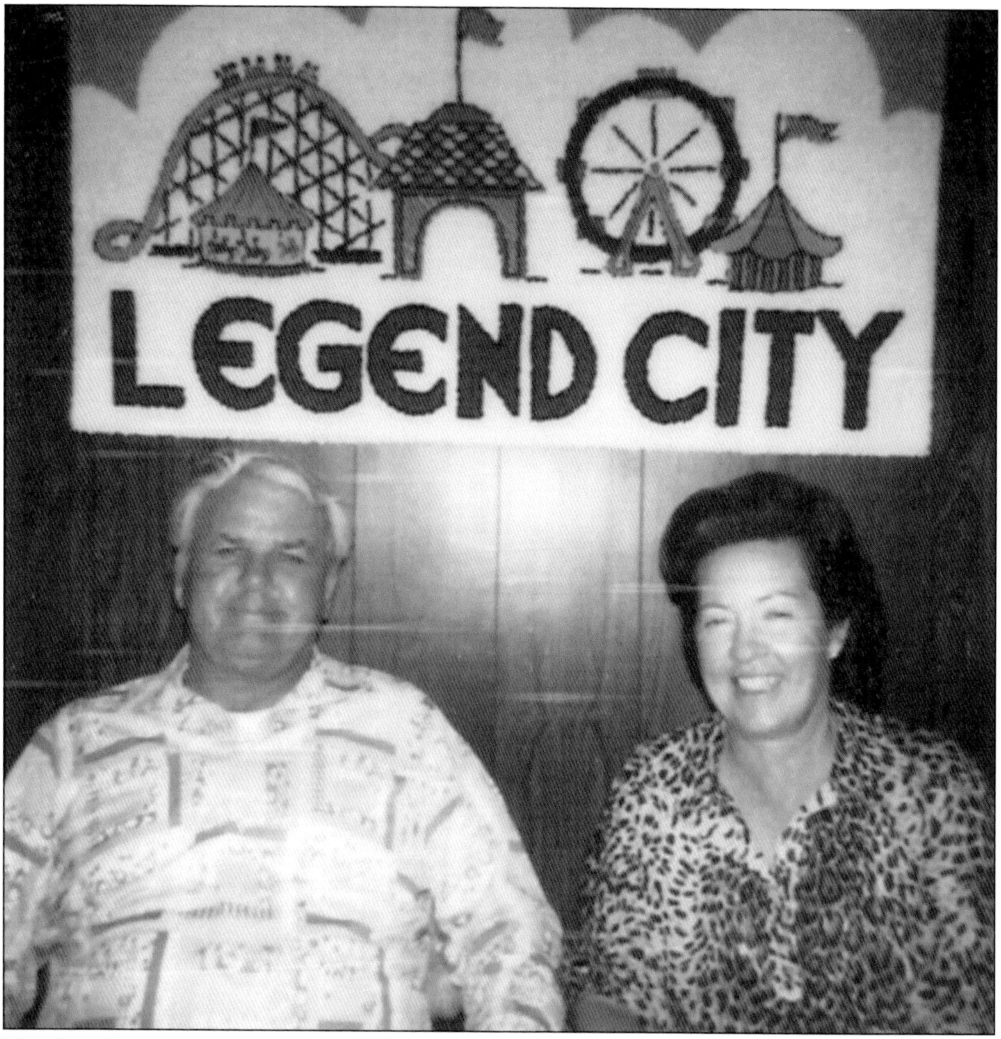

The Capells took over operations at Legend City on May 31, 1976, and opened the park just 12 days later, working around the clock to prepare the facility. Bill Capell immediately brought in a number of carnival-type rides, including a Sky Diver, Zipper, Sizzler, and Twister. He was also conscious of the importance of providing a broad variety of entertainment options. Rock bands, magicians, ventriloquists, actors, and other performers were deployed across the park. Legend City's latest incarnation got off to a good start: a reported 23,000 visitors attended that first weekend. Here, Bill and Dorothy Capell relax in their park office under a special handmade Legend City rug. (Courtesy of Bill Capell Jr.)

Hollywood and Arizona stuntman Ron Nix performed a Wild West stunt show at Legend City for five seasons under both the Shoen and Capell ownerships. He made himself a permanent part of Legend City lore in April 1977 with a record-breaking 106-foot freefall from the Legend City sky ride tower into a pile of flaming cardboard boxes. This photograph comes from the collection of Ivan Henry, a circus man who was the park entertainment director when Legend City reopened in 1976. He became park manager the following season. (Courtesy of www.thecircusblog.com.)

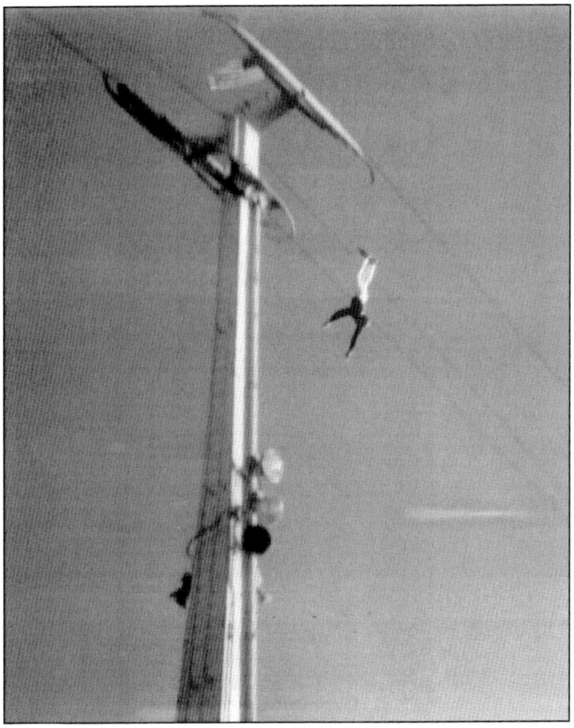

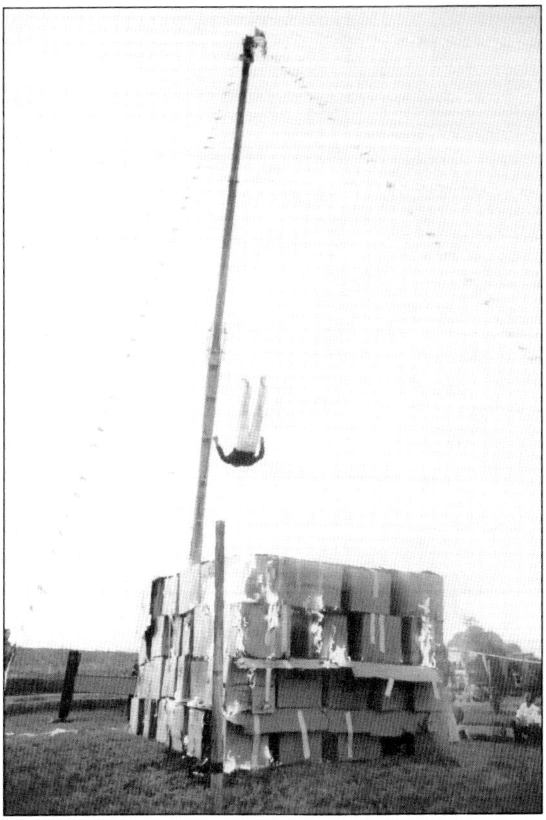

This photograph documents an earlier, 67-foot jump by Nix in 1973, during the Shoen era. These well-publicized jumps attracted people from all over the Phoenix area. Note the flaming cardboard boxes at bottom. (Courtesy of Ron Nix.)

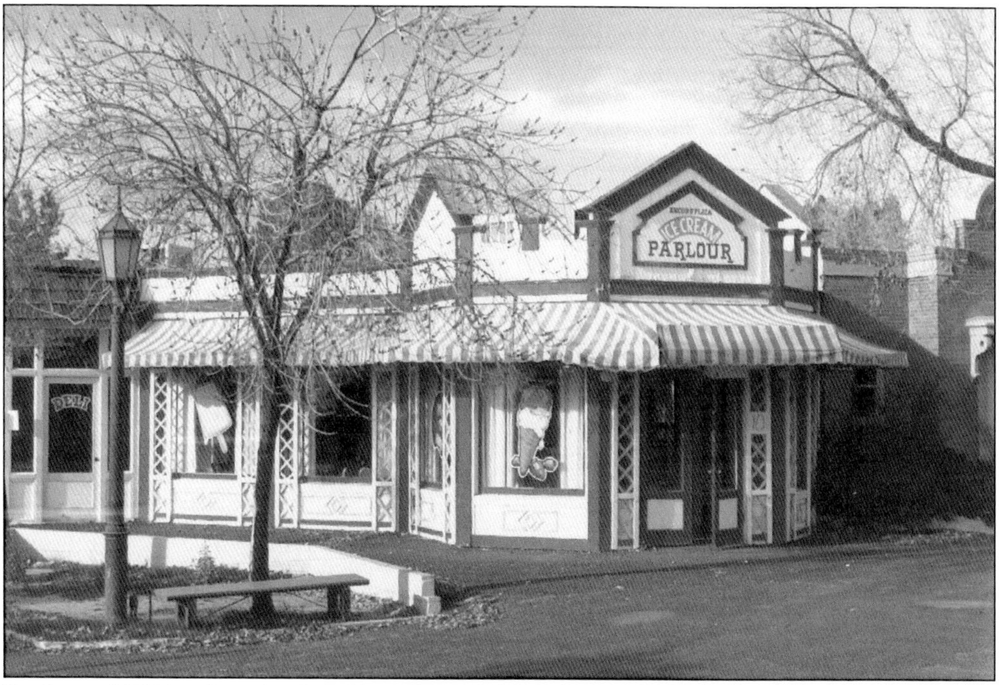

By the mid-1970s, when the Capells took over, the infrastructure at Legend City was beginning to age noticeably. This was a mixed blessing, as it added authenticity to the buildings and rides but also compromised their structural integrity. The old Shamrock Ice Cream Parlor in the Gay '90s section was renamed the Victorian Ice Cream Parlor and began offering Borden products. The building required significant restoration when the park started up again after the Capell acquisition. Sue Ramage, the ice-cream parlor concessionaire at the time, reported, "It was a mess. We had to clean and paint up the best we could in the short time we had to do it." The above photograph shows the parlor after its restoration. Below is a rare view of the interior of the building. (Courtesy of David Doyle.)

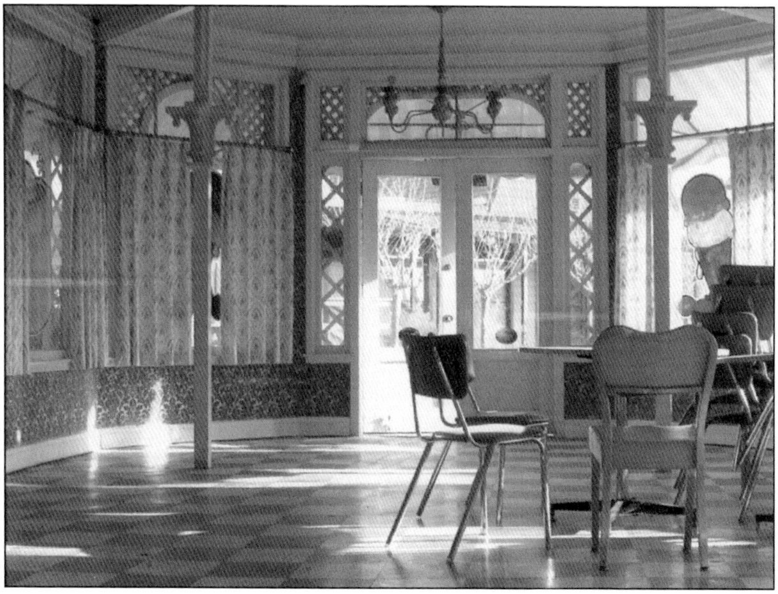

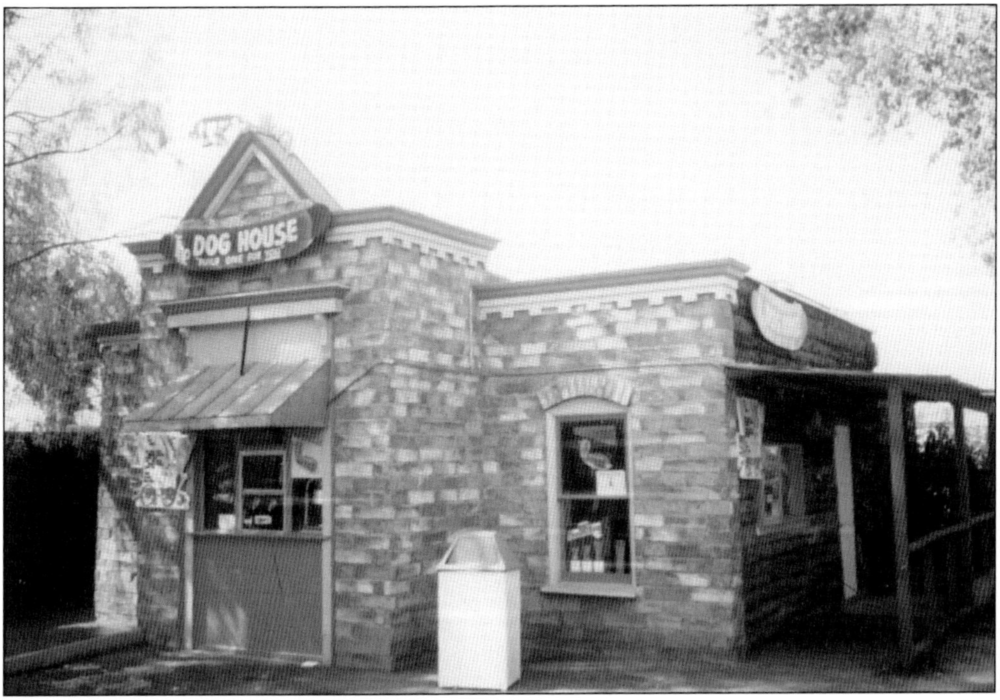

During the 1978 season, Legend City offered 15 shops, 10 fast-food outlets, and 2 restaurants. The old Print Shop building was repurposed as the Dog House (shown here), a fast-food restaurant offering five different styles of dog for the discriminating hot dog aficionado.

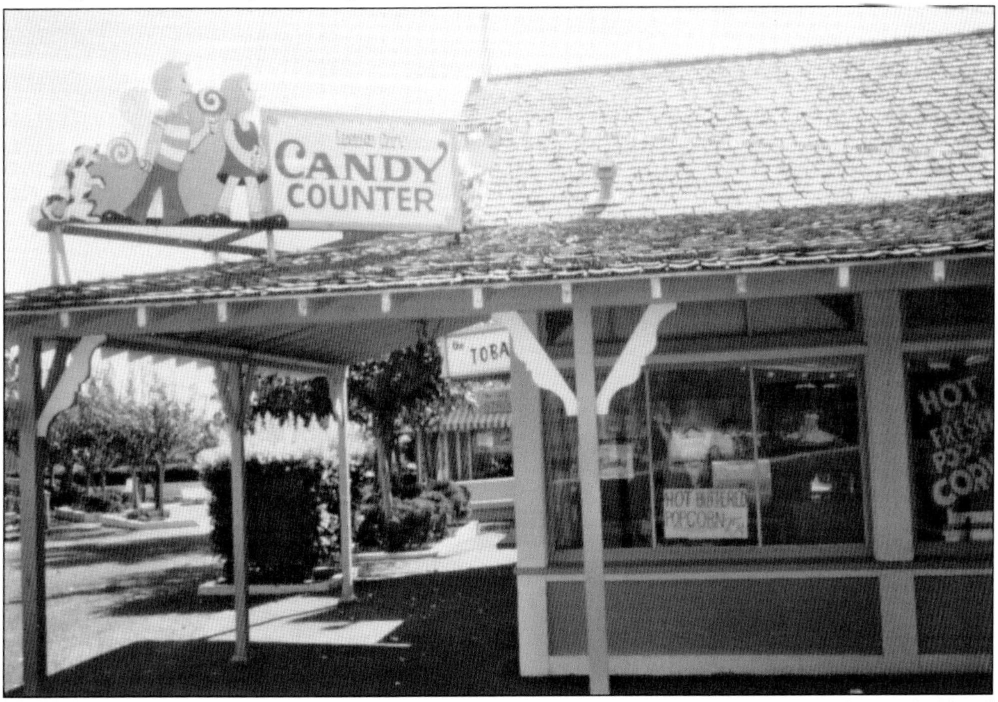

The Candy Counter, another fast-food outlet, was located near the ice-cream parlor and offered homemade candy apples and a variety of other confections.

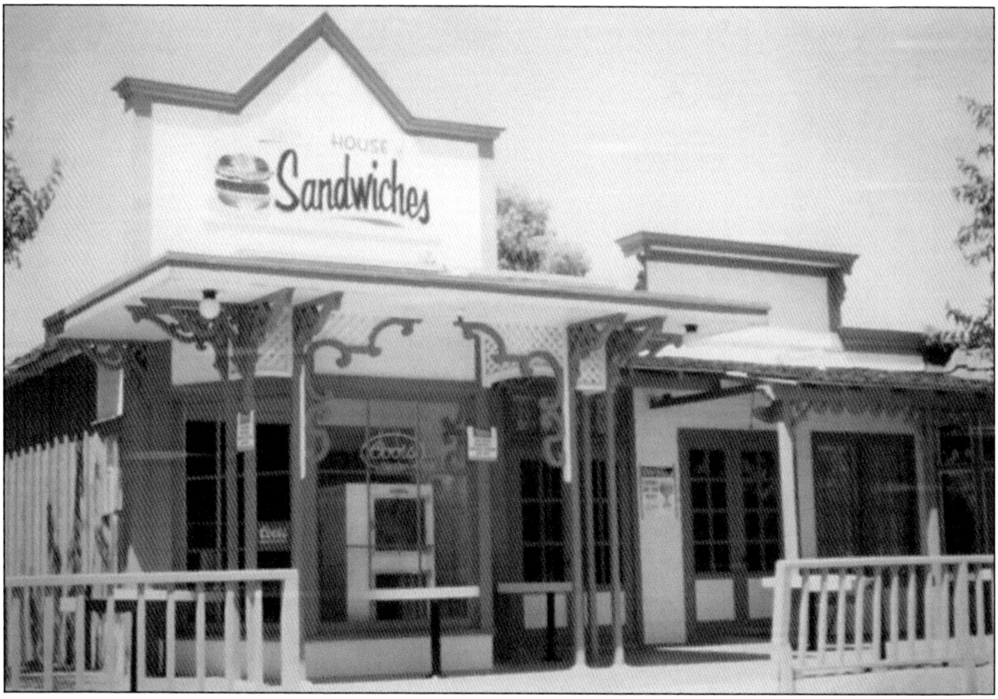

In 1980, Legend City started selling beer, with Coors being vended through a local distributor. A beer sign is clearly visible in the window of the House of Sandwiches (shown here), a small but busy restaurant that was housed in one of the original Victorian-style shops.

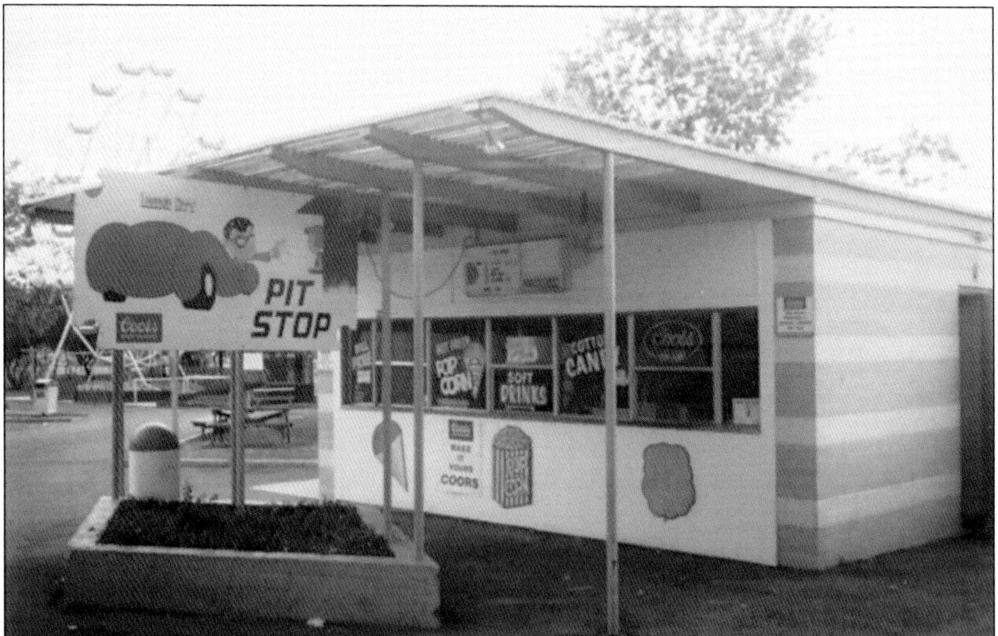

Cold brews were also available at Pit Stop, a freestanding fast-food outlet that specialized in popcorn, cotton candy, and dill pickles.

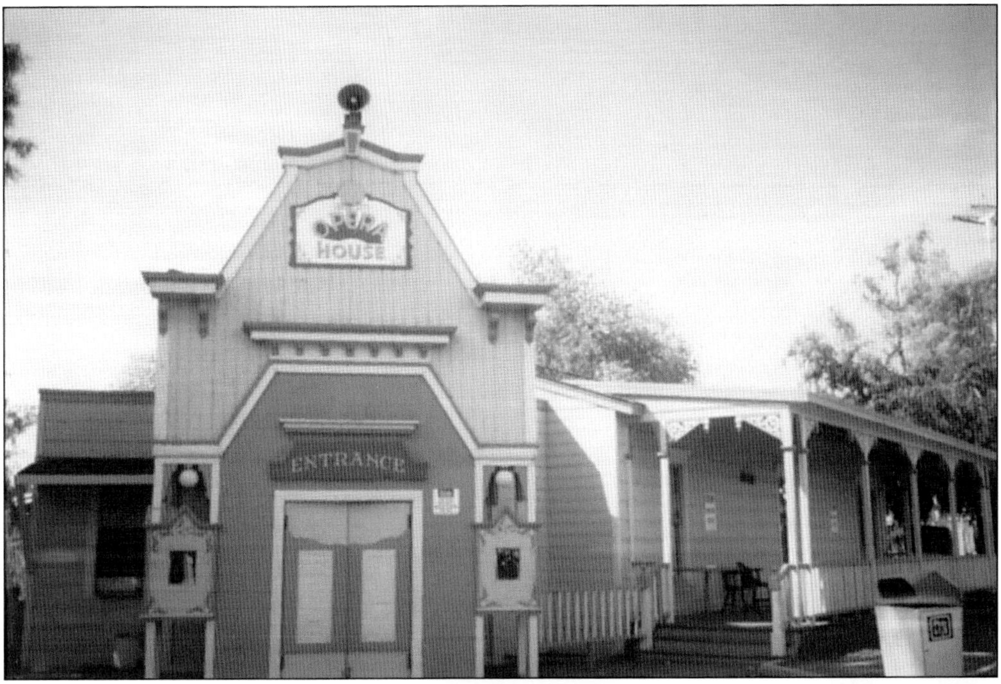

The old Red Garter Saloon, formerly the Golden Palace, had been renamed The Legend City Opera House by the mid-1970s, yet another step away from the original Old West theme of the park. An example of Opera House fare was *The Plight of the Prospector's Daughter*, an original melodrama that elicited cheers and hissing from its audiences in the spring and summer of 1974. Magicians and ventriloquists were also typical acts at the Opera House during this period, with performers rushing from their shows there to the Lagoon stage and back again. Admission to the Opera House shows was included in the park's general admission.

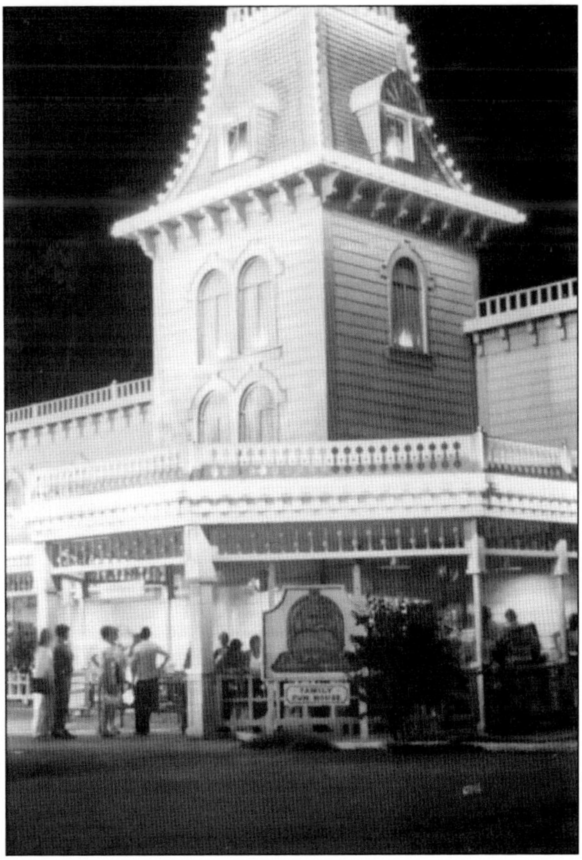

The Turvey Mansion was a two-story, seven-room family funhouse purchased by Legend City in 1978 from the Busch Gardens amusement park in Van Nuys, California. The attraction was a hit with park visitors and drew strong crowds when it opened that summer.

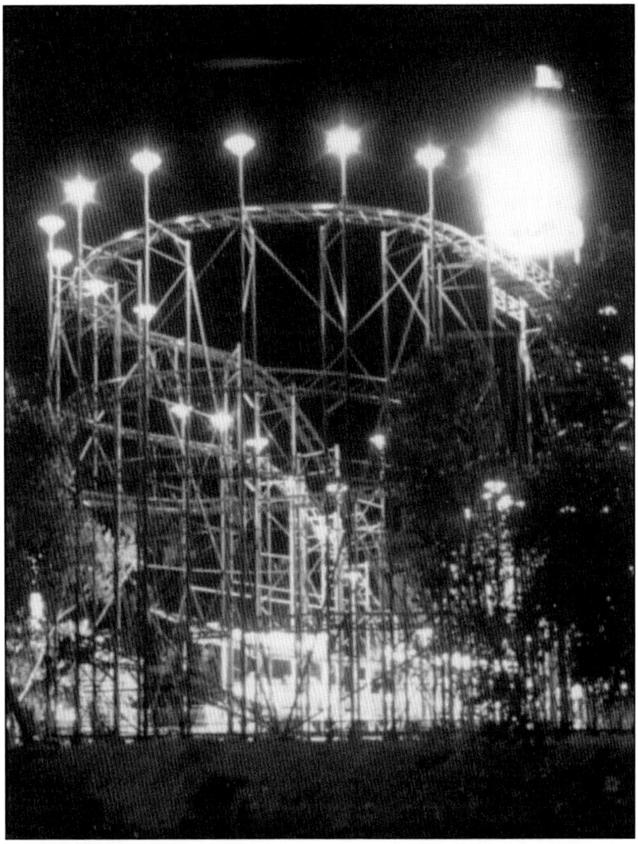

The Capells brought a world-class roller coaster to Legend City in 1978, a 65-foot-high Pinfari steel coaster acquired from the defunct Riverside Park in Chicago. The coaster weighed 100 tons, measured a half-mile in length, and had a working capacity of 1,400 riders per hour. Billed as one of the largest steel coasters in the western United States, it had a 60-foot drop-off at its first hill and was illuminated at night by more than 4,500 light bulbs and tubes. Wallace and Ladmo promoted a "Name the Coaster" contest that brought in up to 1,000 letters a day from young fans hoping to brand the new attraction. The grand prize was a season pass to Legend City and dinner and a ride on the coaster with Wall and Lad. "Sidewinder" opened for business at Legend City in July 1978.

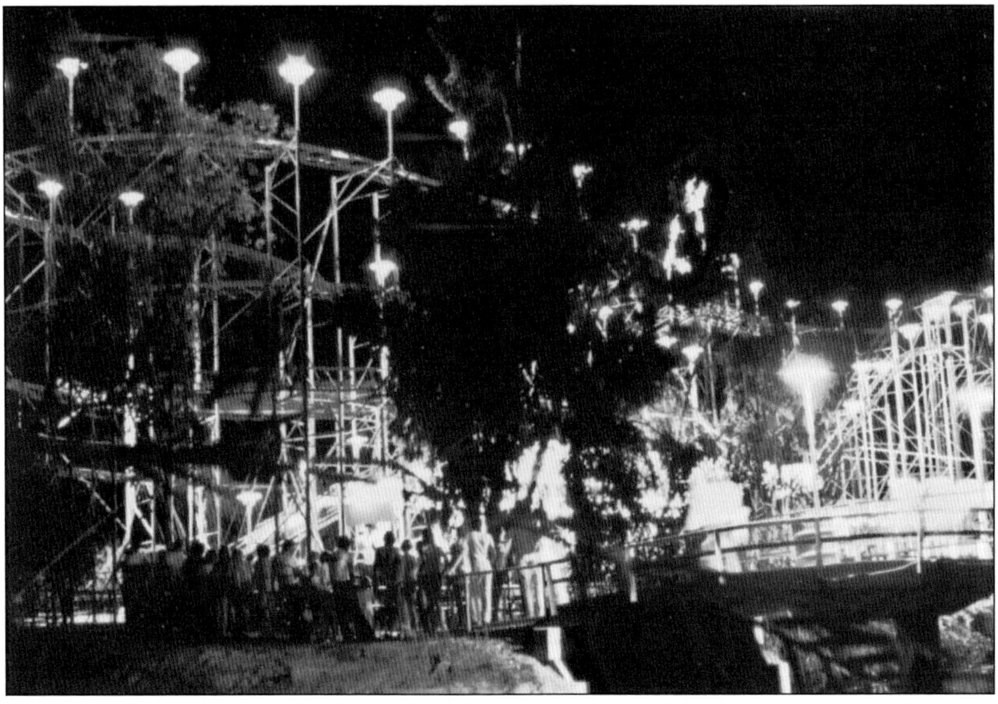

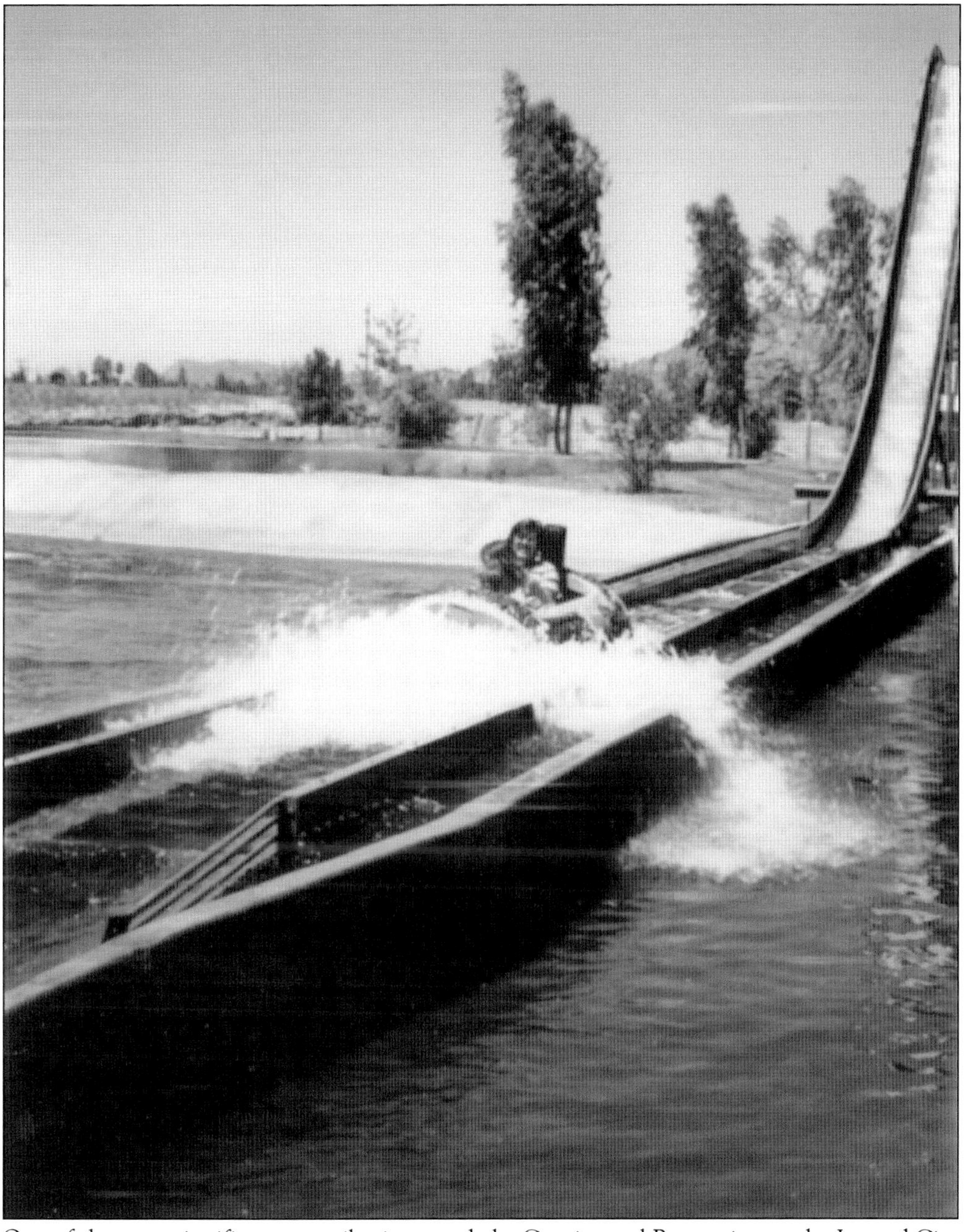

One of the most significant contributions made by Continental Recreation to the Legend City landscape was the Log Ride, or Log Plume ride, which was renamed Log Jammer during the Capell years. The cars, holding four passengers and resembling logs, were propelled through a 1,200-foot winding waterway that culminated in a big, refreshing splashdown. Log Jammer made its way to Santiago, Chile, when Legend City closed.

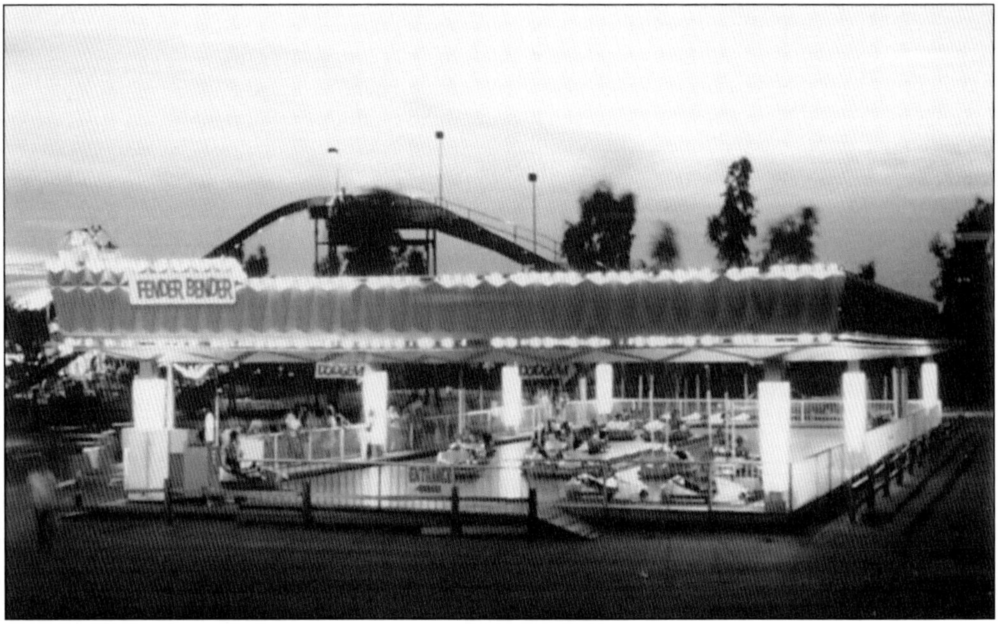

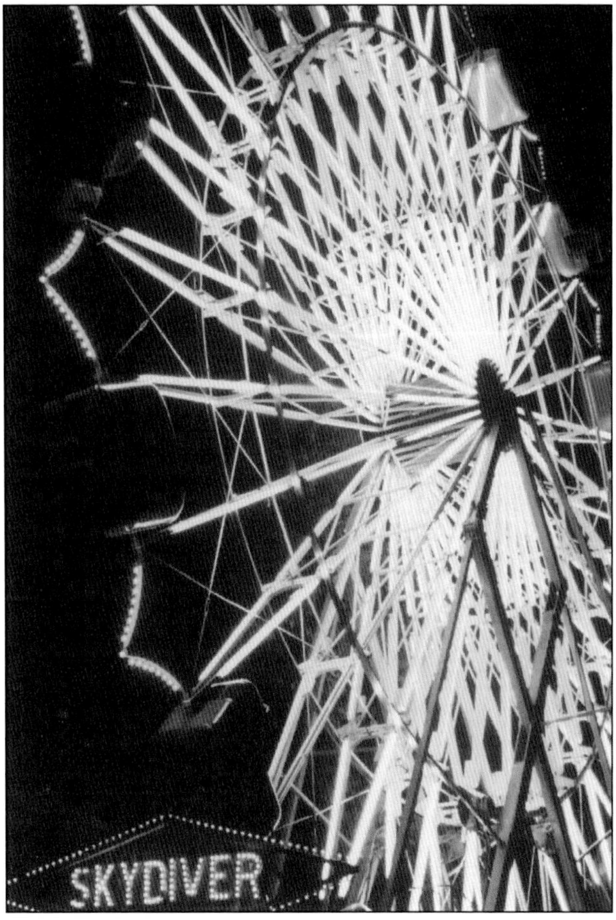

The Crash Cars ride was introduced to the park in 1973 and later dubbed Fender Bender. Note the log plume ride in the background of this photograph, taken in the late 1970s.

Skydiver was one of the original carnival rides that Capell introduced at Legend City in 1976. Manufactured by Chance Rides of Wichita, Kansas, beginning in 1965, Skydiver was a Ferris-wheel-like ride with cars mounted on a front-back axis. Tragedy struck Legend City in August 1977 when a girl was killed and her sister injured after falling from a similar Chance ride, the Zipper.

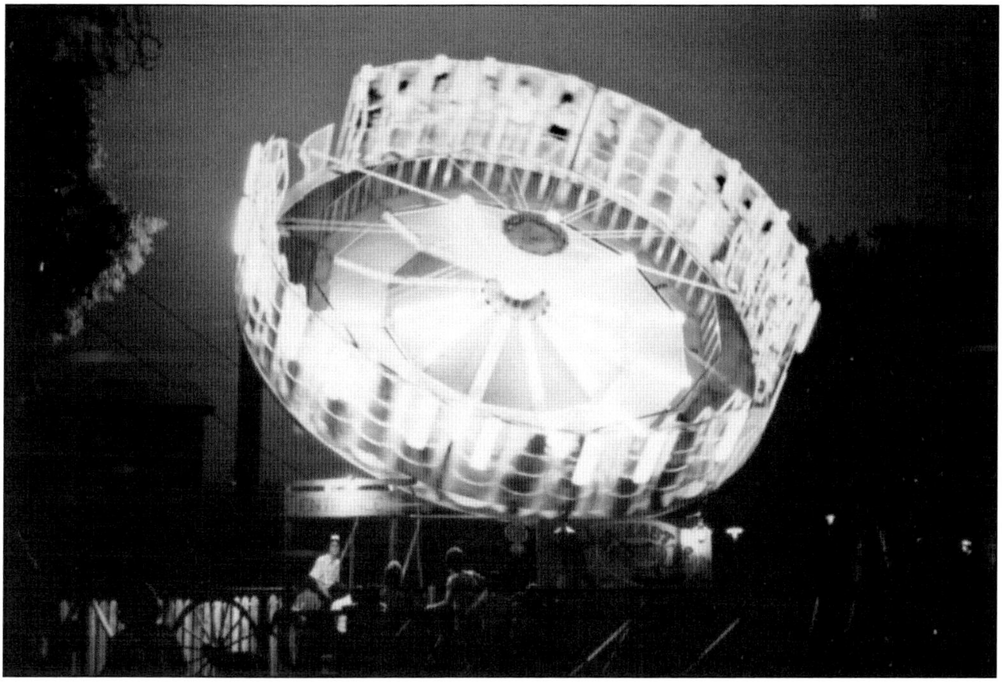

The Last Round Up (above) and Paratrooper (below) were other examples of carnival rides at Legend City in the late 1970s. Round Up consisted of a circular platform with a vertical wall of cages along the edge that held riders in place through centrifugal force while the platform moved from its initial horizontal position to a vertical one. Paratrooper was an "umbrella ride" with cars suspended below a wheel turning at an oblique angle to the ground.

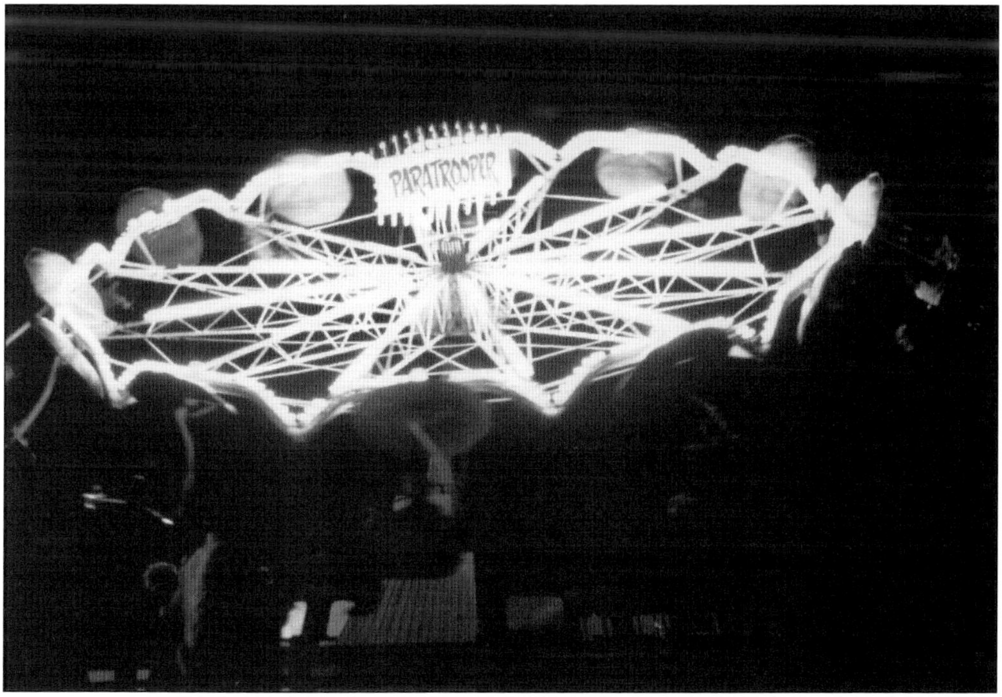

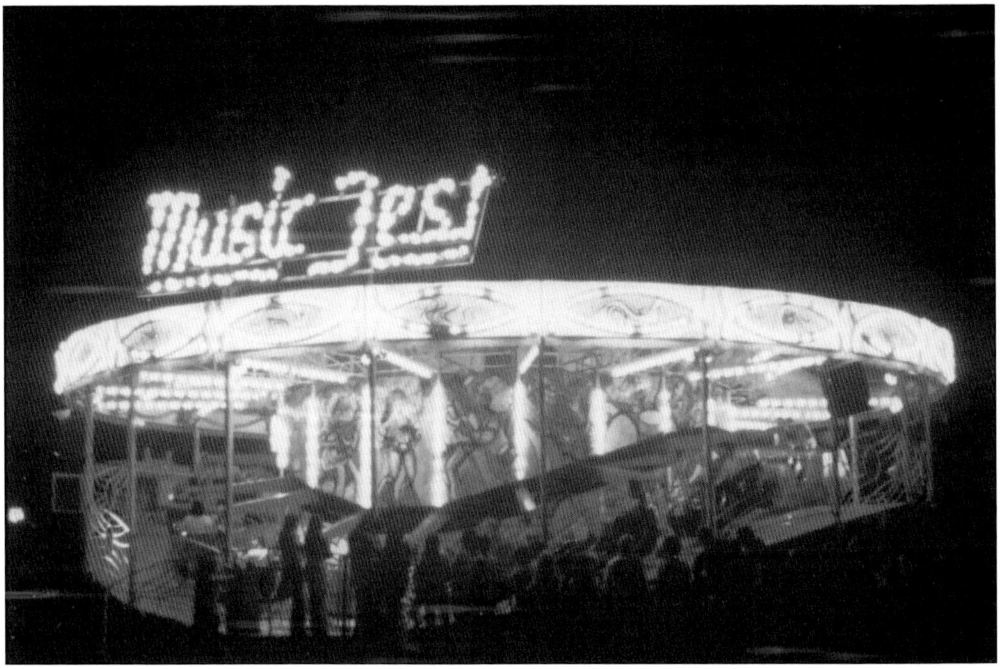

Music Fest and Yo-Yo were two more Chance carnival rides that Capell brought to Legend City when he reopened the park.

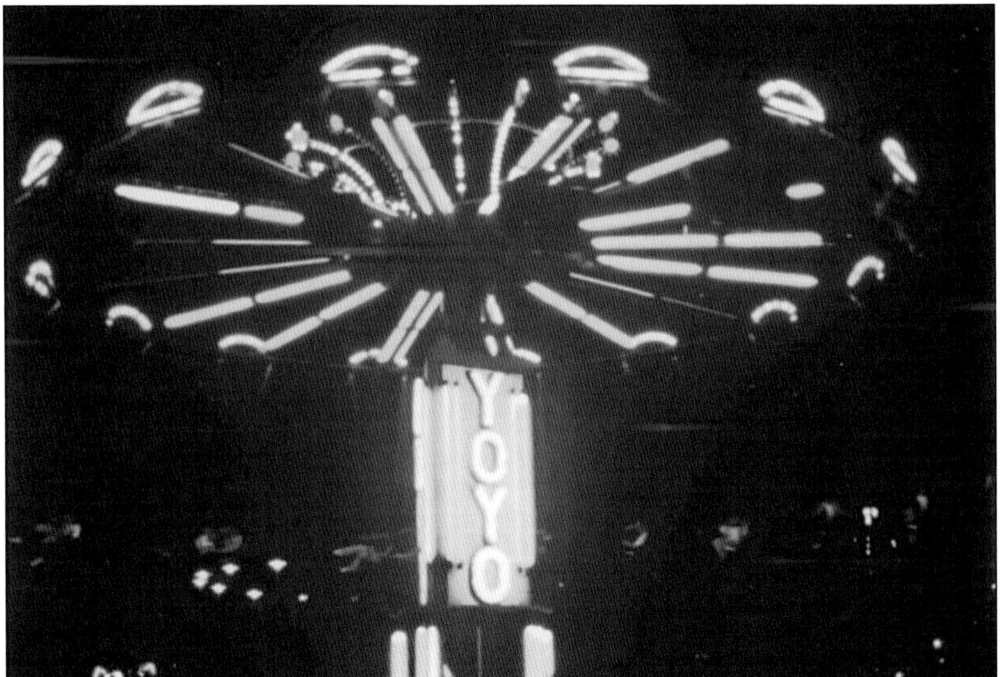

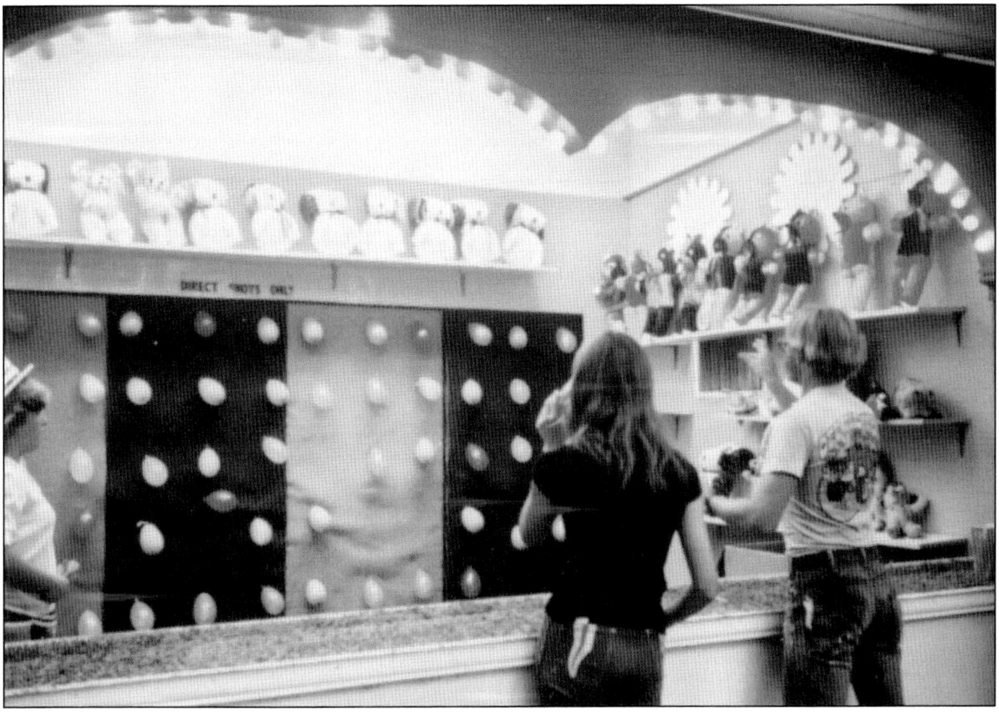

Park visitors try their luck at balloon darts in the late 1970s. This was typical of the carnival-type attractions commonplace at Legend City in the later years.

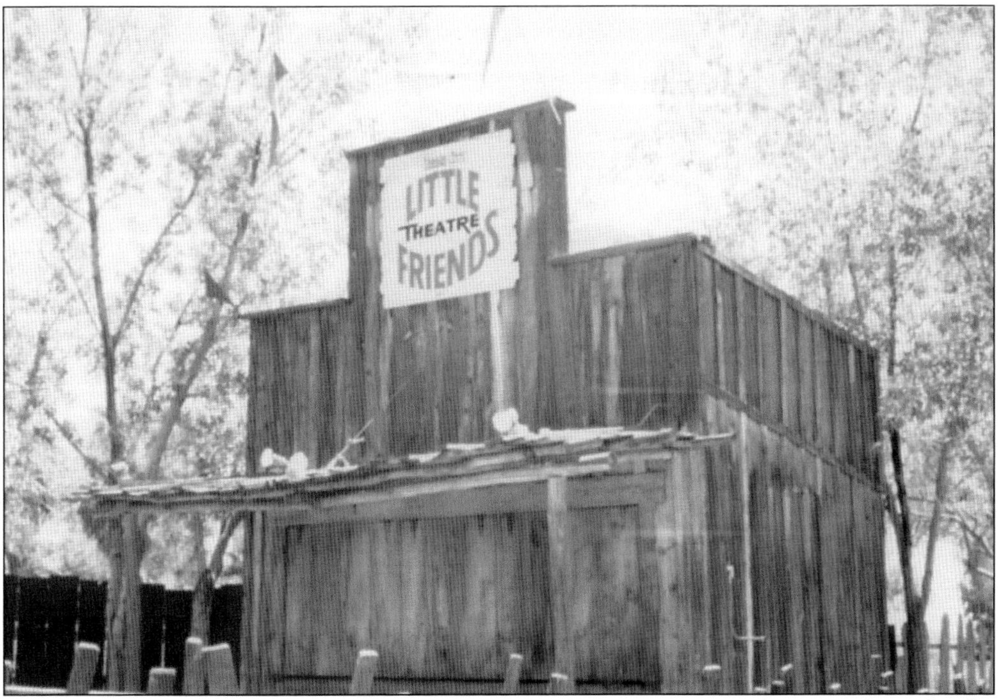

The Little Friends Theatre was a quaint venue for the presentation of puppet shows for the younger park visitors.

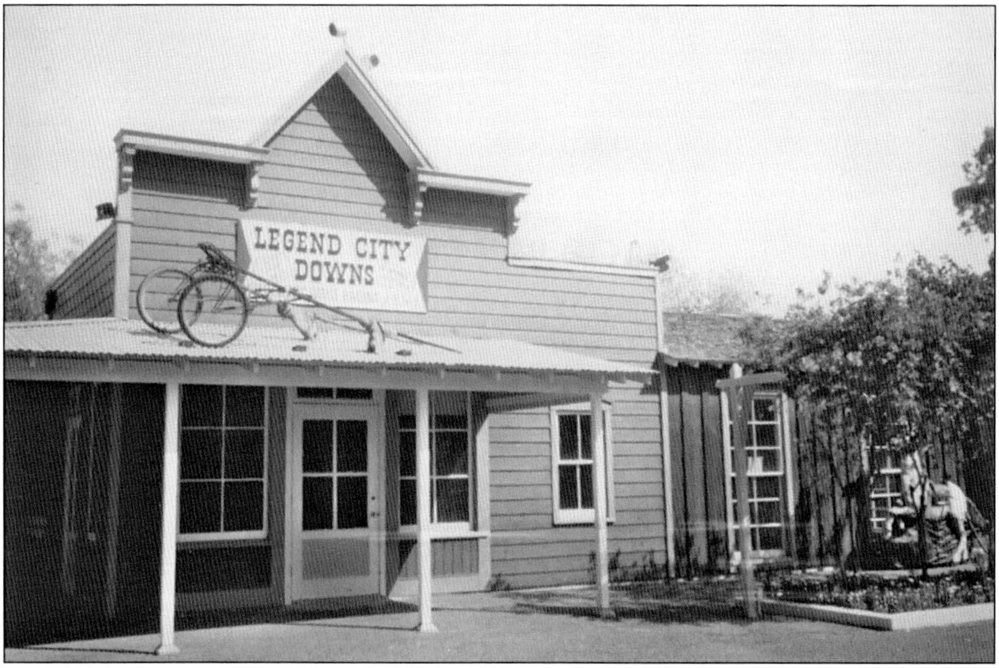

Legend City Downs was a horse-race simulation amusement at Legend City in the late 1970s, housed in one of the Victorian-style buildings in the old Gay '90s section of the park. Competitors sat on stools and advanced their "horses" by means of a pinball-game mechanism. The race could be followed by observing the lighted horses advancing on the large board in the front of the room.

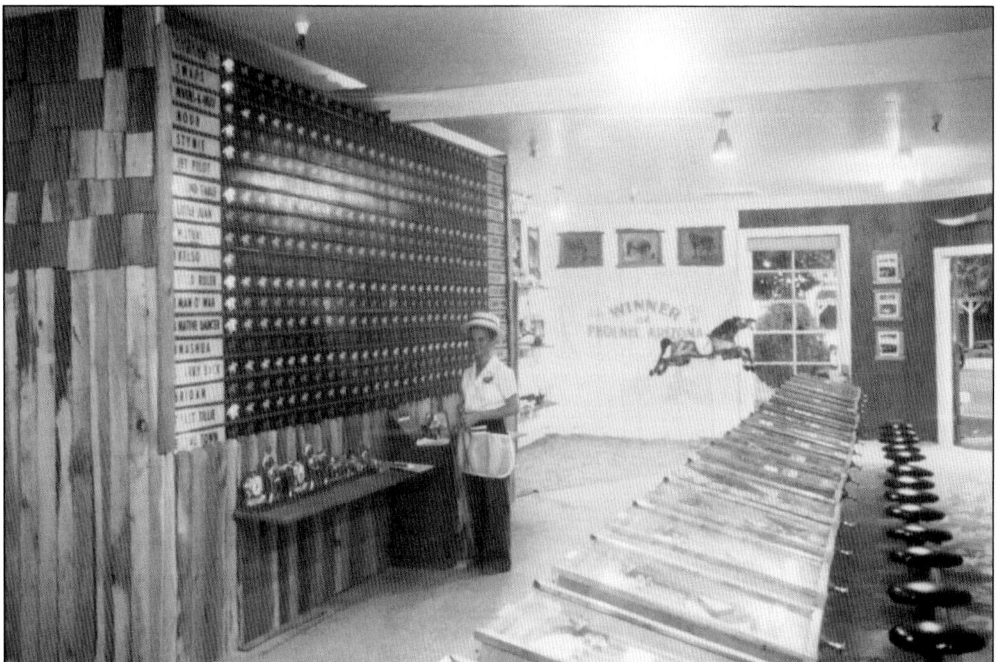

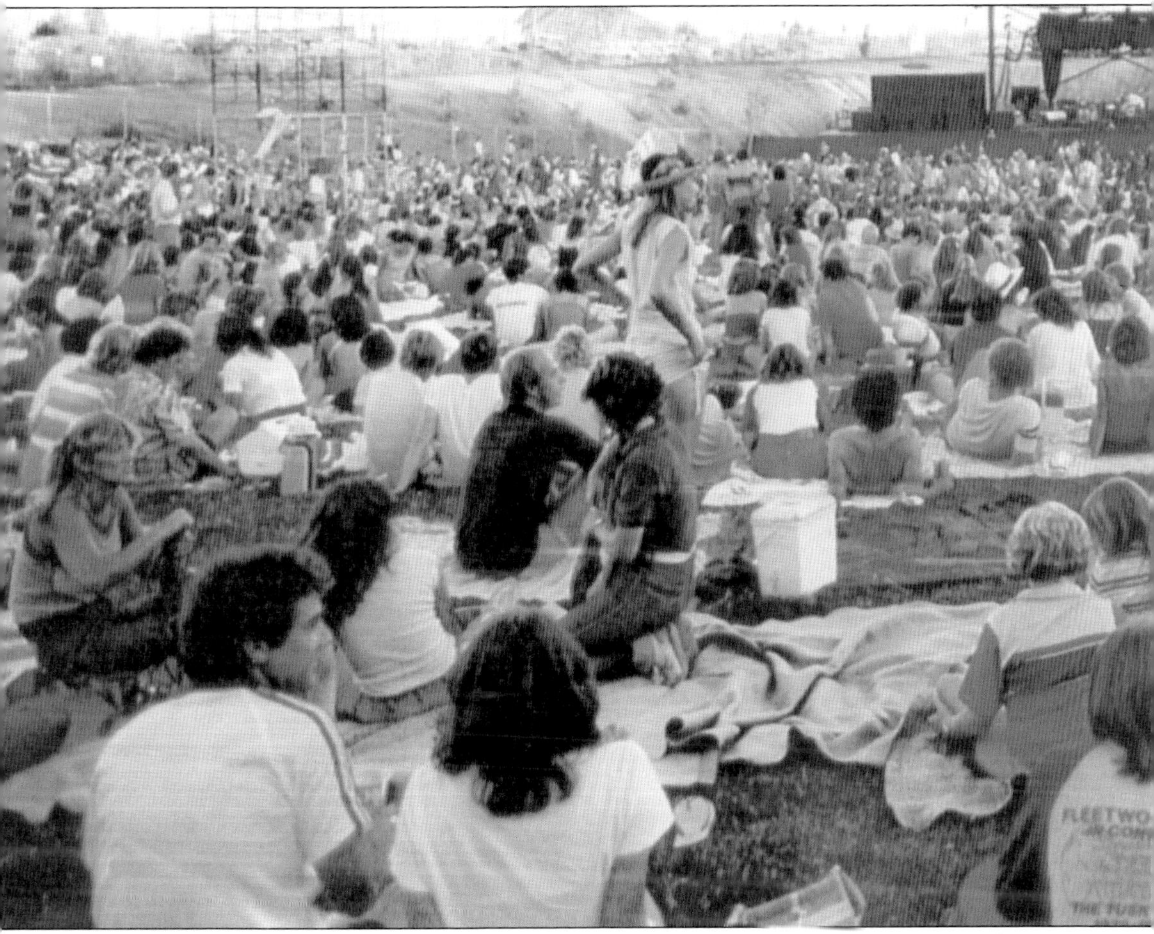

In 1979, concert promoter Doug Clark and Jess Nicks's JBD Corp. entered into a lease-purchase agreement with Capell's Dot Amusement. The agreement enabled Clark to lease land in the unused southeast corner of Legend City and build Compton Terrace (shown here), a musical amphitheater on 30 acres that could accommodate 16,500 people. The lease also contained an option to purchase the entire Legend City property. Compton Terrace brought many changes of lasting consequence to the park. The Antique Car Ride and miniature golf course, two of Legend City's original attractions, were removed to make room for the new amphitheater. The old Gay '90s section was transformed into "Encore Plaza," a common square offering fast food, T-shirts, and entertainment-oriented shops. The idea was to entice concertgoers to patronize the amusement park after the show. It was a nice idea, and, for a time, it worked well. But the acquisition of the Legend City property and the building of Compton carried the seeds of the park's demise.

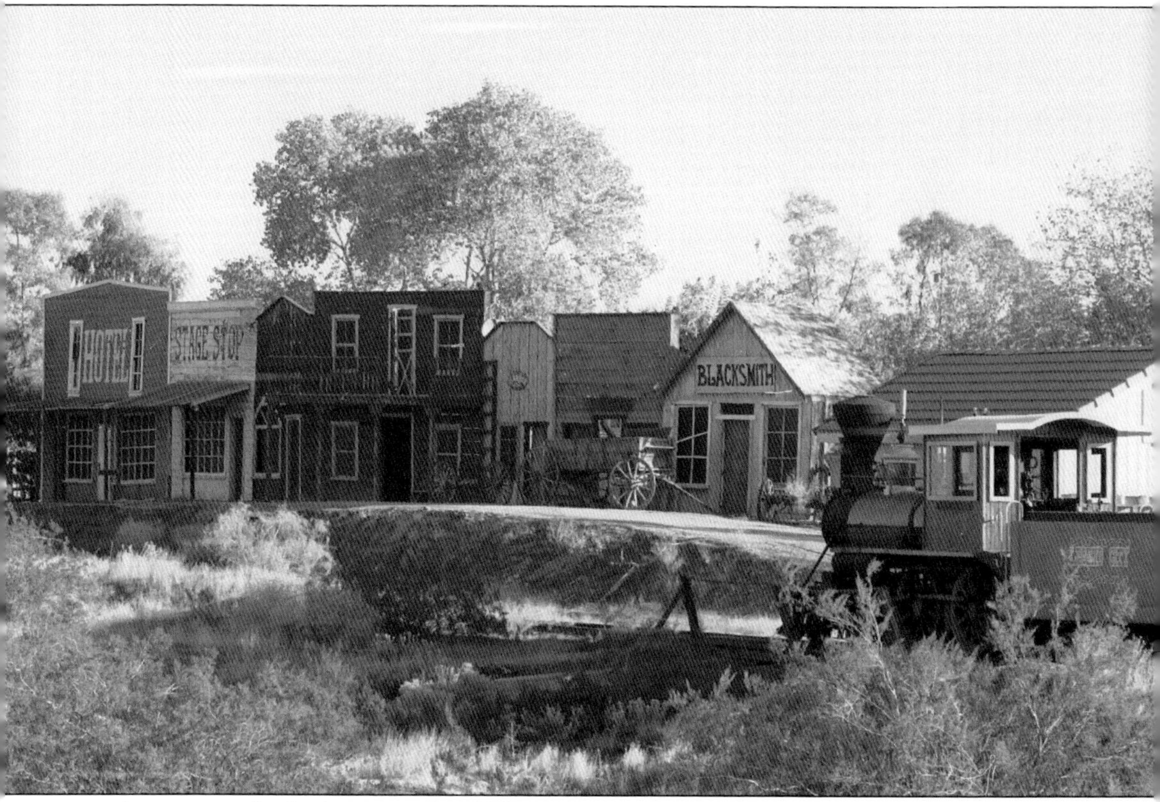

A suspicious fire broke out in the old Boom Town section of Legend City four months after the Zipper tragedy. The blaze destroyed a few of the Western-themed, false-front buildings. The Tempe Fire Department suspected arson, but no arrests were ever made. The Capells attributed the blaze to children playing with matches. The surviving Boom Town buildings are shown here, near the end of the park's run. (Courtesy of David Doyle.)

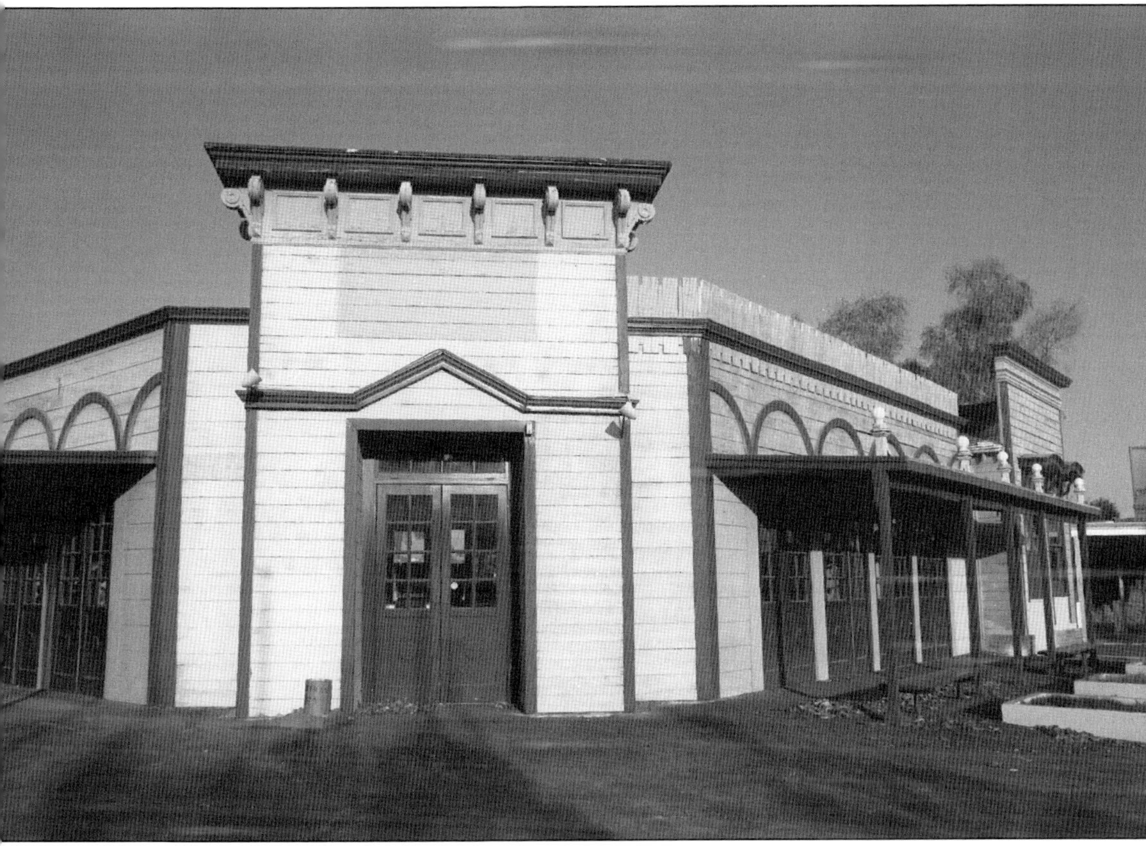

The old Penny Arcade building shows signs of age in this late photograph, taken around 1980. The building bears no discernible identifying signs or lettering, and it may have been unoccupied at this point. (Courtesy of David Doyle.)

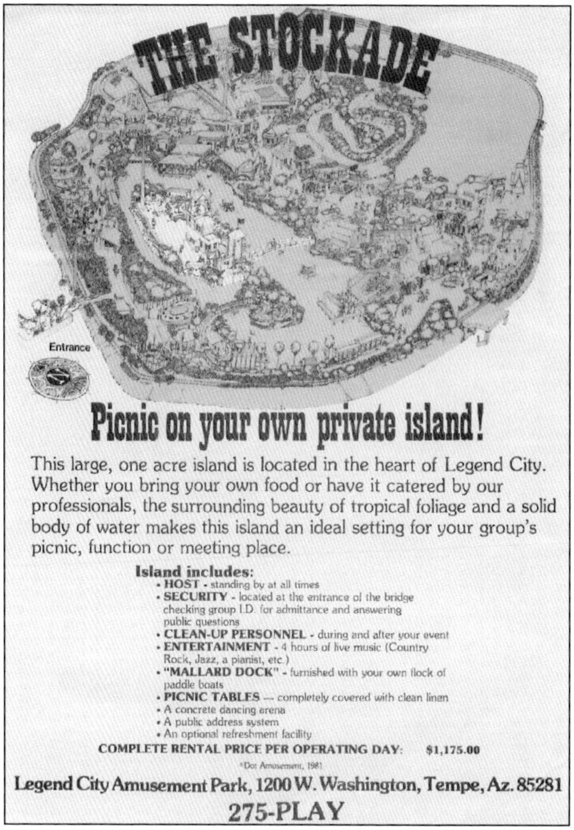

The Stockade and adjoining Indian Island were rented out for company events in the waning years of Legend City's run. Businesses like Honeywell, Motorola, and Western Electric took advantage of the opportunity to treat their employees to a day at Legend City. According to the flyer at left, the one-day rental price of $1,175 included an event host, security, clean-up personnel, picnic tables, paddleboats, and musical entertainment. The photograph below shows a view of the old fort from the island during this later period. (Courtesy of David Doyle.)

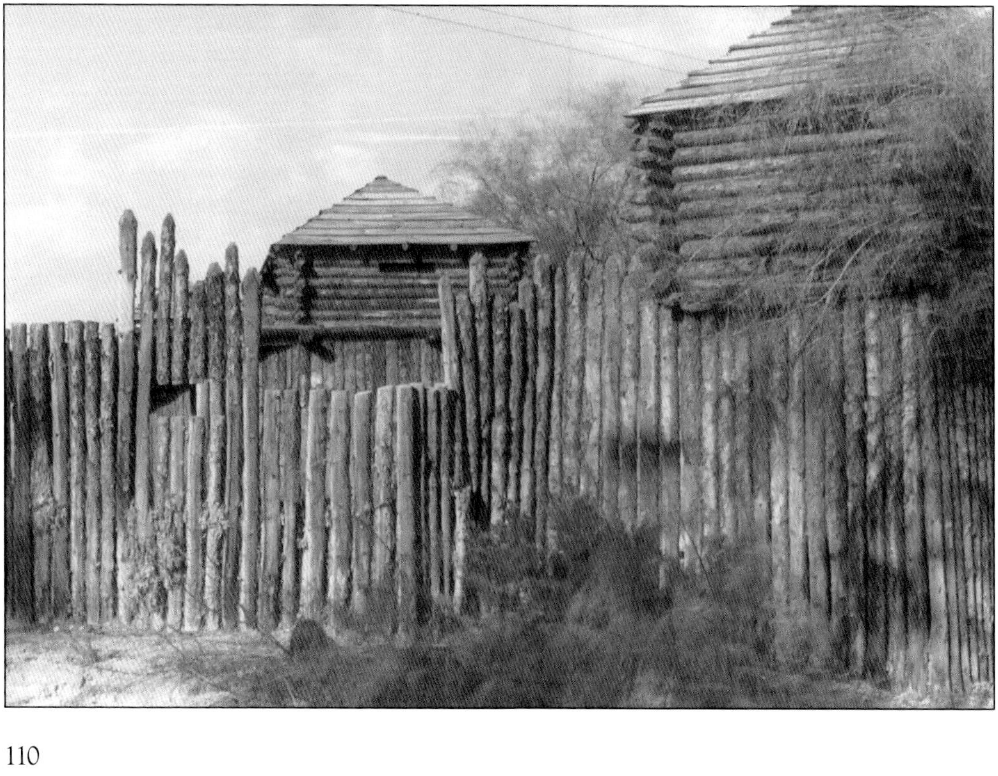

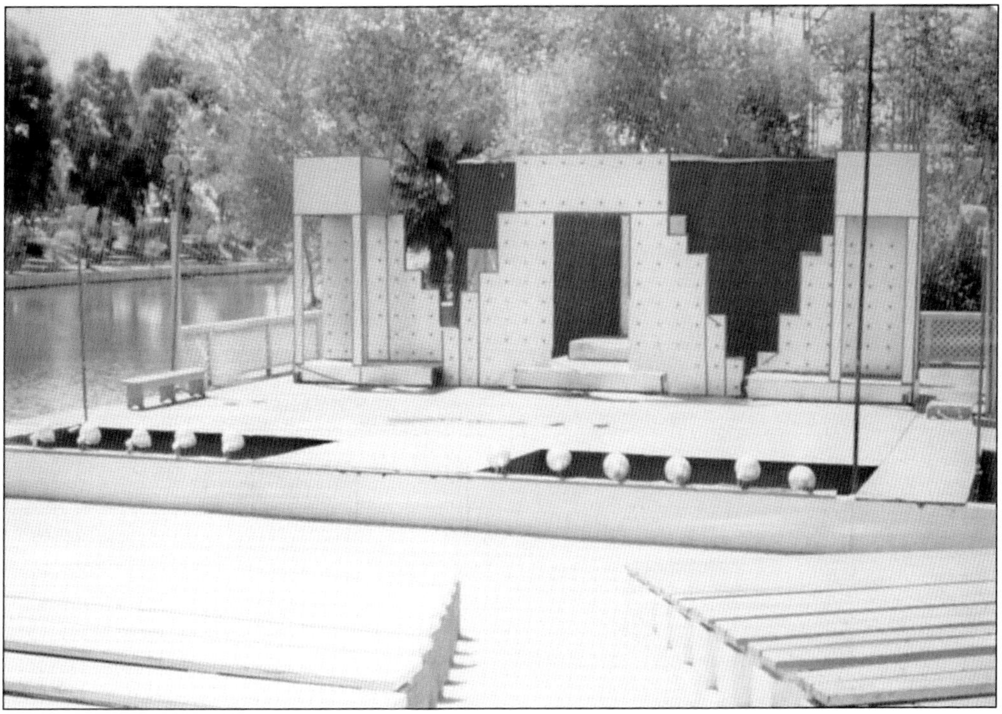

This is a view of the Legend City Lagoon Amphitheater around 1980. It was still a busy venue for entertainment events and various park promotions.

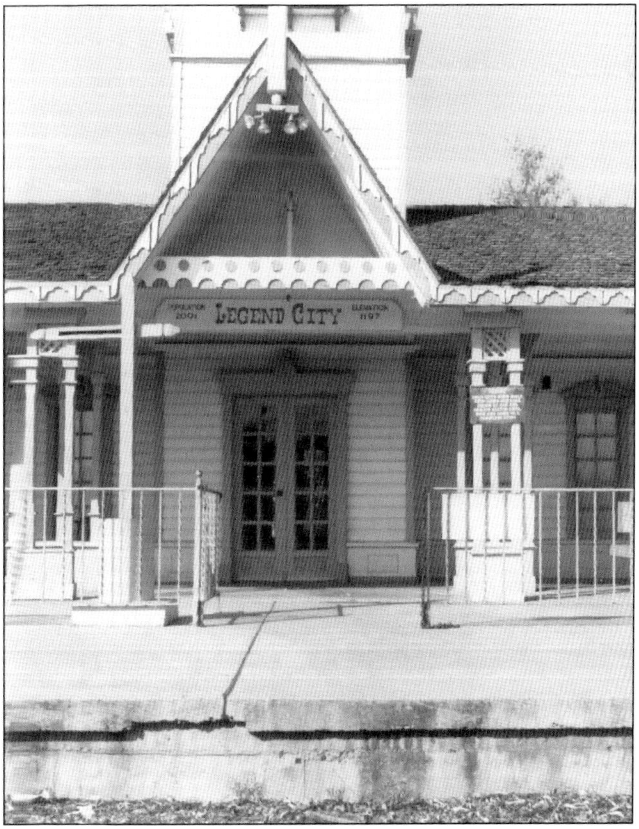

The train station was extensively restored and refurbished by Shoen in 1969, but by the time this photograph was taken around 1980, the building and underlying infrastructure were again showing signs of age and decay. By the end, Legend City was regarded as something of a fire hazard by the Tempe Fire Department. (Courtesy of David Doyle.)

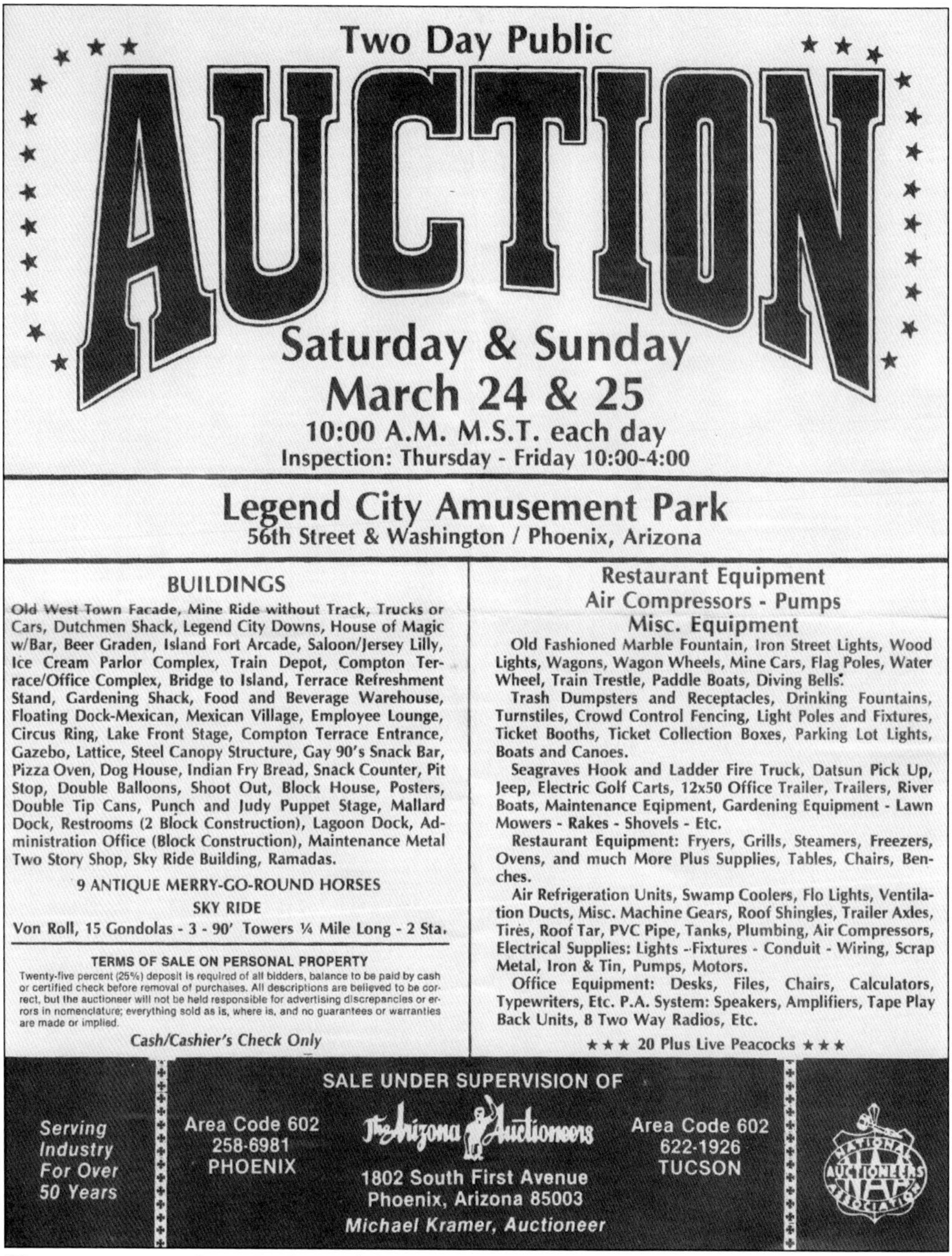
Two Day Public

AUCTION

Saturday & Sunday

March 24 & 25

10:00 A.M. M.S.T. each day

Inspection: Thursday - Friday 10:00-4:00

Legend City Amusement Park

56th Street & Washington / Phoenix, Arizona

BUILDINGS

Old West Town Facade, Mine Ride without Track, Trucks or Cars, Dutchmen Shack, Legend City Downs, House of Magic w/Bar, Beer Graden, Island Fort Arcade, Saloon/Jersey Lilly, Ice Cream Parlor Complex, Train Depot, Compton Terrace/Office Complex, Bridge to Island, Terrace Refreshment Stand, Gardening Shack, Food and Beverage Warehouse, Floating Dock-Mexican, Mexican Village, Employee Lounge, Circus Ring, Lake Front Stage, Compton Terrace Entrance, Gazebo, Lattice, Steel Canopy Structure, Gay 90's Snack Bar, Pizza Oven, Dog House, Indian Fry Bread, Snack Counter, Pit Stop, Double Balloons, Shoot Out, Block House, Posters, Double Tip Cans, Punch and Judy Puppet Stage, Mallard Dock, Restrooms (2 Block Construction), Lagoon Dock, Administration Office (Block Construction), Maintenance Metal Two Story Shop, Sky Ride Building, Ramadas.

9 ANTIQUE MERRY-GO-ROUND HORSES

SKY RIDE

Von Roll, 15 Gondolas - 3 - 90′ Towers ¼ Mile Long - 2 Sta.

TERMS OF SALE ON PERSONAL PROPERTY

Twenty-five percent (25%) deposit is required of all bidders, balance to be paid by cash or certified check before removal of purchases. All descriptions are believed to be correct, but the auctioneer will not be held responsible for advertising discrepancies or errors in nomenclature; everything sold as is, where is, and no guarantees or warranties are made or implied.

Cash/Cashier's Check Only

Restaurant Equipment

Air Compressors - Pumps

Misc. Equipment

Old Fashioned Marble Fountain, Iron Street Lights, Wood Lights, Wagons, Wagon Wheels, Mine Cars, Flag Poles, Water Wheel, Train Trestle, Paddle Boats, Diving Bells.

Trash Dumpsters and Receptacles, Drinking Fountains, Turnstiles, Crowd Control Fencing, Light Poles and Fixtures, Ticket Booths, Ticket Collection Boxes, Parking Lot Lights, Boats and Canoes.

Seagraves Hook and Ladder Fire Truck, Datsun Pick Up, Jeep, Electric Golf Carts, 12x50 Office Trailer, Trailers, River Boats, Maintenance Eqipment, Gardening Equipment - Lawn Mowers - Rakes - Shovels - Etc.

Restaurant Equipment: Fryers, Grills, Steamers, Freezers, Ovens, and much More Plus Supplies, Tables, Chairs, Benches.

Air Refrigeration Units, Swamp Coolers, Flo Lights, Ventilation Ducts, Misc. Machine Gears, Roof Shingles, Trailer Axles, Tires, Roof Tar, PVC Pipe, Tanks, Plumbing, Air Compressors, Electrical Supplies: Lights - Fixtures - Conduit - Wiring, Scrap Metal, Iron & Tin, Pumps, Motors.

Office Equipment: Desks, Files, Chairs, Calculators, Typewriters, Etc. P.A. System: Speakers, Amplifiers, Tape Play Back Units, 8 Two Way Radios, Etc.

★ ★ ★ 20 Plus Live Peacocks ★ ★ ★

SALE UNDER SUPERVISION OF

Serving Industry For Over 50 Years

Area Code 602
258-6981
PHOENIX

The Arizona Auctioneers

1802 South First Avenue
Phoenix, Arizona 85003
Michael Kramer, Auctioneer

Area Code 602
622-1926
TUCSON

National Auctioneers Association NAA

The option to purchase the Legend City property was acquired by a Canadian company and then sold to the Salt River Project, which exercised the option. Legend City closed its doors for the last time on September 4, 1983. The following spring, the remaining rides, signs, buildings, and fixtures went up for auction, and everything that remained was then razed. The Legend City auction was held on March 24 and 25, 1984. As the auction flyer shown here and on the next page indicates, virtually everything was up for sale: buildings, rides, restaurant equipment, compressors, ticket booths, parking-lot lights, air-conditioning units, office equipment, and even a Seagraves Hook and Ladder Fire Truck. (Courtesy of Jim Madden.)

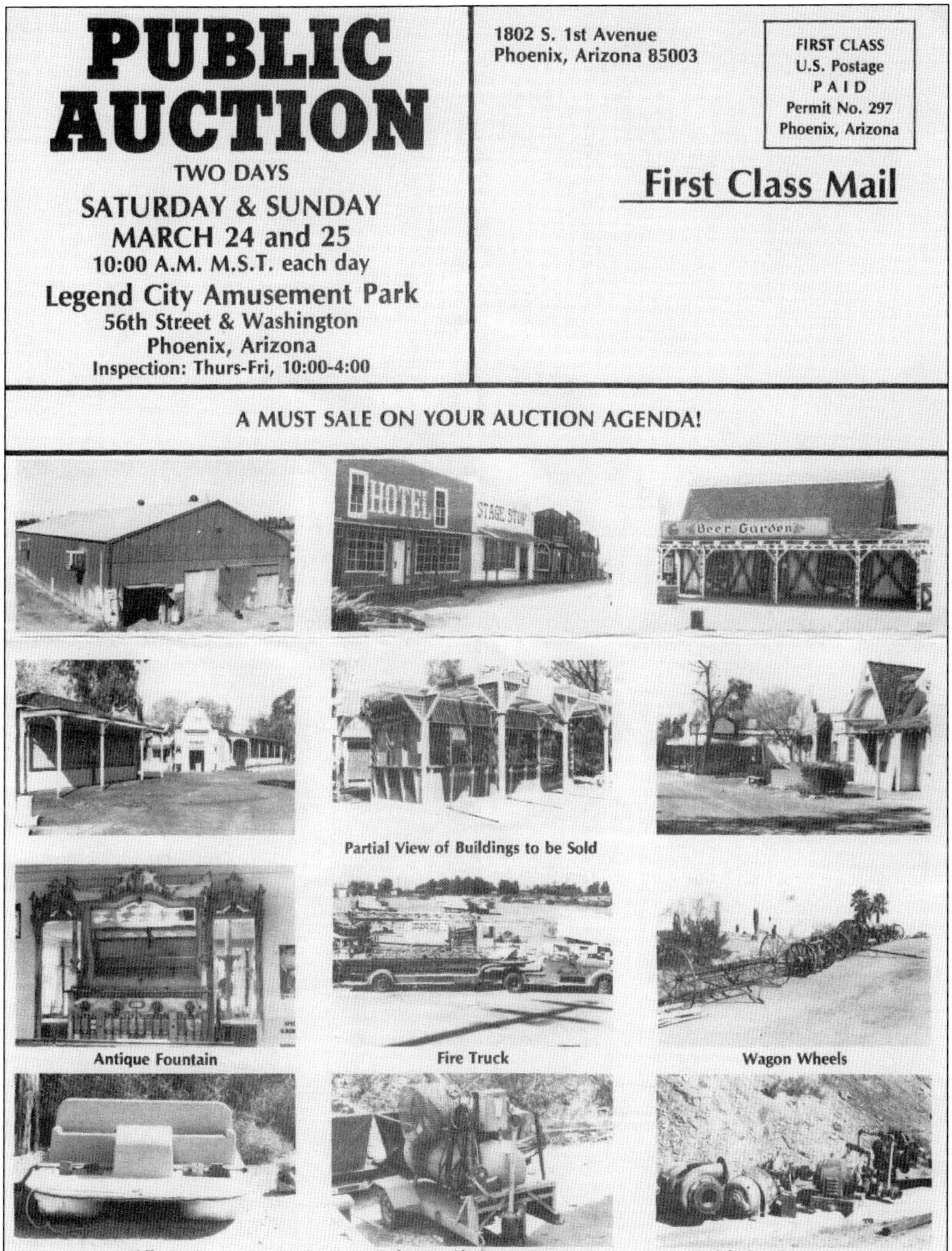

Whatever was not sold at the auction was torn down and carted away. Jim Madden, owner of the nearby Chaparral Speedway, was granted access to the site and documented the park's final days in an extraordinary series of images. (Courtesy of Jim Madden.)

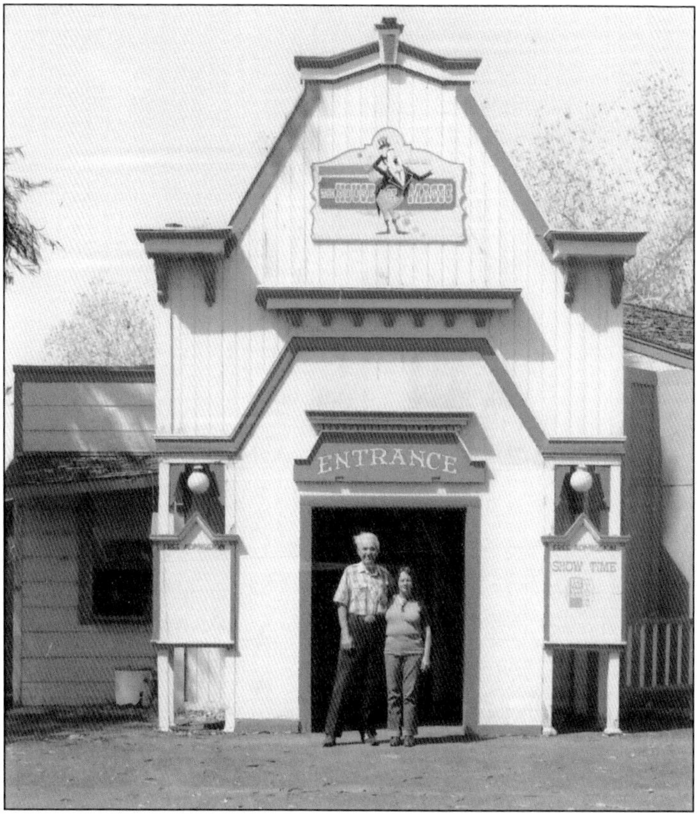

The Capell family retained ownership of the Legend City rides and buildings after the property was sold, and they recruited a firm called The Arizona Auctioneers to conduct the two-day auction of all aboveground assets. At left, Jack Capell, brother of Legend City owner Bill Capell, poses with a friend in front of the House of Magic (originally the Golden Palace Saloon) before the auction. Below, the auction is under way, with some merry-go-round ponies on the block. Bill Capell Jr. has observed that Legend City lives on today in amusement parks throughout the world. (Courtesy of Jim Madden.)

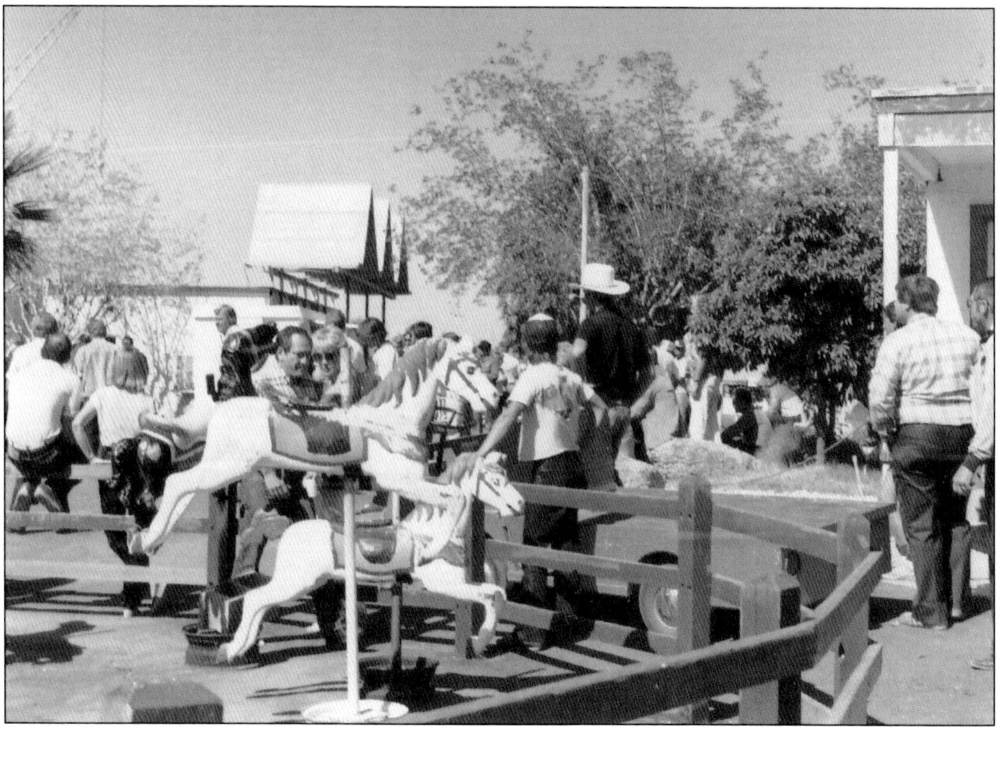

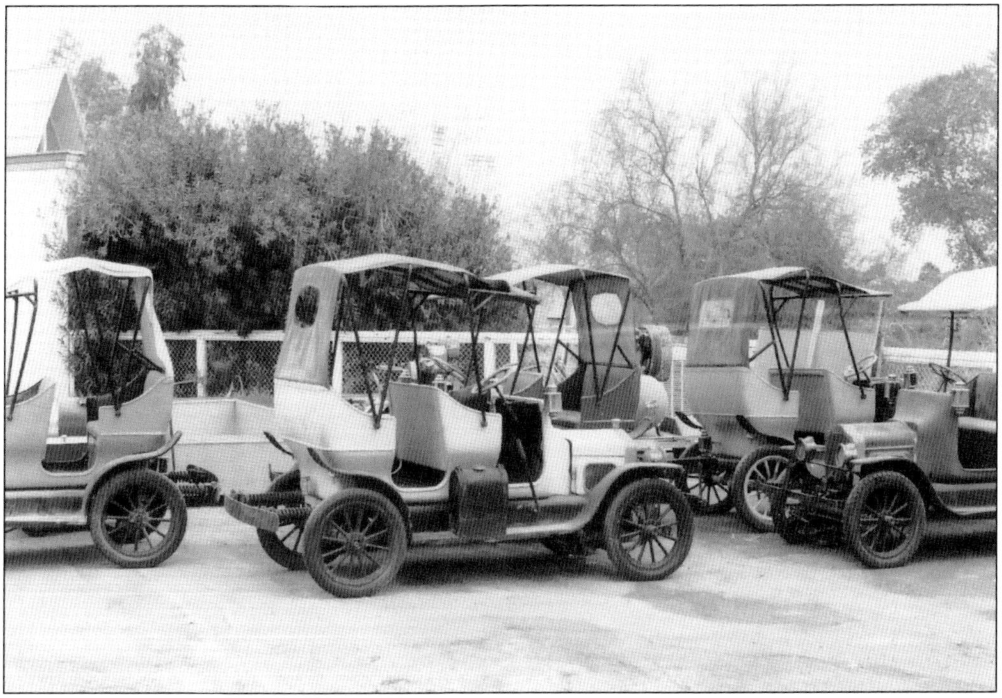

The Antique Car Ride cars await their fate in the Legend City auction. (Courtesy of Jim Madden.)

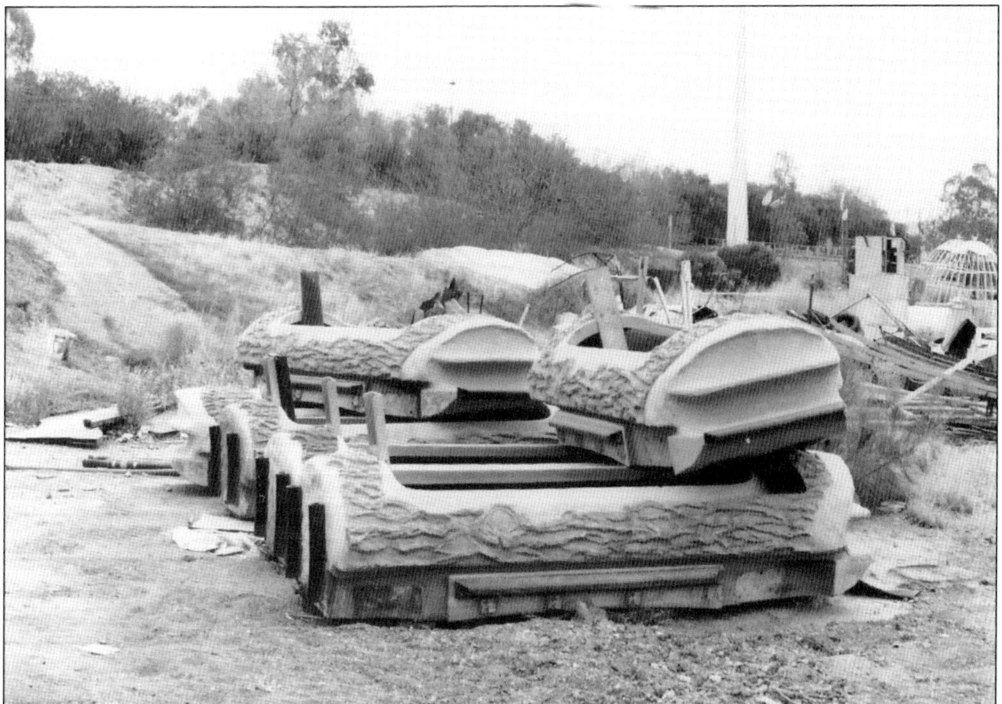

The Log Jammer ride cars are stacked in a pile before their shipment to Chile. (Courtesy of Jim Madden.)

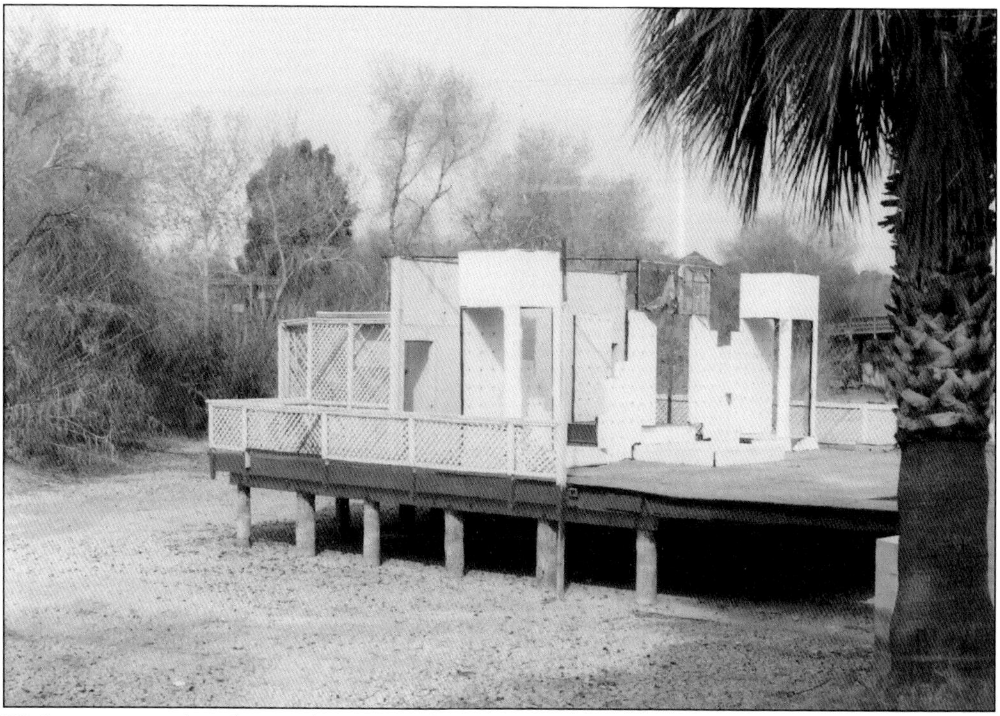

With its surrounding lagoon long since drained, the remains of the amphitheater sit awaiting their final dismantlement.

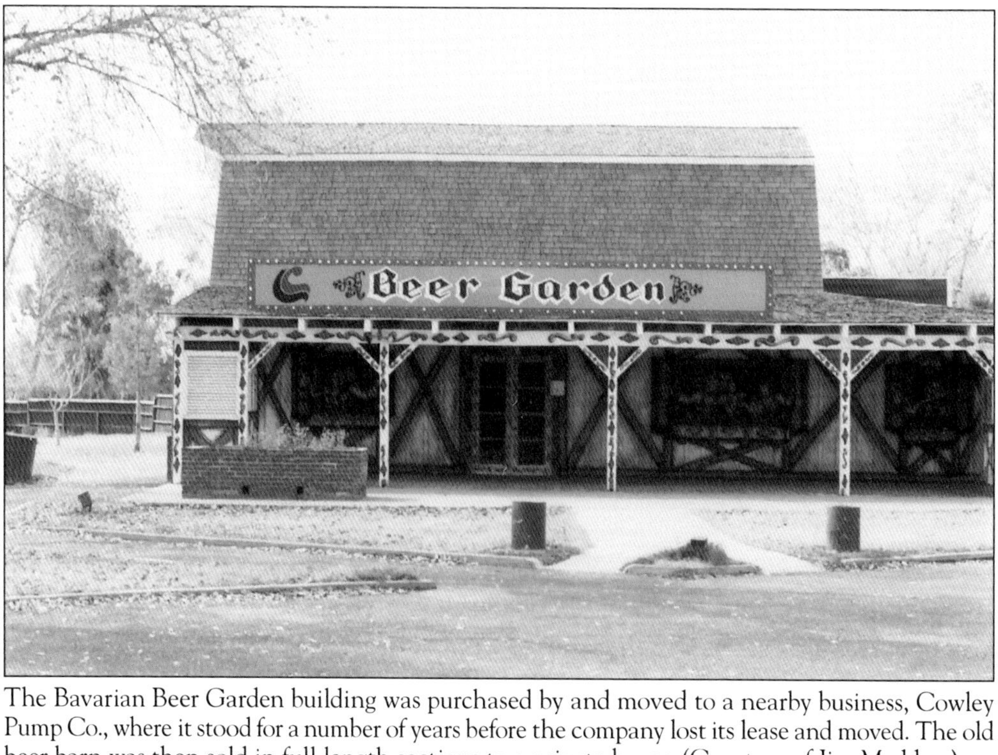

The Bavarian Beer Garden building was purchased by and moved to a nearby business, Cowley Pump Co., where it stood for a number of years before the company lost its lease and moved. The old beer barn was then sold in full-length sections to a private buyer. (Courtesy of Jim Madden.)

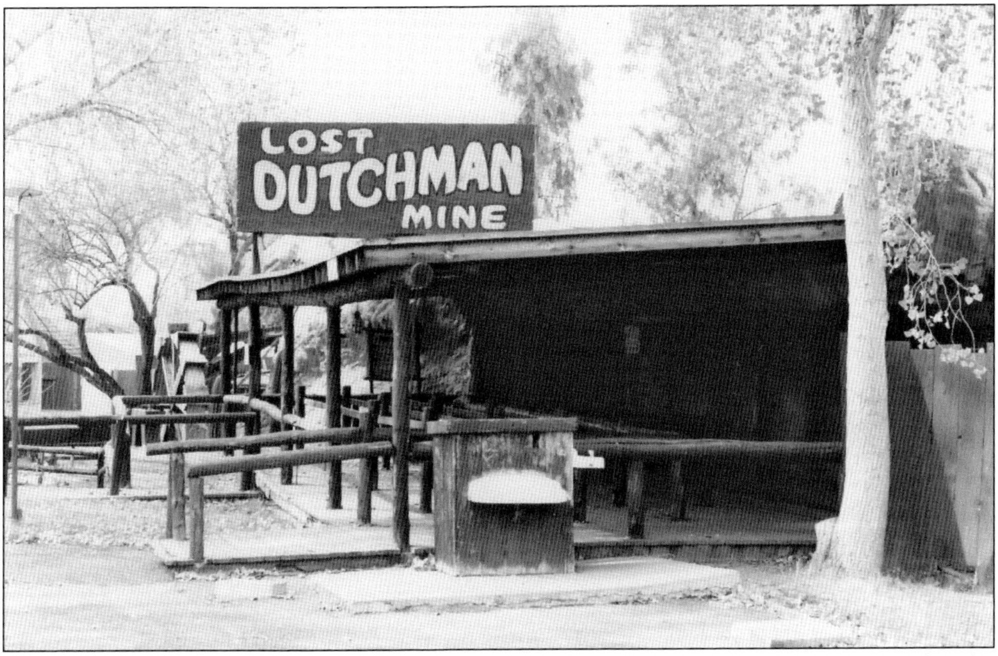

Here we enjoy one final glimpse of the storied Lost Dutchman Mine ride. Like its namesake, the ride is now abandoned and soon to be lost forever. (Courtesy of Jim Madden.)

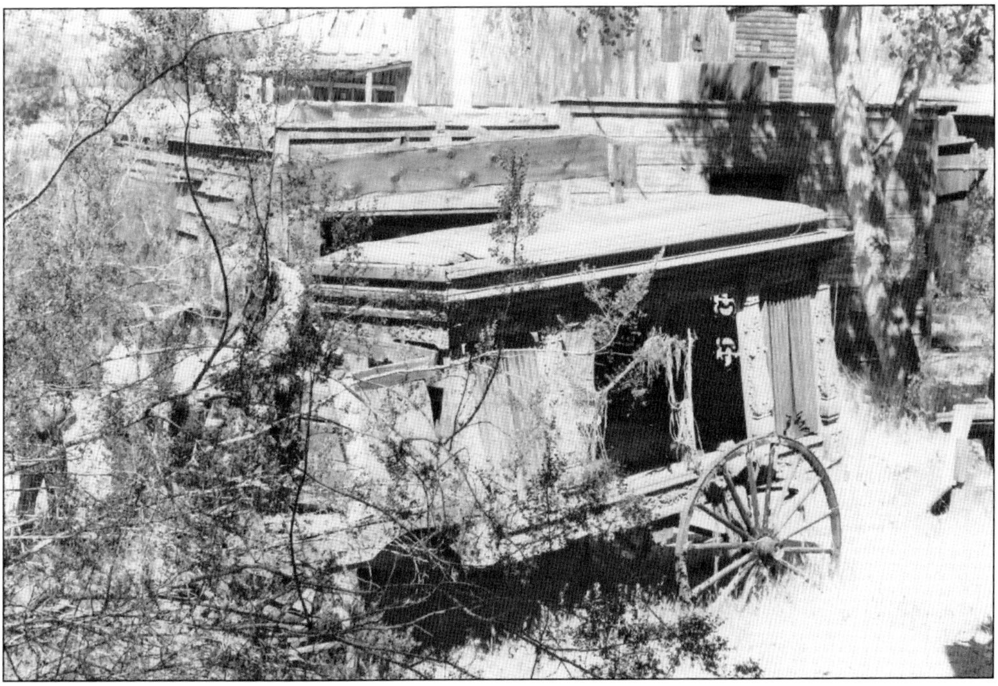

The mine ride graveyard takes on an ironic double meaning as it sits awaiting oblivion, a poignant symbol of the park's unhappy destiny. (Courtesy of Jim Madden.).

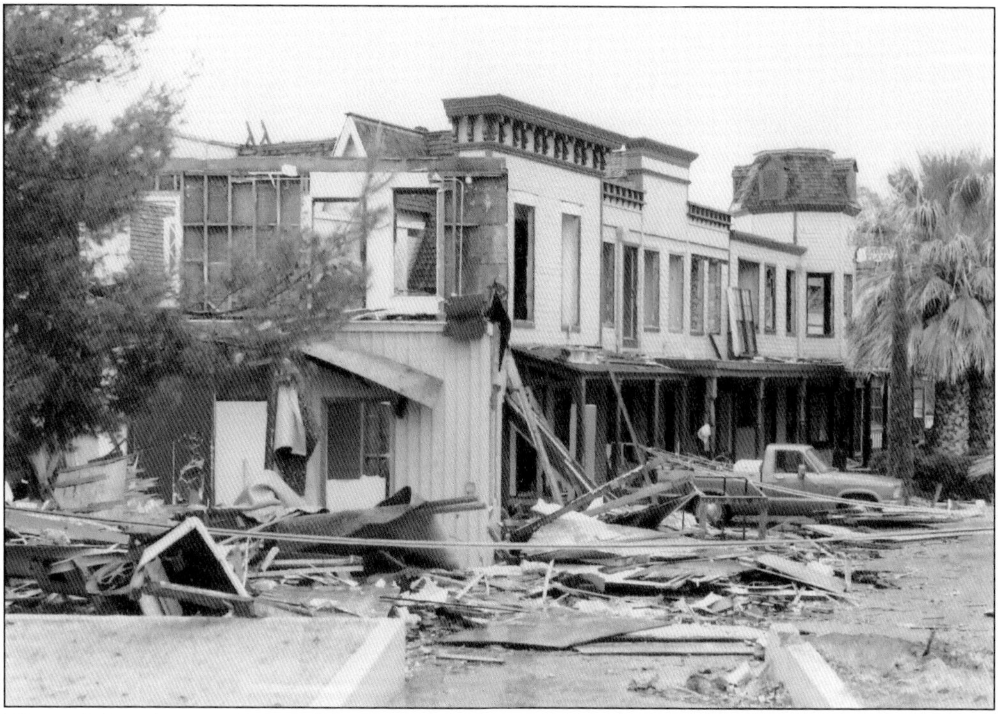

The sad demolition of Legend City's remaining buildings begins even as the auction is being concluded. (Courtesy of Jim Madden.)

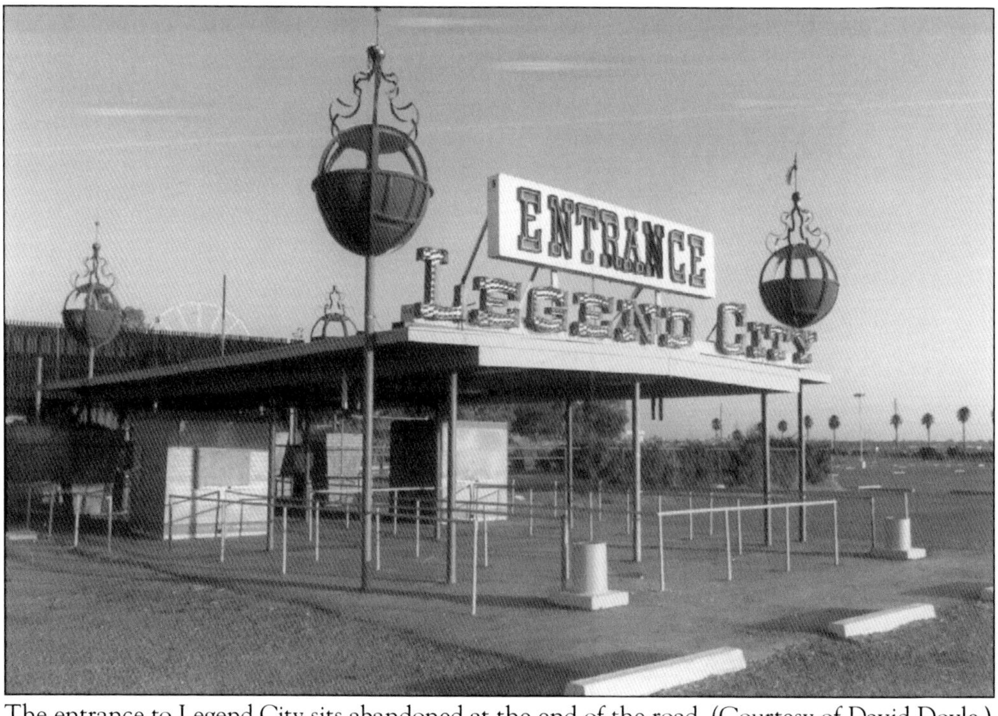

The entrance to Legend City sits abandoned at the end of the road. (Courtesy of David Doyle.)

Five

The Legacy

Perhaps the ultimate legacy of Legend City has been the longstanding reluctance to build its replacement. Periodic calls have arisen through the years to "Bring back Legend City," beginning almost immediately upon the park's disappearance. While various proposals surface from time to time, investors always shy away in the end from pursuing the project. The demise of Legend City continues to cast its long shadow   Phoenix remains by far the largest metropolitan area in the United States devoid of a major amusement park.

But would it even work now? The nostalgia value of a new Legend City for aging Phoenix-area baby boomers would naturally be immeasurable, but is this a realistic business model for an amusement park in the 21st century? There are good reasons to doubt this.

The world has changed quite a bit since 1963. Interest in the Old West has waned noticeably, particularly among youngsters.

Recall the cultural environment into which Legend City was born. Westerns were virtually ubiquitous both on television and in the cinema. Western-themed paperbacks flew off the shelves, and the most popular playtime activity for children was cowboys and Indians. All things Western were phenomenally popular during this era.

The cultural landscape has shifted significantly since that time, however. How many Western television shows are there now? Movies? How many children play cowboys and Indians these days? As always, kids would be the ultimate target population for any new theme park. Legend City was of a particular time and place that has gradually receded into Arizona's past. It will almost certainly remain but a fading memory from a peculiarly rich era of Phoenix history. Yet, three decades after its demise, a certain fascination for this long-gone theme park manages to endure. There is yet some lingering magic there.

Legend City enthusiasts persist in gathering online to reminisce and pay homage to the park's heyday. Television retrospectives air and magazine articles continue to appear. Park memorabilia routinely fetches eyebrow-raising sums on eBay. In June 2013, a sold-out 50th anniversary celebration was held in Tempe. For a failed amusement park that vanished into the desert dust 30 long years ago, Legend City remains a curiously popular place.

It seems Louis Crandall's mission did, in a very real sense, succeed quite well.

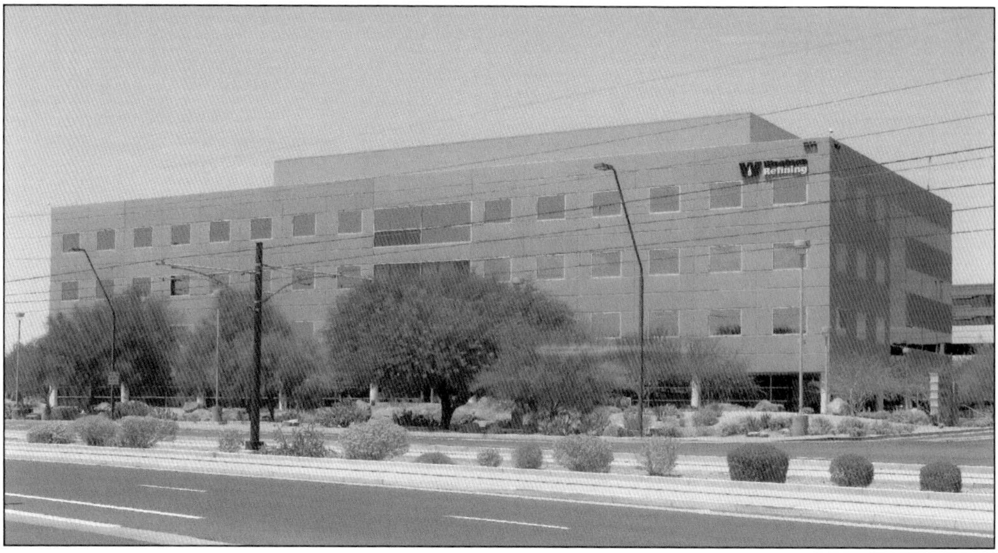

Once the scene of excited youngsters and their parents waiting impatiently in line to be admitted to fabulous Legend City, the location of the park's entrance is today the site of the Western Refining building, at 1250 West Washington Street in Tempe. (Courtesy of Sue Bueker.)

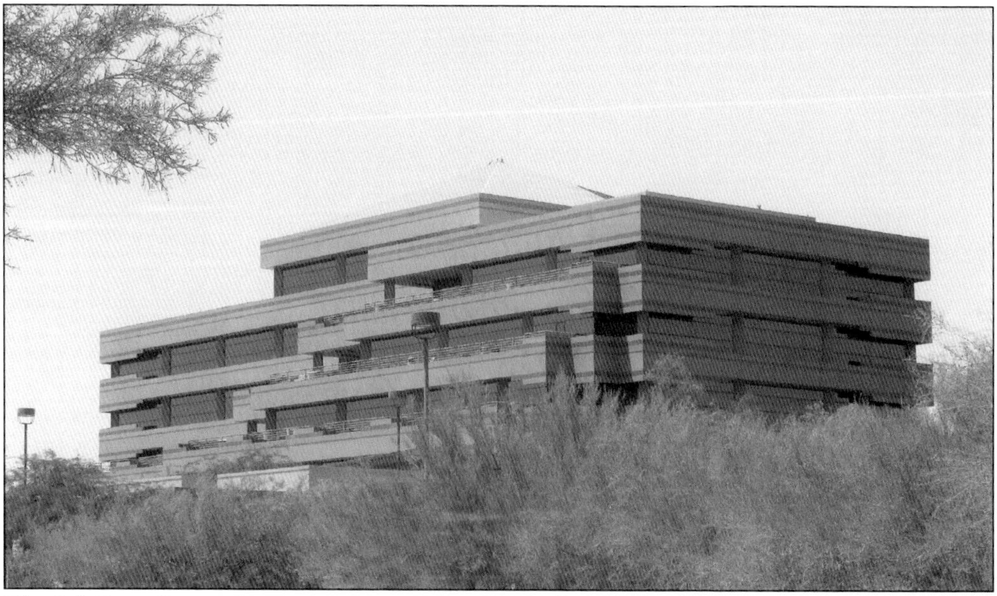

The Salt River Project headquarters now towers over the grounds where Legend City once stood. SRP announced the deal to purchase the land in June 1983, and Legend City had its last hurrah during that summer season. Construction on the SRP corporate headquarters began in 1986. (Courtesy of Sue Bueker.)

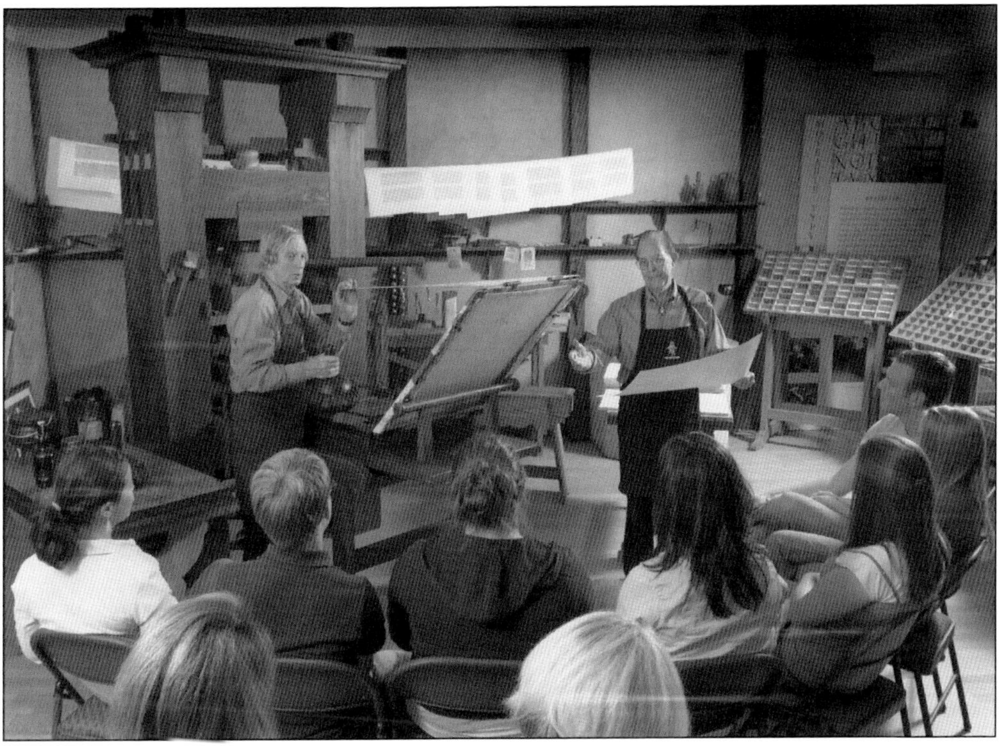

In 1998, Legend City founder Louis Crandall and his wife, Mabel, opened the Crandall Historical Printing Museum in downtown Provo, Utah. Louis began collecting antique printing equipment in 1954, including presses, type cabinets, stones, paper cutters, and other period printing equipment. The same drive for achievement and perfection that made Legend City a reality was now responsible for creating the world's most advanced Gutenberg printing museum. Here, Crandall (right) demonstrates the replica Gutenberg press for a tour group at the museum.

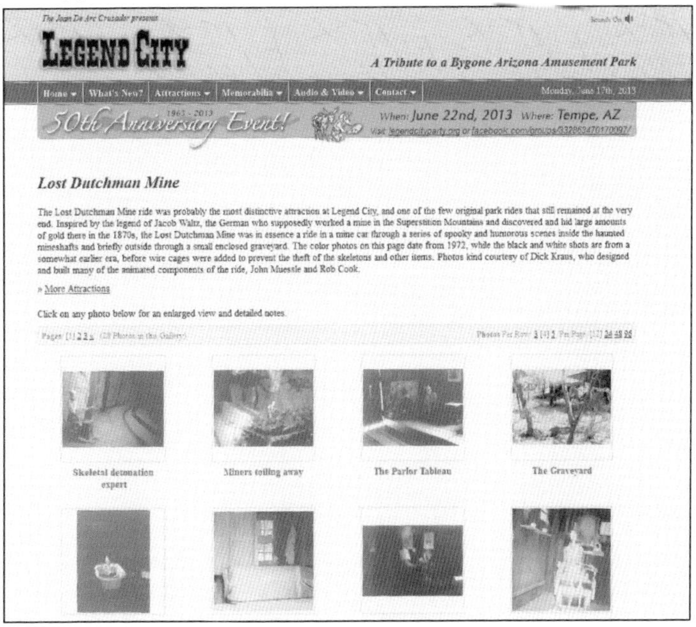

The Legend City website was started in 2001 by the author and originally consisted of a single page containing a handful of postcards and a few ticket stubs. Over the years, nostalgic Arizonans have gradually discovered the site and contributed their own recollections, photographs, videos, and memorabilia in remembrance of the vanished theme park of their youth, making the website a genuinely communal experience. (Courtesy of www.legend-city.com.)

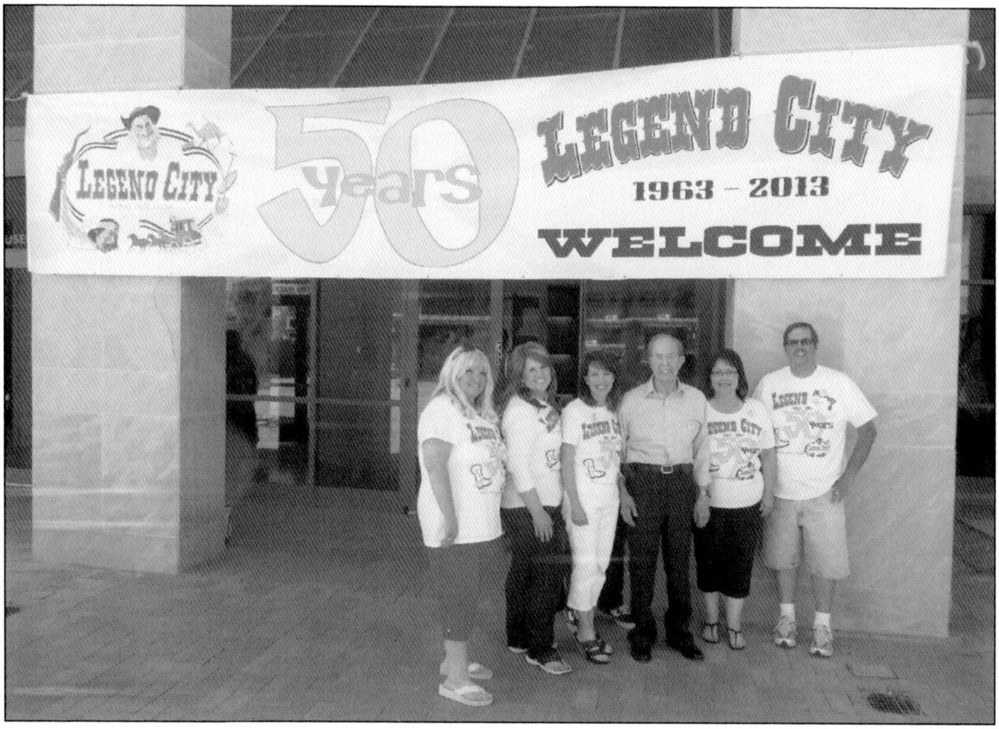

On June 22, 2013, the 50th anniversary of Legend City's grand opening was celebrated at a sold-out event at the Arizona Historical Society Museum in Tempe, Arizona. The event featured exhibits, memorabilia, Legend City celebrities, a show-and-tell activity, a costume contest, and a 90-minute auditorium program. Hundreds of fans, friends, and former employees of Legend City packed the venue. In this photograph, the Crandall family poses outside the museum. From left to right are Janie Crandall Hjorth, Ruthie Crandall Dangerfield, Annette Crandall Olson, Louis Crandall, Mem Crandall Bryan, and Louis Crandall Jr. (Courtesy of Sue Bueker.)

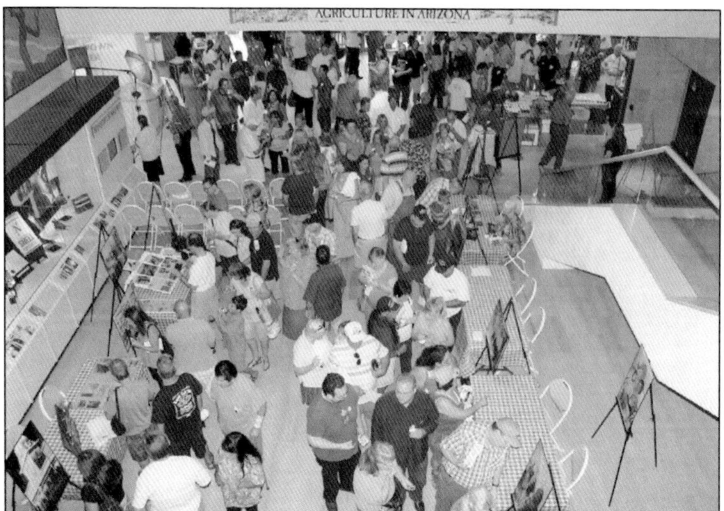

Before the auditorium presentation, the crowd at the 50th-anniversary event files past the various Legend City exhibits and memorabilia displays. Attendees received a 50th-anniversary commemorative pin, purchased T-shirts, and were treated to cupcakes and sno-cones from the original Legend City sno-cone machine. (Courtesy of Louis Crandall Jr.)

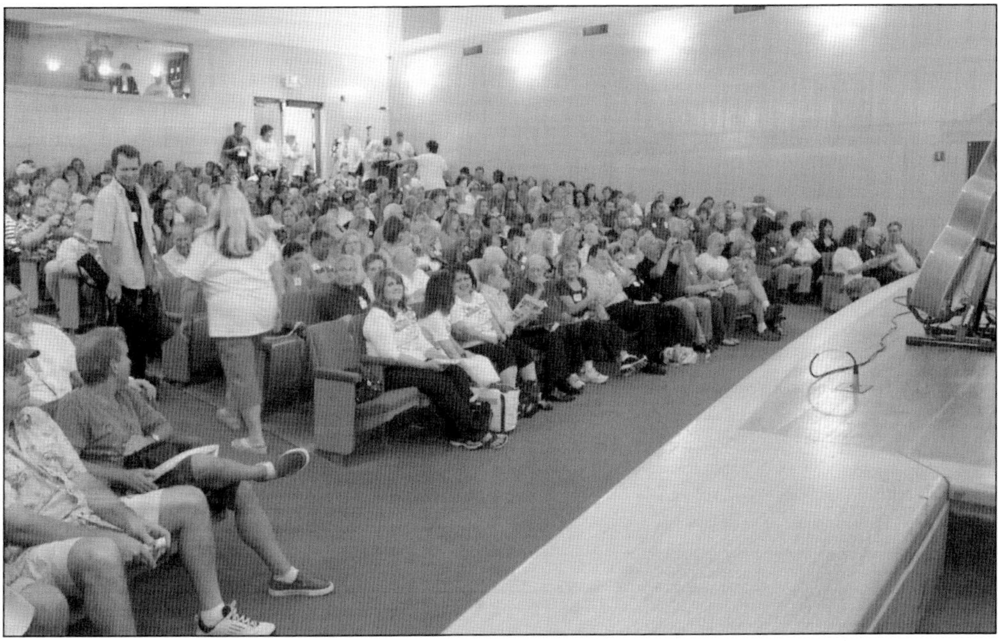

Inside the Arizona Historical Society Museum's auditorium, the crowd awaits the beginning of the Legend City golden anniversary celebration program. The 90-minute program consisted of a series of video presentations, guest speakers, impromptu skits, an audience Q&A, and live performances from Arizona's balladeer and former Legend City performer, Dolan Ellis. (Courtesy of Sue Bueker.)

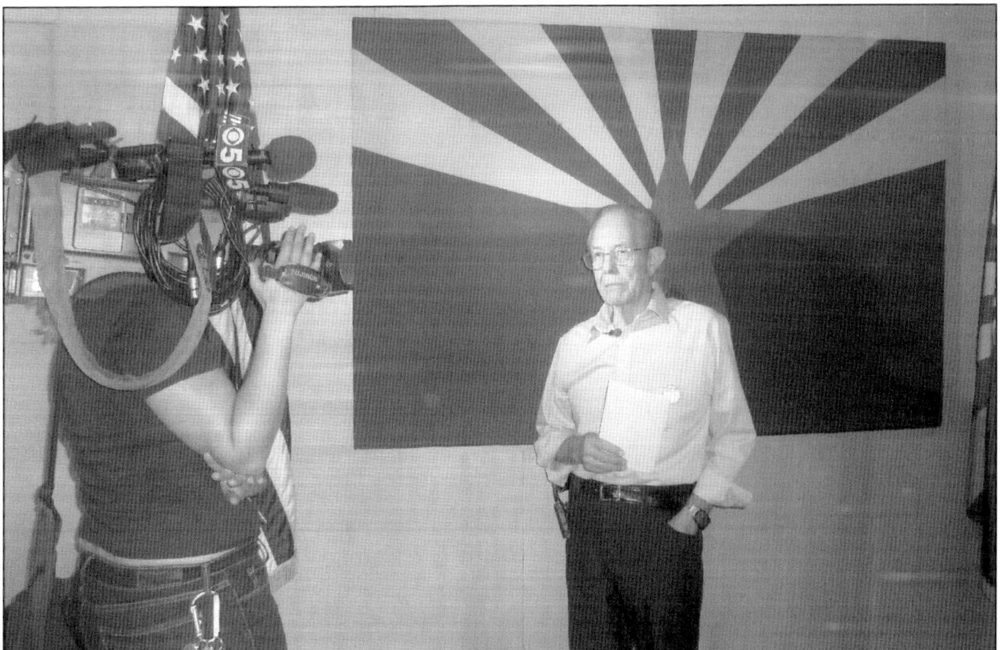

Louis Crandall talks to local media at the Legend City 50th anniversary celebration event. Media coverage of Legend City's golden anniversary and the Tempe celebration included a front-page story in the *Arizona Republic* the day before the event. (Courtesy of Louis Crandall Jr.)

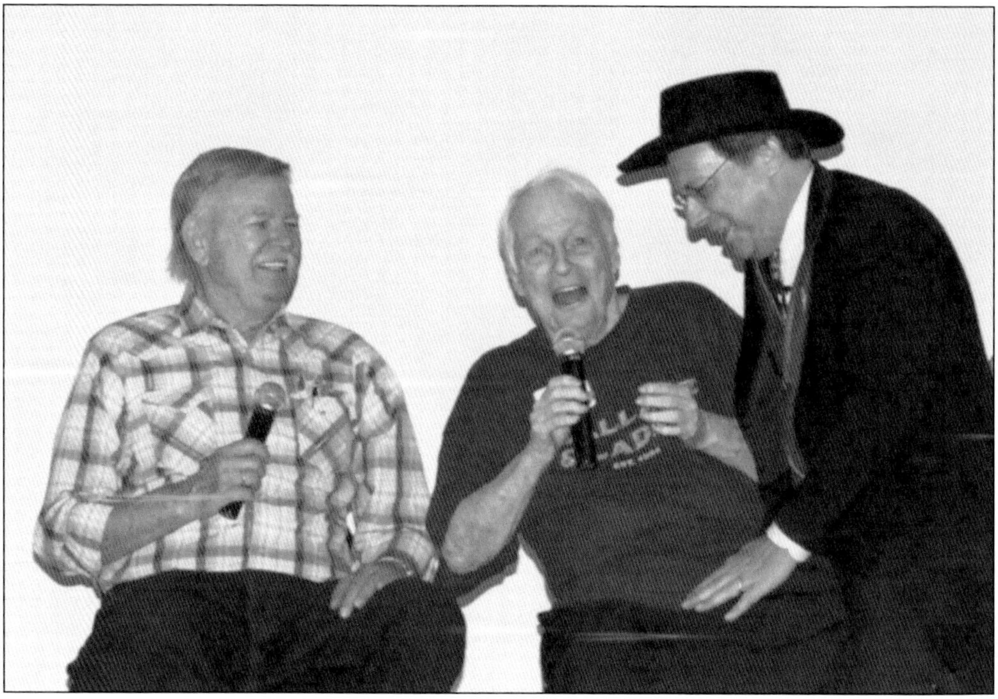

Legend City alumni Sandy Gibbons (left) and Wallace (Bill Thompson, center) share a laugh onstage with emcee Brad Zinn during the auditorium program at the Legend City 50th anniversary event. (Courtesy of Louis Crandall Jr.)

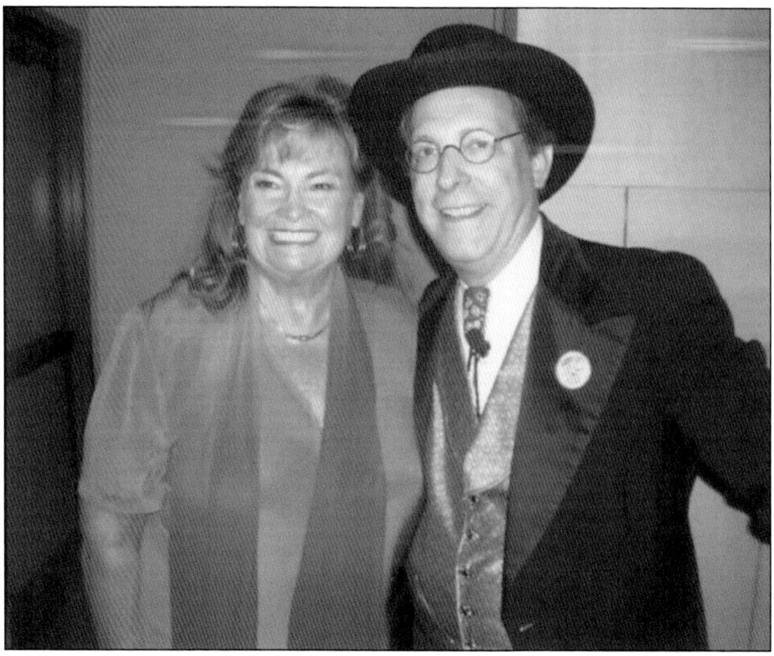

Vonda Kay Van Dyke, Miss America 1965 and former star of the Golden Palace Saloon at Legend City, poses with emcee Brad Zinn after the auditorium program at the 50th anniversary event. (Courtesy of Louis Crandall Jr.)

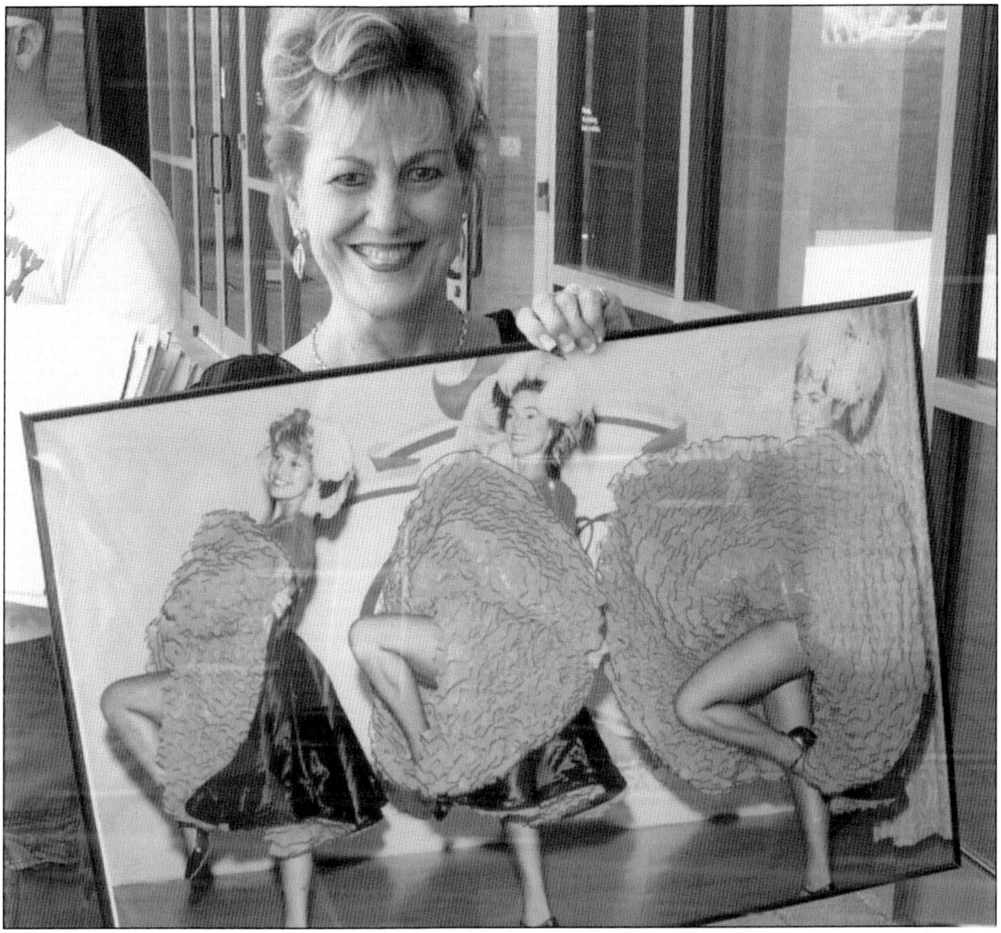

Printy Crandall DeGraff stands outside the Arizona Historical Society Museum after the anniversary event with a poster-sized photograph of herself performing onstage with the other can-can dancers at the Golden Palace Saloon. (Courtesy of Louis Crandall Jr.)

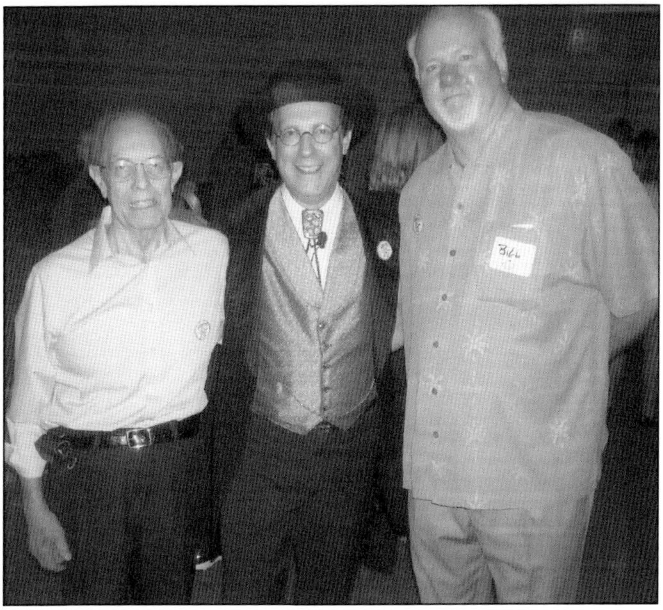

Bookmarked by the beginning and end of Legend City's colorful history, Brad Zinn (center) poses at the Tempe event with park founder Louis Crandall (left) and final owner Bill Capell Jr. (Courtesy of Louis Crandall Jr.)

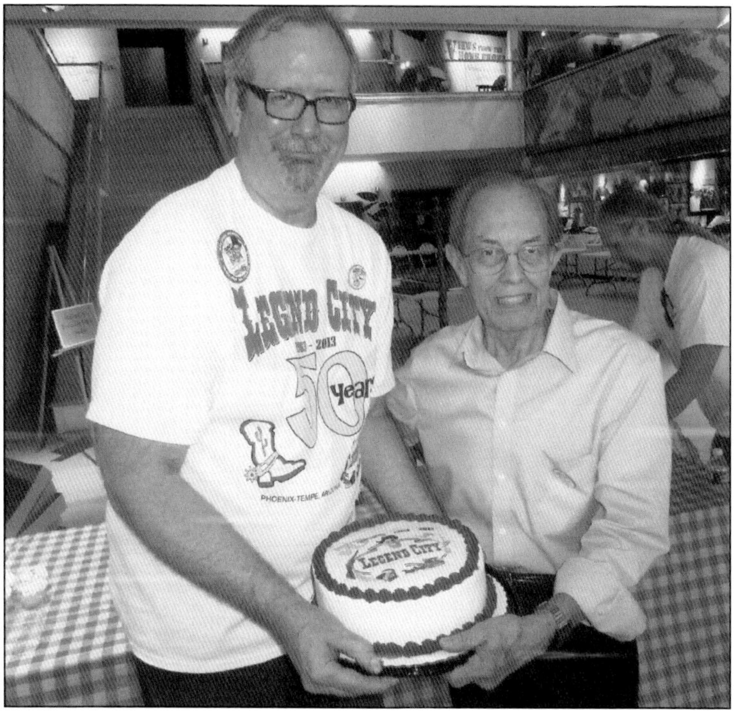

The author (left) and park founder Louis Crandall present the birthday cake at the 50th anniversary event. Their unlikely yet close friendship began in 2003, when Crandall discovered the Legend City website while surfing the Internet with his family during an Easter celebration gathering. (Courtesy of Sue Bueker).

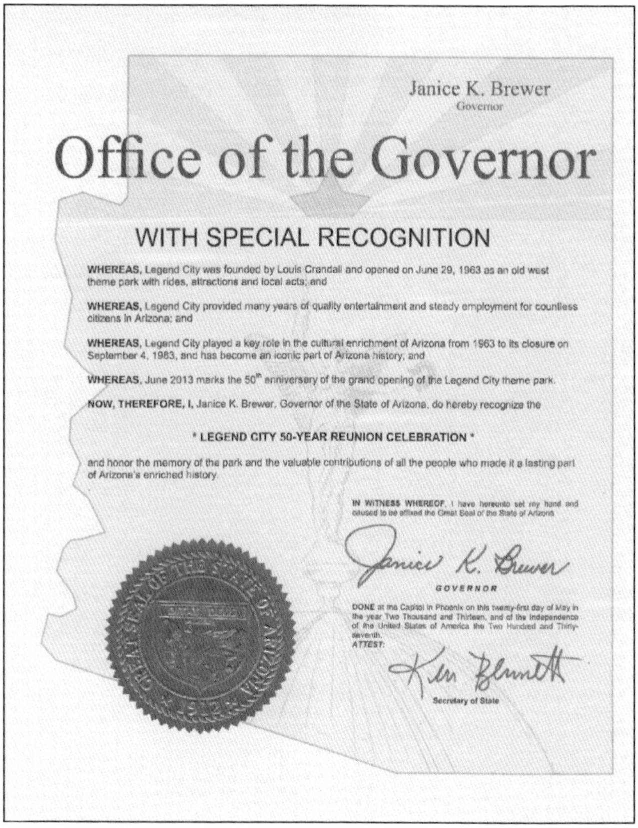

Janice K. Brewer
Governor

Office of the Governor

WITH SPECIAL RECOGNITION

WHEREAS, Legend City was founded by Louis Crandall and opened on June 29, 1963 as an old west theme park with rides, attractions and local acts; and

WHEREAS, Legend City provided many years of quality entertainment and steady employment for countless citizens in Arizona; and

WHEREAS, Legend City played a key role in the cultural enrichment of Arizona from 1963 to its closure on September 4, 1983, and has become an iconic part of Arizona history; and

WHEREAS, June 2013 marks the 50th anniversary of the grand opening of the Legend City theme park.

NOW, THEREFORE, I, Janice K. Brewer, Governor of the State of Arizona, do hereby recognize the

*** LEGEND CITY 50-YEAR REUNION CELEBRATION ***

and honor the memory of the park and the valuable contributions of all the people who made it a lasting part of Arizona's enriched history.

IN WITNESS WHEREOF, I have hereunto set my hand and caused to be affixed the Great Seal of the State of Arizona

Janice K. Brewer
GOVERNOR

DONE at the Capitol in Phoenix on this twenty-first day of May in the year Two Thousand and Thirteen, and of the Independence of the United States of America the Two Hundred and Thirty-seventh.

ATTEST:

Ken Bennett
Secretary of State

Arizona governor Jan Brewer signed an official state proclamation recognizing the 50th anniversary of Legend City's grand opening and honoring "the memory of the park and the valuable contributions of all the people who made it a lasting part of Arizona's enriched history."

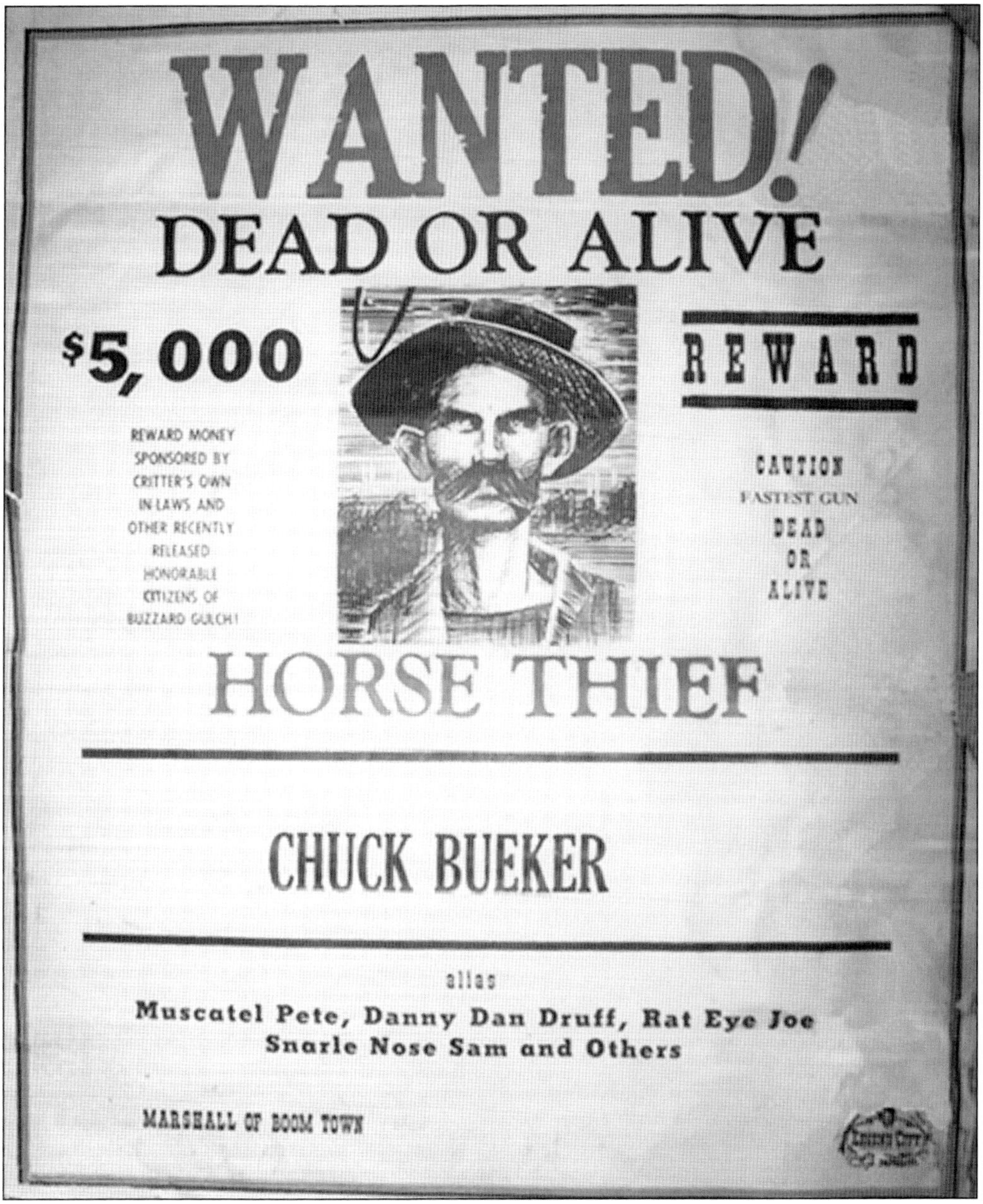

Legend City enthusiasts continue to avidly collect park memorabilia. This rare wanted poster from 1963 was custom-made at the Legend City Print Shop, with the park guest's name printed on it. It was a very popular novelty at the time. (Courtesy of Charles Bueker III.)